Gentle Eminence

MCGILL-QUEEN'S STUDIES IN THE HISTORY OF RELIGION

Volumes in the McGill-Queen's Studies in the History of Religion
have been supported by the Jackman Foundation of Toronto.

SERIES ONE
G.A. Rawlyk, Editor

Gentle Eminence

A Life of
Cardinal Flahiff

P. WALLACE PLATT CSB

McGill-Queen's University Press
Montreal & Kingston · London · Ithaca

© McGill-Queen's University Press 1999
ISBN 0-7735-1846-0

Legal deposit third quarter 1999
Bibliothèque nationale du Québec

Printed in Canada on acid-free paper

McGill-Queen's University Press acknowledges
the financial support of the Government of
Canada through the Book Publishing Industry
Development Program for its activities. We
also acknowledge the support of the
Canada Council for the Arts for our
publishing program.

Canadian Cataloguing in Publication Data

Platt, Philip Wallace, 1925-
Gentle eminence: a life of Cardinal Flahiff
(McGill-Queen's studies in the
history of religion)
Includes bibliographical references and index.
ISBN 0-7735-1846-0
1. Flahiff, George Bernard, 1905–1989. 2. Catho-
lic Church–Cardinals–Biography. 3. Cardinals–
Canada–Biography. I. Title. II. Series.

BX4705.F52P63   1999   282'.092   C99-900348-8

This book was typeset by Typo Litho
Composition Inc. in 10/12.5 Palatino.

CONTENTS

For all the friends of Cardinal Flahiff
and for those who would become such by reading his story

FOREWORD

This volume is an eloquent and satisfying account of the life and record of a quite extraordinary Christian, churchman, scholar, and Canadian, His Eminence George Bernard Cardinal Flahiff. I regard it as a high privilege to offer a brief introduction to such a distinguished biography.

When George Flahiff was consecrated Archbishop of Winnipeg in St Michael's Cathedral, Toronto, on 31 May 1961, I had my first occasion to meet him. I attended in a representative capacity as Premier of Manitoba in the company of a large contingent of his well-wishers from that province. The ceremony, so expressive of the spiritual nature of the consecration, moved the congregation as it certainly moved the new archbishop.

Afterwards, when we had an opportunity to speak, the impression of his personality was immediate. Here was a wise pastor, well furnished with ability, who by his modest demeanour and obvious interest in people, attracted the respect of all who met him. Yet there was sufficient of a twinkle in his blue eyes to put you at your ease. Here was a man of deep spirituality with a gift for human relations. He was the shepherd of his own flock, to be sure, but at the same time an open and sympathetic friend to others around him. There was a natural courtesy, a kindliness of manner, and a sincerity of interest that demanded a response.

It is not my part to advert to his high calling as a priest and prelate of the Roman Catholic communion. That task has been faithfully discharged with grace and sympathetic perception by the author of this work and record. But I can observe that the province was soon to take note of the strong and generous spirit of ecumenism he brought to bear in his dealings with the community around him. He touched us all.

That ecumenical spirit has a particular resonance among Manitobans. After all, we can usually count no less than five archbishops in Winnipeg, representative of the different languages and rites. In one sense, we are a province of minorities. Differences often divide but Cardinal Flahiff could also see them as a source of strength. He did not seek to water down belief but he sought to rejoice in what we have in common. It was not a question of concession and compromise but of charity and cooperation. Father Platt offers an illuminating quotation from the cardinal himself when he said do not "set aside the precious differences of inspiration in favour of a bland conformity." In this context, he made ecumenism a principle of community relations.

It may be expected that as an Anglican I took particular notice of his practical interest and support of the establishment of the Assiniboia Christian Centre. This came about when two parishes – one Roman Catholic, John XXIII, and one Anglican, St. Chad's – joined together to share one physical facility but within which each parish would continue to have its own independent existence and follow its own rule. The experience has been a happy one.

Until I left the legislature in Manitoba in 1968 there were opportunities for congenial meetings. On occasions of state or family life I could expect to receive from the cardinal a special card of concern. His handwritten and perceptive reference to the matter at hand was a sign of personal interest and encouragement that so endeared him to his friends. One does not forget such acts of consideration.

Now this volume commemorates his life. In the character of priest and pastor he ennobled his flock. In the character of archbishop and cardinal he ennobled our community. This book celebrates his handiwork.

The Honourable Duff Roblin

ACKNOWLEDGMENTS

In writing a biography one becomes indebted to many. The contributors to this present work, all friends of George Bernard Flahiff, found a good deal of pleasure in remembering him, and I as much in recording their memories. In imitation of my subject, who was the most grateful of men, I wish to acknowledge and thank all those who helped me along in this labour of love.

My Basilian superiors permitted, encouraged, and facilitated the work; my confreres showed interest at every turn, pleased that the life of a great Basilian was being recorded, however imperfectly. Kevin Kirley, archivist of the Basilian Fathers, not only helped enormously in my research, but was an ever patient and wise mentor and sounding-board during the writing. Many Basilians read chapters and/or shared anecdotes and memories of the cardinal: Claude Arnold, Robert Barringer, George Beaune, Fred Black, Victor Brezik, James Carruthers, Michael Fallona, Hugh Foley, George Freemesser, Jack Gallagher, Harry Gardner, Patrick Gorman, James Hanrahan, David Katulski, Robert Madden, Frank Mallon, Armand Maurer, Peter Mosteller, the late Raphael O'Loughlin, Ulysse Paré, Ambrose Raftis, Richard Schiefen and Joseph Wey. To Terence Forestell and Peter Swan I am especially grateful for their reading of the entire manuscript and for their perceptive comments.

Terrence J. Flahiff, the cardinal's brother, and his wife Françoise received me several times at their home in Montreal and contributed much to my knowledge of the Flahiff family background. Mary Murray, an honorary member of the Flahiff family, also gave me many hours of conversation about George in his relationship to the family which was so dear to him. Terry Flahiff and Mary Murray have since gone to God. Simone Flahiff, Norman Flahiff's widow was also very helpful. Other members of the Flahiff family, Professor Fred Flahiff, John Cleary, and Mary (Flahiff) Smith, kindly provided information about the cardinal as they knew him.

Among the members of the hierarchy, where Cardinal Flahiff was a friend and esteemed colleague, I must acknowledge the interest shown and the help given by Cardinal Aloysius Ambrozic, the late Cardinal Joseph Bernadin, Archbishop Carlo Curis, apostolic nuncio to Canada, Bishop Alexander Carter, Bishop Remi De Roo, Archbishop James Hayes, Bishop Eugène LaRocque, Archbishop Joseph MacNeil, Archbishop Aurèle Plourde, and Bishop John Sherlock. From the beginning of this project, Cardinal Gerald Emmett Carter has shown a special interest in the biography of his good friend, and has been wonderfully helpful with suggestions, information, and encouragement.

In Winnipeg, where the memories of their former archbishop are as strong as they are dear, I found warm hospitality, warm memories, and redolence of the man I was studying. I am grateful especially to Archbishop Wall for a western welcome and for full accessibility to the archives of the Archdiocese; to Roy Larrabee for hospitality and reminiscences of the cardinal; to the persons at the chancery, especially Ward Jamieson, Michael Moore, Joseph ("Jakey") Driscoll sj, and all the staff both at the chancery and at the cathedral. Viola Specht, the cardinal's secretary for twenty-one years, has helped in many ways; I am most grateful to her. I came to understand why the cardinal appreciated Viola's services so highly. Other friends of the cardinal in Winnipeg shared time, memories, and reflections. I should like to mention John Currie, the late David Hockman, Jacob Hollenbach, Gary Killen, Debra Kohen, Sterling Lyon, Arthur Mauro, Duff Roblin, and Gary Ward.

The interviews I had with persons who knew the cardinal and the letters I received from many of these are what have given life to the bare bones of chronology. I hope I have faithfully reflected the thoughts confided to me. I gratefully acknowledge the contribution of these persons: Gregory Baum, Margaret Brennan ihm, Jim Conley, Bernard Daly, Caroline Dawson ibvm, Thomas Day, Dan Donovan, Helen Flannery, the late Marie Garvey, Lorraine Griffin rpb, Agnes Hearn ss, Augustine Kalberer osb, Sheila Madden rmdn, Rita McCormack, Pauline McGibbon, the late Jack McGoey sfm, James O'Brien, the late Jack O'Farrell, Olga Warnke ibvm, Aileen Richard rpb, the late Edward Synan, and David Tough. To Marc Lerman, archivist of the Archdiocese of Toronto, to Mary Martin sc, archivist of the Sisters of Charity of Halifax and to Fred Power sj, editor of *The*

Canadian Messenger of the Sacred Heart, I also express my thanks for assistance, as well as to Karen Dinsdale, secretary of the Pontifical Institute of Mediaeval Studies in Toronto. Don Akenson and his colleagues at McGill-Queen's University Press, especially Joan McGilvray and Diane Mew, have been ever helpful and encouraging.

There are four persons I must single out for special thanks. Helene Darte sc, whose friendship with the cardinal began in 1937 and continued until his death, allowed me into the sacred and highly personal realm of Flahiff's spiritual direction and has been most gracious in sharing her reflections. Norman Chartrand, chancellor, friend, companion and faithful assistant to Cardinal Flahiff for twenty-one years, has been extremely generous with his time, his information, and his interest in the life of the man he admired and served for so long. Lenore Sullivan ibvm, not only by the correspondence which she placed at my disposal, but also by many hours of sharing recollections and reflections, has enriched and guided my writing in a unique way. Irene McDonald csj, who attended the cardinal in his last months, has shown by her careful reading and re-reading of my manuscript and her ever-encouraging interest a love for the subject equal to my own.

If I have overlooked anyone in these acknowledgments, or if I have expressed the thoughts of any of my contributors clumsily or inadequately, I ask pardon.

P.W.P.
26 October 1998

ABBREVIATIONS

CCC   Canadian Catholic Conference

CCCB   Canadian Conference of Catholic Bishops

CSB   Congregation of St Basil (Basilian Fathers)

IBVM   Institute of the Blessed Virgin Mary (Loretto Sisters)

IHM   Immaculate Heart of Mary

OP   Order of Preachers (Dominican)

OSB   Order of St Benedict (Benedictine)

RMDN Religieuses de Notre Dame des Missions

RPB   Religious of the Precious Blood

SC   Sisters of Charity

SJ   Society of Jesus (Jesuit)

SCCE   Sacred Congregation for Catholic Education

SCRSI Sacred Congregation for Religious and Secular Institutes

SFM   Scarborough Foreign Missions

SS   Sisters of Service

TOR   Third Order Regular (Franciscan)

Gentle Eminence

PROLOGUE

But the wisdom from above is first pure, then peaceable,
gentle, willing to yield, full of mercy and good fruits,
without a trace of partiality or hypocrisy. And a harvest
of righteousness is sown in peace for those who make peace.

– James 3: 17–18

In the city of Rome on 11 October 1971, in the presence of Pope
Paul VI, a seven-minute speech was given which reverberated
around the world and made the speaker a hero to some and something of a heretic to others. The occasion was a meeting of the Roman
Catholic Synod of Bishops, whose members represented the Church
throughout the world, and whose themes for this second synod of its
kind were the Catholic priesthood and social justice. The person who
gave the speech was a tall, dignified cardinal from western Canada.
He was not speaking in his own name, but in the name of the Roman
Catholic bishops of Canada with whom he had prepared the speech
with great care. He had no idea of the effect his words would produce. The speech drew enormous attention and gave him a reputation which he carried uneasily but probably with some satisfaction
for the rest of his days.

George Bernard Cardinal Flahiff, one of the four Canadian bishops
at the synod, was speaking to the question of ministries in the
Church. He recalled that the speakers before him had suggested
extension of these ministries, even of the priesthood itself, to other
categories in the Church such as married men. He went on to say that
all the previous speakers had spoken about these various ministries
as applying only to men; no one had mentioned the place of women
in ministries. He suggested that to neglect such a consideration was

to exclude one-half of all believers, and that the traditional arguments for male exclusivity for ministries no longer held. As his speech drew to an end he proposed: "That the representatives of the Canadian Catholic Conference urge the ... Synod of Bishops to recommend to the Holy Father the immediate establishment of a mixed commission (that is, composed of bishops, priests, laymen and laywomen, and religious men and religious women) to study in depth the question of *the ministries of women in the Church.*"[1]

This carefully honed and modestly presented speech turned out to be a bombshell. It was immediately, irrevocably, and erroneously interpreted as an appeal for women priests in the Roman Catholic Church. The reactions to the speech were both positive and negative, and all of them strong. The cardinal was amazed and disconcerted by the furor he had caused, for, scholar that he was, he had chosen his words very carefully, assuming that they would be taken at face value. From that moment on, however, he was willy-nilly the champion for the cause of women in major ministries. The role into which he was cast was not always easy and was the cause of considerable embarrassment to him. In the opinion of some, it put an end to any further advancement of George Bernard Flahiff in the hierarchy of the Church – more to his relief than to his chagrin.

In his own description of the sequel to his speech we catch his surprise, his frustration, and his admirable capacity to see the humour of the situation. He wrote: "[I was] proposing quite simply, not to say naïvely, that a Commission be established to *study* the further question of the *possibility* of ordination of women or of a part in new ministries that might be created. I could not watch [Pope] Paul as I was delivering [my speech] so I cannot guess his reaction. Many came up after to express their satisfaction that the question had been raised." But then the media got hold of the matter: "I am not quite sure what the present image is, but there are echoes of 'knight in shining armour,' (nobody has seized on the name 'George'), liberationist, champion of the downtrodden, 'women's voice in the Synod,' and what not. All I asked for was a commission to begin a study! Yet some of the Italian papers are speculating about the possibility of women as bishops and even pope!"[2]

A few days after the speech, the *Osservatore Romano*, the official Vatican newspaper, published an article by their theologian Gino Concetti, which stated that the cardinal had been misquoted and that the ordination of women was theologically impossible. Flahiff commented, with just a hint of untypical sarcasm: "Simple, isn't it? It's nice to know, in any case." He spoke of articles in *Le Monde*, the most influential daily in France, and on the front page of the *Herald Tribune*, the popular American daily published in Europe and widely circulated there.[3] These clippings he sent to his correspondent, together with a copy of his speech. "I think you will agree," he wrote, "that the content of what was said is hardly revolutionary or epoch-making. Not that that matters: it is so often the story of what is said *after* a fairly innocent talk or statement that becomes an interest and an end in itself." The publicity was overwhelming; he asked playfully in the same letter, "Could you possibly take a week off and come help me look after the letters, telegrams, telephone calls, interviews and requests for pictures that are making these days all but impossible?"[4]

Cardinal Flahiff was beseiged by media agents from Ireland, Germany, Switzerland, Italy, France (*Paris-Match*), and the United States (*Newsweek*) with requests for interviews. He had to be shielded by the members of the communications agency of the Canadian bishops from a number of other requests. He wondered what the reaction was in Canada: "You will have to tell me, when I see you, what was reported in Canada. Two telegrams make it evident that something was said."[5] Warming up to the preposterousness of it all, he wrote: "One Spanish lady has offered herself for ordination. An Italian has written to say that 'in this day of charisms and recognition of the Holy Spirit's influence, *Sua Eminentissima Reverendissima* (G.B.F., I take it) must have been inspired by the Holy Spirit, and probably through the archangel Gabriel; nothing else could explain the intervention in the Synod!' I must check with my Jesuit friends on the discernment of spirits."[6]

The irony is that George Flahiff was identified with something he never proposed. He was a highly trained scholar and a careful one, with an exquisite sense of precision in the examination of a text, and a scrupulous discipline in his own presentation of facts or ideas. These qualities of his thought and word, however, were entirely lost in the wave of sensationalism which followed his speech. A further irony lies in the tremendous publicity following the words of a person who was rather shy, reserved in his expression of opinion at all times, and naturally adverse to any kind of acclaim. He became a hero in spite of himself. He also became an object of suspicion and even of hatred. There were elements in both the hierarchy of the Church and among lay Catholics who took umbrage, to say the least, at what the cardinal said, or at what they thought he said, or at what they thought his words implied.[7] It is quite possible that Flahiff's intervention at the synod effectively killed any possibility of his being named to the Vatican post of Prefect of the Sacred Congregation for Religious,[8] a position for which he was apt and for which he was thought destined, but to which he had not the slightest pretension.

The synod of 1971 was, for better or worse, one more crucial moment for George Bernard Flahiff, whose life was marked by unusual and surprising events. As at other stages in his life where there was upset or change, Flahiff met this turn with equanimity. He did not feel himself overwhelmed or victimized by the event, though he knew that there was now the burden of a new role to be played. He was actually at the zenith of his career. He had been Archbishop of Winnipeg, esteemed and beloved, for ten years. He had achieved world status by being named to the College of Cardinals two years previously. He was well known and highly respected in Canada and the United States as an open-minded, inspiring speaker. He had the esteem of his fellow bishops in Canada and in various parts of the world. From October 1971 he took on the new enforced roles of hero and suspect liberal and assimilated them by his faith, his intelligence, his love of humanity, and his saving sense of humour.

Every life is unique and mysterious. Not every life, however, is as fascinating as that of an innkeeper's son from a small Ontario town, who passed his boyhood and youth in the ordinary round of school, sports, and large-family life, tending the bar in his father's hotel, and who became successively a noted scholar, superior general of an international religious order, an archbishop, and ultimately a prince of the Church. At every turn he distinguished himself and seemed to move easily through these remarkable phases, maintaining and developing a manner of being in which fidelity, friendship, wisdom, holiness, and humour worked in harmony. George Flahiff was a man who loved greatly. The loves of his life – God, family, friends, his religious community, sport, studies, travel, nature, poetry, conviviality, French cuisine – were harmoniously ordered. He was a man at home in the world and conscious of heaven.

While his public image was that of a person who was serene, open, and confident, Flahiff had his share of uncertainties and failures. These were hardly discernible, for he seldom complained and he never wore his heart on his sleeve. The self-discipline which he learned early and cultivated all his life hid a good deal of suffering and self-doubt. The man who spoke out in 1971 on the place of women in the ministries of the Church and on social justice was the same man who agonized over decisions and eschewed conflict of any kind. The man in whom many found strength and encouragement was a man deeply dependent on friendship and keenly sensitive to the comments and attitudes of others. The man who seemed to walk in an aura of achievement and acclaim, listened to and respected for twenty years as a spiritual leader in the Church in Canada, was to know considerable suffering and heartache in the last decade of his life, when age, infirmity, and the thoughtless pace of time came to claim their due.

Yet overall his life was splendid. He was a man who lived by faith and illuminated the world around him by that same faith. He achieved in himself a harmony of the divine and the human which Thomas Aquinas or Thomas More would have praised. He left no monuments, at least none in bricks or books. His monument is his memory in the hearts of hundreds, at the service of which are the following pages.

CHAPTER ONE

Youth in the Sunshine

The contours and quiet beauty of Paris, Ontario, the prettiest town in Canada, as the "Parisians" have called it for generations, are much the same today as they were when George Bernard Flahiff was born there, in his father's hotel, almost a century ago. The pretension of the town to a particular beauty was not unfounded; even today Paris maintains an aura of charm and peace in a busy, noisy world. The centre of the town lies on a level area between two rivers, the Nith and the Grand. From the centre the town rises gently to the east and to the west on lush green hills and melts into the rich surrounding farmland. Paris has the distinction of being the place where the first long-distance telephone call in the world was received, on the evening of 10 August 1876.[1] It also has the distinction of being the birthplace of both a famous Canadian athlete, Sylvanus Apps,[2] and of a cardinal of the Holy Roman Church.

Michael Flahiff, George's paternal great-grandfather, emigrated from Annascaul, County Kerry, Ireland, in 1847 to escape the famine. He settled in the Kenilworth–Mount Forest area of Ontario. One of his sons, Terrence, moved to Paris, Ontario, sometime between 1867 and 1870. There his son John, born in 1871, went into the hotel business, acquiring the New Royal Hotel in the centre of town in 1900.

William Waller of Castle Waller, George's maternal great-grandfather, was born in Newport, County Tipperary, Ireland, of a prominent Irish family (the Wallers of Castle Waller fill seven pages of the 1977 edition of Burke's *Irish Family Records*). He sold the family estate, including the dilapidated castle, and emigrated to Canada in 1851, settling in Paris, Ontario. He and his wife Bridget had four children, of whom Mary was the eldest. She married a man named Pierce Fleming, a blacksmith and carriage repairer in Paris. They had

John and Eleanor (Fleming) Flahiff on their wedding day,
17 April 1901, in Paris, Ontario. (Basilian Archives, Toronto)

ten children, four boys and six girls, of whom Eleanor Rose Marie, the youngest, married John Flahiff, the hotel-keeper, in the Church of the Sacred Heart on 17 April 1901.[3]

The notice of the wedding on the front page of the Paris *Star Transcript* of 17 April 1901, very much in the style of the time, spoke of the couple being "united in the holy bonds of matrimony," and identified the best man with the expression, "Mr. David Brockbank supported the groom." The article continued: "As both the contracting parties are very highly thought of and extremely popular, the wedding was of particular interest to a great many people, and large numbers of the fair sex were at the Church to witness an event so rare and interesting. Many and handsome were the presents received, a striking testimony of the esteem in which the young couple are deservedly held by their friends."

John and Eleanor Flahiff and their children would be well-known citizens of the town of Paris for the next thirty years. Their home in the New Royal Hotel put them physically in the heart of the town. Their family life, civic spirit, religious fidelity, and simple goodness put them in the hearts of their fellow citizens. It was a happy household which ultimately counted six sons and three daughters. Frequent correspondence among the Flahiff family members during more than fifty years after the death of John Flahiff testifies to their strong family ties and to the affection and gratitude they had for their parents.

Eleanor Rose Marie Flahiff was a person of refinement. She was beautiful and she was accomplished, having graduated from the Toronto Conservatory of Music. She was adored by her husband, who would sometimes refer to her, even when speaking to his children, as "the beautiful lady."[4] From the scant information we have of her it is evident that she was devoted and self-sacrificing. The family lived on the top floor of the hotel.[5] Eleanor hated the living arrangements and longed for a regular house and home where one would not have to pass through a beverage room to get to the family quarters. Loyally she went along with the situation for the sake of her husband, for he had asked her to do so for a period of ten years. When the ten years had passed the hotel was prosperous and the family already numbered six children. John asked his wife to continue living in the hotel for another five years. She consented, recognizing how much their livelihood depended on it, though all the time holding on to her dream of the day when they could move into a real home of their own. Sadly that day never came.

The first child of John and Eleanor was born in 1902 and christened John Joseph. The boy died at the age of eighteen months, choking to death on the pits of some cherries he found in the room next to where his mother was chatting with a friend. The second son, Edward Waller, born in 1903, became a doctor. He began his medical career with the Rockefeller Foundation as Caribbean medical chief. In 1932 he married Helen Dudley Parsons, a member of a prominent Toronto family. He served in North Africa during the Second World War, when at the Battle of Tobruk he once tended the wounds of a German soldier who proved to be Field Marshal Erwin von Rommel. Rommel is said to have cited the young Canadian doctor to Flahiff's superiors in London, who awarded him a decoration as a result.[6] After the war he became medical officer of the Canadian Mining Association.

James Norman was born in 1904. He joined the Canadian Bank of Commerce at the age of seventeen and stayed with the bank for fifty-nine years, ending as chief foreign exchange executive. He married Simone Martheleur, the daughter of a Belgian diplomat, who after living in various parts of the world, had settled in Cape Breton. They had one son, Terence.

The fourth son, George Bernard, the future cardinal and subject of this book, was born on 26 October 1905. He was followed in the family by Terrence Fleming who was born in 1907, had a distinguished career as a lawyer in Toronto, as a soldier in the Second World War, rising to the rank of brigadier general, as a public servant in Ottawa, and then as a business executive living in Montreal. He married Françoise de Sevigny, the daughter of the former Chief Justice of Quebec. They had two sons, Robert and George.

After the birth of five boys, it must have been a great joy to the Flahiffs when in August of 1908 the first daughter, Eleanor Rose, was born. A strikingly beautiful girl, Eleanor went into nursing at St. Michael's Hospital in Toronto, where she nursed for a time after her graduation. She married George Cleary and they made their home in Brantford, Ontario. They had two sons, Michael and John.

A second daughter, Margaret Mary, born in 1911, graduated from the University of Toronto in 1939 and then entered the Sisters of Charity of Halifax, where she was professed as Sister Thérèse Carmel. Besides serving her community in important positions, notably in New York and Vancouver, Margaret became professor of history at Mount St Vincent University in Halifax. Later she became the first librarian of the Atlantic School of Theology, by which institution she was awarded an honorary doctorate in 1987. An exceptionally beautiful reading room in the library has been named for her. She received the "Pro Ecclesia et Pontifice" medal from Pope John Paul II for her services to ecumenism. Margaret died in Halifax in August 1990, six months after her golden jubilee as a religious, and one year to the day after the funeral of her cardinal brother.

Another daughter, Catherine McEllistrum, was born in 1914. Because of the difficult financial situation of the Flahiff family in the mid-1930s, Catherine was unable to go to university, a disappointment which she felt keenly all through her life. She undertook office work in Toronto and became secretary to the assistant attorney general of Ontario. Later she went to work in New York where, at the time of her retirement, she was executive secretary to one of the vice-presidents of Standard Oil. Catherine returned to Toronto in 1970.

The last child in the family was John Benedict, born in 1916 and named for his father and for the first-born son who had died, as well as for Benedict XV who had become pope two years previously. Jack became a sales agent and then a federal public servant. Like three of his brothers, he served his country in the war, spending a year and a half as a prisoner of war in Germany, but returning safely to the great joy and relief of his family. Jack married Louise Smith, a native of Newfoundland and lives in Mississauga, Ontario.

The first fifteen years of the Flahiff family were busy, happy, and prosperous. The children were healthy and active. They had come in quick succession: nine births in fourteen years. Eleanor Flahiff was well occupied, though she found time to participate in parish and civic activities as well. One year, probably about 1910, John Flahiff bought a Cadillac car, the first in Paris. His wife was uncomfortable with the extravagance but soon found the car was useful in a special way. On summer evenings she would pack her brood into the car and, with her husband driving, set off for a spin in the country. Gradually, as she knew would happen, the children would drowse and fall asleep. When they got home the neighbours taking the summer air would help her carry the sleeping children to the top floor of the hotel.

The family's religious practice was regular and accepted by all: Sunday mass and sometimes weekday mass, family rosary after supper, and charity to all at all times. All the boys served on the altar; everyone took part in parish activities and projects. There seems to have been an admirable spirit of peace and love in the Flahiff home. It is hard to imagine so large a family without the usual quarrels and bickering of children, but if they did exist, they were minimal, as anyone who has had acquaintance with the members of the Flahiff family would testify. Many years later, some months after George's death, and just a month before Margaret's, Terry reflected on their family life: "In a way, we were *born* lucky – eight (nine actually) children born to have a childhood of love and companionship with each other – something which is as active today as it was over 80 years ago for me!! Large families are a heavy responsibility for a mother and father, but they are a godsend to the kids who grow up in the circle of family love. And who also, as I believe in our case, grow into maturity with a solid, unshakeable, belief in our religious faith. Dad and Mother started it, but we, all of us, kept it going." [7]

George Bernard was by nature gentle and considerate, and disposed to help others. His "charge" in the family buddy system was Terry, the brother immediately younger. (Ed for Norman, George for Terry, Eleanor for Margaret, and Catherine for Jack.) Terry remembered well the bond that developed between him and George, and the lessons of kindness he learned from his brother. He also remembered how, when the two of them were serving midnight mass one Christmas Eve, George, who had been working in the stationer's shop, fell soundly asleep, safely out of view of the congregation in a convenient corner of the sanctuary. Terry joined the priest for the offertory, but George slept on, and had to be roused to duty. It became a family joke, one which George did not appreciate. Another great embarrassment for young George was the accident of breaking his fast on the morning of his First Communion, which meant that he could not receive communion on that day. Nor did he care to be reminded of this catastrophe in his young life.

Along with his brothers and sisters, George did his primary education at the convent school attached to the Parish of the Sacred Heart. His facility for learning and his natural diligence marked him from the beginning. He did the eight grades in seven years, and moved on to Paris High School. There he was consistently first in his class. He seemed to do this effortlessly; no one would have described him as studious, much less bookish. With this natural and easily carried brilliance went a steady conscientiousness in his duty; nor would he avoid the difficult or unpleasant.

He gives his own account, many years later, of his early school days in a charming letter, dated 12 May 1977,[8] to Laurie Burns, a little girl from Paris, Ontario, who evidently has written to the cardinal with a questionnaire on his remembrances. He writes that he is "delighted to receive [her] questionnaire and to be asked to recall memories of Sacred Heart School." He tells her (repeating her name several times in the letter, as was his wont) that he began school in September 1910 and remained there until 1917, when he passed his entrance examination. While he was there, the school building was renewed, and the children found the new premises "palatial." (One wonders how Laurie coped with "palatial."). In the new premises, there were only two classrooms, with four grades in each. There was one teacher in each classroom: Sister Anselm (who was also principal) for the senior grades, and Sister Perpetua for the lower grades. He talks about the close relation between the parish and the school, and how everyone loved the pastor, Father George L. Cassidy. He comments on the smallness of the yard, in which they could not have a "real" game of baseball, how there were no organized sports, and how periodically during the day they would throw open the windows and do exercises. He concludes: "My recollections are of very happy years at Sacred Heart, Laurie. I think I can honestly say that I have no sad or painful memories at all of the school or of my experiences there, even though I did get the strap occasionally. We were a close-knit group of pupils. We all knew one another; families were also well acquainted and we all felt very much like an over-all family. As I said in regard to Father Cassidy, school life and parish life were closely tied up."

The letter speaks well for the cardinal's memory, as it does for his kindness in replying to the child's letter with such care and interest. While he does not get away from a certain formality which characterizes much of his correspondence, he does speak to the child warmly

The Flahiff family about 1917. The future cardinal is the boy on the extreme
left of the picture. (Basilian Archives, Toronto)

and without condescension, as respectfully as though he were writing
to one of his peers. The letter is two full pages of single-spaced type.

From his earliest days, George was a keen athlete, and his brothers
and sisters had a similar interest in sports. Baseball, soccer, hockey,
and swimming were the chief sports available. The Flahiffs were able
to muster a complete hockey team from their own family. Nor was it
unusual for three Flahiff boys to be playing on the same baseball
team. The proximity of the two rivers made swimming easily accessible. (George derived much pleasure from swimming and diving; he
practised these sports all his life.) The Flahiffs were all good swim-
mers and ran the normal risks of that sport at that time. Places for
swimming around the mills could be hazardous, and of course there
were no lifeguards. Edward, the oldest of the boys, on one occasion
by his presence of mind and swiftness to act, saved his younger
brother Terry, seven years old at the time, from what would have
been sure death. Terry began to cross a spillway to join his brothers.
The cement bottom was slippery with seaweed, and the rush of the
water swept the boy off his feet and over the edge into deeper water.
Edward was in the water and at his brother's side in seconds. Terry
never forgot this, and liked to recall it as an example of what each
owed to the other members of their family. Edward was reluctant to

go home after the event for fear of being scolded for his wet clothes. Another time the boys with their friends assembled a raft and, mounting a sail, attempted to cross the broad space of water where the rivers meet. The raft was ungovernable; the sailors had to be rescued and, since this could be viewed from the bridge near the centre of town, they suffered great shame.

Though Catholics were in a minority in Paris, and the Flahiffs were obviously very much attached to their religion and to their parish, there seems to have been no divisions in the community along religious lines. Paris had a tradition of tolerance and mutual respect, except for charlatans and fanatics, a tradition which certainly entered into the education of George and his brothers and sisters. He would become well known in later life for his respect for the religious beliefs and practices of others and an openness to dialogue on religious differences. In fact, when Archbishop of Winnipeg, he would become a leader in ecumenism, though people there thought of it simply as friendship. He could easily enter into a cause that was good, no matter what the label. David Tough, a boyhood companion, and a member of the Tough Hardware family prominent in Paris, recalls how, on an excursion to Port Dover, where the Flahiff boys and their friends were headed to spend some days at the Tough cottage, George investigated a nearby Kiwanis orphanage, saw they needed assistance, and organized his companions into an auxiliary force, during their vacation time.

John James Flahiff faced a sorrowful and daunting challenge soon after the birth of his last son when, on 23 November 1916, his wife died after a short struggle with pneumonia. Being eager to get back to her duties in the family and the parish, Eleanor Rose did not allow herself sufficient time to recover from her last pregnancy and childbirth. She sacrificed everything for her husband and family: the finer things of life to which she was accustomed, a normal home, and years which might have been hers under different circumstances. She gave her children a deep faith and a spirit of sacrifice; they bore witness in their own lives to her goodness and refinement. Nor was she forgotten. George was only eleven when she died, and though there is rare mention of her in family letters, he writes of celebrating an anniversary mass for her sixty-seven years later,[9] which would suggest that he did so annually. Her husband had a beautiful marble statue of a sorrowing female figure imported from Italy to adorn her grave. Her death devastated him. His older children remembered how he drew them close to himself at the graveside, unable to speak for his tears. It was 26 November 1916, Margaret's fifth birthday.

Good Christian father that he was, John James Flahiff met his challenge admirably. He invited his unmarried sister to come into his household to help him raise his children. Teresa Flahiff left her home in the United States to come to his aid. She was strict but good, and she carried on the Christian family traditions as the Flahiff parents had established them. John James took an active part in the education of his children. Since his own education had been limited, he wanted them all to go to university, and he assured them that support for this would be forthcoming. Unfortunately he did not live to fulfil his promise. When the older ones left home he would write to each one every week, sometimes mixing up the envelopes, so that the away-from-homes had the fun of redirecting the letters to the proper person. While he wanted them to follow their various careers, he missed them keenly, even to the point of frequent tears. Terry, who stayed home with the girls and young Jack, once inquired of his father the reason for his silent tears. "I miss my family," was the brief reply. He was also fiercely defensive of his children, once dunking a man in a horse trough when the man dared to administer a kick to one his sons who brought his bike too close. Many years later in a CBC interview about Cardinal Flahiff, Sister Margaret Flahiff made a moving statement: "I have come to realize over the years that the qualities I admire in my brothers are the qualities I admired in my father."[10]

George entered Paris High School in 1917. He consistently led his class and did so with ease and modesty. The *Paris Star* of 25 April 1919 reported a prize essay on the Victory Loan written by George Flahiff, and made a prophecy about this young Parisian "going far."[11] There also survives from the same year a bronze medal for excellence in rifle drill inscribed with George's name. Perhaps because he discerned signs of religious vocation in his son, and likely urged on by the pastor of the parish, Monsignor Cassidy, John Flahiff decided to send George to St Jerome's College in Kitchener when he passed into what used to be called Fourth Form. Probably he wanted to give his son a wider experience or a religious environment or both. At St Jerome's Flahiff was awarded the Motz Gold Medal for excellence in English Literature. But young George was dreadfully lonely away from his family and remained at St Jerome's only one year. Of course there were financial considerations as the hotel business was declining, and it was only the theatre which John Flahiff built onto his hotel, and opened in 1919, that kept the family afloat. No doubt the boys bore some of the burden with summer jobs, and by helping in the hotel, which they all did, taking their turns at bar-tending in the popular beverage room of the New Royal.[12]

George did his senior matriculation back in Paris, and in the fall of 1922 went to Toronto to be enrolled at St Michael's College in the University of Toronto. This was what his father wanted. The two older boys had already left, Edward to study medicine in Toronto, while living at the Newman Club on St George Street, and Norman to join the Canadian Bank of Commerce. This left Terry, the three girls, and Jack at home, to live through the hard times of the declining hotel business of the 1920s, the onset of the depression in 1929, the death of John James Flahiff in 1930, the selling of the hotel in 1931, and the struggle with poverty during the following years. It was Terry who postponed his education to sustain his father, his sisters, and younger brother. Edward and Norman sent money home to help the family during those difficult years. George appears to have been favoured, for he was supported by the family during the time of his studies in Toronto, and later by his religious community. He did not directly experience the financial difficulties other members knew, though he was aware of the situation. Of course, all the family were proud of George and happy with his vocation.

After George left his home town at the age of sixteen, he would return only for the summer holidays during his university years, and after that, only rarely. To the great joy and pride of all the people of Paris, he would come back in 1961 when he visited as archbishop, and again in 1969 after being named cardinal. Despite the rarity of his visits, he liked to drive there in his retirement years, just to recall his happy youth. He was proud to be from Paris and from the Diocese of Hamilton, and never missed a chance to say or show as much, should the occasion present itself, consistently with his loyalty to friends and to memories.

Paris, Ontario, and the early years of his life, were for George Flahiff the source of those things which he loved most: his family and his faith, the things which formed him deeply. He was ever conscious of what he had received in these two gifts and no achievement or honour in his lifetime ever meant so much to him as did they. Those who knew and loved him perceived that these were the things that made him, and that family and faith were the basis of whatever else was admirable in the man who came to occupy positions of leadership and dignity, but who is remembered chiefly for being a wonderfully *human* human being.

CHAPTER TWO

The Mind and the Heart

When George Flahiff went up to St Michael's College in the University of Toronto in September 1922, he was not yet seventeen years of age. He was consistently a bit under the average age of his peers at the various stages of his life, finishing grade school at age eleven, five years of high school at sixteen, and graduating from university with an honours BA at twenty. But the sixteen-year-old who began university was already tall and well built. He was full of face, not yet characterized by the somewhat long countenance of later years which gave him a slightly ascetic look. His hair was dark, slicked down, and neatly parted on the left side. He had striking blue eyes, which added greatly to his attractiveness to women, eyes which would maintain their clarity and their colour to the day of his death. Pictures of him taken during his university years show a mild expression, slightly shy, but not fearful. Though younger than his peers, he knew his own ability and was endowed with the social graces both by nature and by his upbringing. He was reassured in his new environment by the presence of his older brother, Edward Flahiff, the eldest of the family, who was enrolled in the Faculty of Medicine at the university. George visited him regularly at the Newman Club on St George Street where Edward was staying.

Young George does not seem to have come to the university with any fixed idea about his career. He was interested in study, *very* interested in sports, and was looking forward to university life as an adventure. He certainly did not know or even dream of the remarkable life that lay ahead of him, nor where the decisions he would take in the next few years would lead. The first of these decisions was the choice of courses. He could not have done better, even had he known the future, than he did by choosing Honours English and History. He was following his tastes and continuing in the areas of study in which he had excelled in high school. He was also fostering his natural catholicity of mind. His academic record indicates that in his first year he enrolled in both English and History, and Philosophy, English, and History.[1] In subsequent years his record indicates English and History only. During his four years at the university, Flahiff took six courses in history, four in English, three in religious knowledge, three in French, two in Latin, one in philosophy, and one in Greek. Physical training was obligatory, but for him it was pure enjoyment.

Flahiff came into contact with some outstanding men at the university. One of these was Father Henry Carr (1880–1963), Superior of St Michael's College and Professor of Philosophy when Flahiff arrived there. Carr was a man of ideas and convictions whose intellectual curiosity and unorthodox views stimulated others. He was responsible for the federation of St Michael's College with the University of Toronto in 1906 and influential in the renewal of the Basilian Congregation which began in 1922. He was Flahiff's superior in the seminary for one year (1927–8) and in 1930 he was elected superior general of the Basilian Congregation. Flahiff caught from Carr an excitement for ideas and a passion for excellence in education. Much of Flahiff's later work and writing in education bore the stamp of Henry Carr, the most outstanding educator the Basilians have produced and the one who has had the most influence on education on a national level.[2]

Another Basilian priest who had considerable influence on Flahiff was Father Edmund McCorkell (1891–1980), a personality quite different from Carr, but someone who was congenial to Flahiff for his literary knowledge and interests, and for his sensitivity to the beauty and what one might call the glory of literature. McCorkell was an excellent speaker as well as an outstanding teacher. He became superior of St Michael's in 1925 and thus was in that position during the last three years of Flahiff's stay at St Michael's. It was McCorkell to whom Flahiff spoke about his interest in the priesthood, and it was he who suggested to Flahiff that he consider the Basilians. McCorkell succeeded Carr as superior general in 1942, and Flahiff would succeed McCorkell in that same office in 1954.[3]

Among the professors whom Flahiff encountered at the university, was Lester B. Pearson, the future prime minister. As Flahiff's tutor in history, Pearson perceived the talents and the potential of his student and suggested to him that he consider a career in diplomacy. Years later when Cardinal Flahiff heard of Pearson's death in 1972, he commented: "I did admire that man and my feelings toward him were always warm. I had seen him with a certain frequency over the years and I cannot recall any least unpleasantness from student days on. I have rarely met a man whose good humour and integrity impressed me more. May he rest in peace!"[4]

University life was not all books; Flahiff managed a nice balance between studies and non-academic activities, which might have tipped slightly in favour of the latter. He excelled as an athlete, and was sought after for football and hockey. Twice (in 1924 and in 1925) he played for the St Michael's Intercollegiate Intermediate Championship football team, which won the Shaw Trophy and came within an ace of winning the Dominion Championship in 1925. He played hockey for the St Michael's Junior A team in the Ontario Hockey Association, distinguishing himself in speed and team play. He rarely body-checked; he relied on his skating skill, his speed, and his stickhandling – in a word, on the art of the game – rather than on the advantage of weight and size. Whatever the sport, he played exceptionally well. A silver medal in the Basilian Archives attests that he was a member of a championship softball team, probably in Paris, Ontario, in the summer of 1925. It is reported that during vacation time one year he took up tennis. He was a learner in June and champion of the club in August. It is also reported that the first time he went out for golf he lost the ball he had hit. Incredibly, the ball was found in the hole. Skill or accident, it was nevertheless a hole-in-one first time out.

Along with his participation in sports went his participation in literary and cultural activities at St Michael's and within the university at large. During all four years of his course he was on the staff of the St Michael's College *Year Book*, and in his last year he was on the board of editors of the *Torontonensis*, the university yearbook. At St Michael's he was librarian of the Historical Society for one year and secretary of the Literary Club, also for one year. Twice he was a member of the Students' Parliament, once as "Minister for Jewish Affairs" and once as "Minister of Education." This group was a mock parliament which would discuss current events, echoing or criticizing or parodying the federal parliament. For the last two years of his course he was a member of a rather exclusive club at St Michael's known as "Quindecim" and limited to fifteen members. This also was a forum for political discussions, though of a more serious kind. In his last year he was a member of the Library Committee at Hart House as well as a member of the Oratorical Club at St Michael's. He developed considerable forensic ability, winning in his final year the gold medal for oratory sponsored by the Newman Club, a prize his brother Edward had won two years previously.

St Michael's College championship football team, 1925. Twelve members of this team became Basilian priests. (St Michael's College *Year Book*, 1926)

Not surprisingly, Flahiff was popular with women. He had it all: looks, charm, intelligence, achievement, athletic prowess, affability, and goodness. The only thing he lacked was an abundance of money. He was a superb dancer, had no trouble finding partners, and loved to dance. One young lady whom Flahiff had dated on several occasions remarked on his decision to go into religious life: "What a waste of a good pair of dancing feet!" The girls would vie with one another to put his jacket over his shoulders when he came back to the bench during a hockey or football game. Doubtless he enjoyed the popularity as he enjoyed the social life; he was welcome in any gathering. His decision to go to the Basilian novitiate was a disappointment to some. Hoping to see him back in Paris, one girl from the home town asked David Tough, Flahiff's boyhood friend, about George's plans after graduation, only to be told that he was going to enter religious life. "That's the trouble with Catholic boys," commented the young lady, "they are either in the seminary or in the cemetery." Doubtless she was thinking of those eligible young men who had not returned from the war.

Flahiff's contemporaries among the students at the university, some of whom were good friends, include notable names. One of these, a fellow athlete and companion at St Michael's, was David Trottier who made a name for himself as a hockey star.[5] Another was Morley Callaghan (1903–90) who became one of the best-known Canadian writers, and who maintained his friendship with Flahiff through the years. Paul Martin (1903–92), who distinguished himself in Canadian politics, was also Flahiff's good friend from university days. Probably Flahiff's closest friend and the one who accompanied him into religious life was Terence McLaughlin (1903–70) from St Andrew's, Ontario, of whom we shall have more to say later. McLaughlin died prematurely in 1970. In the passing of this close companion, Flahiff felt that something of himself had died.[6]

Flahiff's academic record at the university is not outstanding. He obtained first-class honours only in his first year, ranking second among the firsts. He obtained second-class honours in the three subsequent years, ranking fifth, tenth, and seventh respectively among the seconds. In two particular courses he fell to third-class honours. The results seem not to be an indication of his talents, if one considers the brilliance he showed in his graduate studies and in later life. But seen in the light of his youth, his remarkable athletic record at the university, and his participation in university life in all its dimensions, his academic results reflect a balance of interests and attitudes which went to form the well-rounded man he became.

The playful blurb which accompanied his graduation picture in the *Torontonensis* of 1926 reads as follows: "George B. Flahiff – 'Clever, consistent and congenial, too.' Oct. 26, 1905 – Paris, Ont., puts George on the map. 1922–1926 – George reciprocates. Intermediate rugby. O.H.A. hockey – playing and managing – Hart House committees. *Year Book* and *Torontonensis* editing, all helped. Works hard, plays hard – and enjoys both. Takes as much fun out of English and History as at Columbus and the Hipp. Nuff sed!" Indeed enough said to characterize the young man very well, though not completely. "Columbus" refers to Columbus Hall, run by the Knights of Columbus, on Sherbourne Street, and the locus of weekly dances, popular with the university students. "Hipp" refers to Shea's Hippodrome on Bay Street just north of Queen Street, where the new Toronto City Hall is now located, and where, in the twenties, one could enjoy vaudeville and movies. The light-hearted words of the blurb hit on the essential in Flahiff: his integrated character, his ability to enjoy the people and the world around him, his grasp of the art of being human.

What is not alluded to by his fellow students, nor would one expect it to be, is the spiritual aspiration of their young friend. During his final year at the university Flahiff was thinking about the priesthood. Judging from the surprise with which the announcement of his decision was met, he did not communicate what he was thinking to many, if to any. The atmosphere and discipline of St Michael's College at that time would have favoured thoughts and aspirations concerning the priesthood in any student so disposed: life in close association with a community of priest-professors, obligatory daily mass, and night prayers in common in the residence, with an annual retreat of three days in Holy Week. It is interesting to note with regard to the championship football team on which Flahiff played in the fall of 1925 that twelve of the twenty-two players became Basilian priests. Thus he was in no way odd man out, but rather one moved by his circumstances and his friends.

Sometime in the early months of 1926 Flahiff approached Father McCorkell, then superior of St Michael's[7] and inquired about application to St Augustine's Seminary in the Archdiocese of Toronto. His original intention, it seems, was to enter the secular priesthood and give his life to parish ministry. He had great admiration and affection for his parish priest in Paris, Monsignor Cassidy, and very likely associated vocation to the priesthood with his pastor rather than with his professors, the Basilians. He admitted some years later that when he first came to St Michael's he thought he was meeting the "Brazilian Fathers," and he wondered why there were no tawny-skinned persons among them.[8]

Father McCorkell gave him the information he wished. Then, in what seemed like an off-hand suggestion, but which was probably fathered by an ardent wish, he asked young Flahiff whether he had ever thought of the Basilian Fathers. What conversation ensued is not known. The upshot was that George did not apply to the archdiocesan seminary. Instead, he made application for the novitiate of the Basilian Fathers. McCorkell, and probably a good number of the Basilians, knew that Flahiff's talents would find their scope more fully in religious life and in a teaching community.

Though Flahiff could hardly have been aware of the fact, the Basilian Fathers at this time were undergoing a kind of renaissance. The year 1922 had seen the separation of the Basilians in North America from the Basilians in France. At the request of the French confreres, Rome had set up two distinct congregations, one in France, and one in North America with headquarters in Toronto. There was concomitantly a tightening of structures with regard to religious life itself, the Canadian and American branch opting for more rigid adherence to the norms of Canon Law for Religious, as stated in the *Code of Canon Law* of 1917. One of the results of these developments among the Basilians in Canada was a marked increase in the number of new members. The year Flahiff went to the novitiate twenty-seven young men entered, of whom fifteen persevered to the priesthood as Basilians. Up to that time this was the

largest class ever to enter the congregation. It was the first of consistently large classes of novices which were to follow during the next four
decades. The future superior general joined the Basilians at the beginning of what might be called the golden age of the congregation's
growth in numbers. He would temporarily leave the congregation to
take up the duties of archbishop in 1961 on the eve of the Basilians' precipitous decline in numbers in the 1960s.

St Basil's Novitiate in Toronto was situated on Kendal (now
Tweedsmuir) Avenue just north of St Clair. Dating from 1892, the
building contained a large chapel which filled the whole of the
ground floor, with three floors of residence above. The dining room
and kitchen jutted out from the back of the building. Behind the novitiate was a generous section of the Spadina ravine, which provided
good walks in all seasons. A few acres near the building had been levelled for a baseball diamond and vegetable garden, thus providing
both play and work for the novices. The area was not so built up as it
is today; there was a certain country atmosphere about the place.

Life in the novitiate was frugal and strictly ordered: silence for
most hours of the day, prayer, classes in scripture and spirituality,
manual labour, and private study. For one aspiring to the religious
life the novitiate was intended to be a time of trial and discernment; it
was not intended to be easy. But the schedule also included sports,
long walks twice a week, and the comic relief which might naturally
develop among a group of young men whose high-mindedness did
not exclude high jinks. Visits from one's family were allowed once a
month, except in Advent and Lent when no visiting was allowed.
Flahiff found himself with a good number of his friends, and those
who were not yet his friends quickly became so. A group picture
taken at the end of the year shows a tall, slim George Flahiff, with a
good head of wavy hair which he was destined soon to lose. His
expression is just on the edge of a smile, though he has lost the fullness of face that is observed in the team photographs of his university
years.

The master of novices was Father Wilfrid Clarence Sharpe (1891–
1976), at that time thirty-five years of age, a man of cultivated manners and prayerful habits. Sharpe was a classics scholar as well as an
ardent baseball player. It was said of him that he considered himself a
mediocre classicist and an excellent second baseman. In reality, it was
just the other way round. He was probably the best classicist among
the Basilians at that time, having done his studies at the University of
Toronto and at the Catholic University of America in Washington. He
was also an accomplished pianist and an enthusiast for comic opera,

knowing scores, actors and actresses, dates of composition of the various works, and the merits of each. Even into old age he had a prodigious memory for baseball players, games, scores, and memorable moments in sports. His pedagogy of example and encouragement rather than of obligation and compulsion, and his interest in sports and music, would have set up sympathetic vibrations in Flahiff, who was fortunate to be under the direction of this wise and good man at the beginning of his religious life.[9]

The novitiate year ended with the profession of first temporary vows on 30 September 1927. Flahiff was appointed to St Basil's Seminary at 21 St Mary Street in Toronto, for theological studies. It was customary in those days to combine theological studies with some teaching and pedagogical training. The theology classes were given in the early morning and in the late afternoon. During his theological studies Flahiff taught high-school English at St Michael's College School on Bay Street, probably two or three periods a day. He also attended classes at the Ontario College of Education and obtained his teaching certification. One wonders about the wisdom of this kind of crowded schedule, which might tend to produce mediocre results in all areas of activity. The system was ultimately abandoned by the Basilian Fathers in favour of more concentrated attention to theology. But Flahiff seems to have met the challenges with equanimity and success. Father Louis Bondy (1894–1985),[10] superior of the seminary at the time, and a person who had a great influence on Flahiff, recommended him for graduate studies in theology, hoping to make use of his fine intelligence and obvious seriousness in religious life to bolster the seminary staff. There were other plans afoot, however, which would set him on a different course.

With the founding of the Institute of Mediaeval Studies in 1929, the Basilian Fathers selected a group of younger members to be sent on graduate studies with a view to constituting a qualified staff for the new venture. Flahiff was one of those chosen.[11] His theological studies were shortened to three years instead of the usual four which necessitated a dispensation from Rome for his ordination to the priesthood. With his good friend Terry McLaughlin, Flahiff was ordained on Sunday, 17 August 1930, in St Basil's Church, Toronto, by the Most Reverend Neil McNeil, Archbishop of Toronto. His family were present in force, his father getting out of his hospital bed to witness the event which meant so much to him. A week later Flahiff went down to Paris to say his first mass. When the young priest entered his father's room at the hotel, the dying man insisted on rising from his bed and standing to receive his newly ordained son. In spite of his critical condition, John Flahiff also attended the first mass. It was a time of keen emotion for both of them: of happiness in the ordination, and of sadness in the knowlege of parting very soon, the young man for a new life of studies in another country, the older man for a new life in another world.

This was the only shadow on an otherwise joyous occasion, for all Paris rejoiced with the Flahiffs. Even Mrs Tough, a staunch Presbyterian but a life-long friend of the family, found it in her heart to swallow her prejudices sufficiently to attend the first mass – in a Catholic church! Everyone was immensely proud of George. The financial straits of the family were forgotten for the moment. A few days after the celebrations in Paris, Flahiff set out with his brother Terry by car for Toronto. It was a custom among the Flahiffs to stop on the hill going out of town to wave a last time before continuing on their way. George said to Terry as they got into the car: "Don't forget to stop." Then as he stepped out of the car and looked back he saw the curtain of his father's room drawn back and his father half hidden behind it. He waved once more then got back into the car mumbling "Our Father," in prayer or from emotion, Terry was not sure. One month later, as he was settling into his new residence in Strasbourg, Flahiff received a telegram from his brother which read simply: "Dad died this morning."

CHAPTER THREE

A Parisian in Paris

Though Flahiff's study venture in Europe began under the shadow of his father's death, it was to be a time of adventure and enrichment for the young priest. He was not yet twenty-five when he set out for Strasbourg with his classmate and good friend, Terry McLaughlin. Professor Gilson[1] had directed him to go to the university there, because of his own attachment to a place where he had taught, because of persons there who would be of great help to the two future professors, and because of the growing reputation of the University of Strasbourg as one of the leading schools of Europe. The university had been founded in the previous century when Alsace was under the domination of Germany. After the First World War, which brought Alsace back to France, the French government had made considerable effort to affirm its influence in Strasbourg, and considerable attention had been given to the development of the university. An added attraction was the particular beauty of the university buildings.

Thus Flahiff found himself in congenial surroundings with a purpose and a challenge. He was enthused about the adventure of the new Institute of Mediaeval Studies being established in Toronto and pleased to be a part of it.[2] He would, of course, like any young person who is sent away to study, undergo the usual trials of loneliness, separation from his religious community and his friends, and distance from his family. This last was particularly keen for him, especially at the beginning when he could not be with his brothers and sisters in the sorrow of their father's death. He knew it would be a long time before he would return to Canada. He does not seem, however, to have been daunted at the prospect of what he was beginning, nor to have flagged during the years of his studies. We do not have any of his letters from this time. One can only surmise from his lecture notes, from some personal notes, and from his success, that it was a peaceful and enriching time for him.

The first thing that strikes one about the young priest-student at this time is his facility with languages. His notes taken in class reveal that he is soon at ease with Latin, French, German, and Greek. He would have had an introduction to these in earlier studies, of course. Latin he would have first met as an altar boy, giving the responses to the priest at mass and hearing the liturgy celebrated in that language, with greater comprehension being acquired as he studied Latin in high school. Latin was also much used and much demanded during his seminary years, when theology texts were studied in that language. French he would have had from high school, from university, and from the familiarity with French that any interested Canadian enjoys. German and Greek would have come in smaller doses from his university and theological studies. But knowing a language is one thing; using it is another. Flahiff soon acquired the ability to read, write, and speak French, German, and Latin. Facility in Italian was to come somewhat later with his numerous visits to Rome and the need to read documents in Italian and deal with the members of the Roman Curia, where Italian was the lingua franca. Flahiff obviously had a gift for languages and was placed in circumstances where he could learn and perfect them.

French, of course, was the predominant language in his studies. He obviously subjected himself to a rigid discipline in leaving aside his native English to speak and write as much as he could in French. He and McLaughlin took on the services of a tutor, and they covenanted to speak only French to each other. Flahiff took his lecture notes in French, and did so in complete sentences, carefully verifying and correcting them afterwards. He acquired not only facility and correctness in French, but also eloquence. He loved the language, which made the acquiring of it that much easier. His facility in French would serve him in good stead, especially as Archbishop of Winnipeg, where the French-speaking element was considerable. French was necessary, too, in his work with the Canadian Conference of Catholic Bishops (cccb), and in his international dealings. He spoke and corresponded readily in French, although he ultimately distrusted his ability to speak correctly, and in his later years he would answer letters written in French in English, from a quite unfounded fear of making a mistake and thereby offending his correspondent.

His hand-written lecture notes, taken during his courses in both Strasbourg and Paris, which he preserved carefully and which still exist, are remarkable for their clarity, their order, and their complete-

George Flahiff during studies in Strasbourg, a photo taken
on Sunday, 8 February 1931. (Basilian Archives, Toronto)

ness. They could be printed as they stand and would serve as splendid
texts. They represent painstaking hours of work. Flahiff obviously
took pleasure in writing. He made it a work of art, at times even deco-
rating or illustrating his text. His writing is a pleasure to read, not only
for the substance, but for the splendid calligraphy. This gift accompanied him into old age. The marvellous evenness of his hand-writing
diminished with time but the clarity was never lost.

According to the plans that Professor Gilson had worked out with
the Basilians for the staffing of the Institute, Flahiff was intended to
teach mediaeval history. No one at that time could know how valuable the courses he took in history and canon law would be for his future work, but there would be few among his contemporaries who
would have so rich a background for understanding the Church
through the ages and the Church in the modern world.

After one year at the University of Strasbourg, Flahiff moved to
Paris to enrol in the École des Chartes. This institution was the best to
be found for the study of mediaeval writings of all kinds: charters,
wills, treaties, treatises, commentaries, business transactions, and literature. It was the focus of the history of the Middle Ages, the place

where one could find access to the rich deposit of this knowledge as
well as method for its acquisition. The standards were high and the
course of study demanding. Flahiff himself describes the school some
years later to the editor of *Liturgical Arts*, a journal out of New York to
which Flahiff contributed from time to time. Flahiff's pride in his
place of study is evident:

As to the École des Chartes, I was there from 1931 to 1935, graduating in the
latter year. As you are undoubtedly aware, it is a special school founded by
the French government in 1821 for the training of mediaeval research scholars, and many of the French mediaevalists, as well as some in Austria and
Germany have been among its products ... The École was founded for the express purpose of carrying on the work of the great Benedictine scholars of the
School of St. Maur at St. Germain-des-Prés in Paris, which had been inter-
rupted by the Revolution. Directly inspired by their traditions, the École has
always regarded itself, and has been regarded as the lineal descendant of the
monks like Mabillon, Montfaucon and many others, who, for well more than
a century did that great pioneering work which more than any other contribution has made possible the critical historical scholarship of modern times.[3]

Flahiff's scholarly habits and tastes found full scope in the program
of the École, and he was sustained by the thought of his future participation in the work of the Institute in Toronto. Gilson must have
struck all the right cords in outlining for his protégé the path of his
studies and his destiny as professor. As time went on, there developed a great bond of friendship between the two men, something
that went beyond mere common interest in study. It was a spiritual
relationship based on a love of the Church, which they both desired
to serve, and a love of learning itself.

One of the courses which Flahiff took at the École was the *Explication de Textes*, a rather banal title for something which involved much
more than a mere "explanation" of a text. This course, an integral
part of French education from quite early grades, and honed to a fine
art in the lycées and universities, involves the minute and thorough
examination of a text of philosophy, theology, history, or literature,
from every possible point of view: subject, author, content, context,
origin, meaning, relation, implications, diction, nuance, imagery, syntax, and so on. The text need not be long, sometimes just a paragraph.
The idea is that by concentrating on one small selection of an author's
work one may obtain an appreciation of the whole. It is a remarkable
discipline and a valuable one, though some find fault with it for being so analytic as to compromise synthesis. Be that as it may, there is

no doubt that the analytic approach of the *Explication de Textes* is an invaluable training for any scholar. Flahiff was one who benefited immensely from this practice. His manner of scholarship, of teaching, of examining documents, of explaining texts, all show clear evidence of sharp and thorough analysis. Whenever he wrote or spoke as he moved on to the different phases of his life, the effect of this scholarly training was evident. Details rarely escaped him. And, happily in his case, he never left the body dissected, but always returned it to its beauty as a whole, better understood and appreciated for having been seen in its parts. We shall see some examples of this, particularly in his work as professor and as bishop.

This rigid training in analysis and perception had another effect. It worked to make Flahiff a careful and painstaking writer. He wrote well, and with seeming ease, but the end product, when it came, was the result of a good deal of revision, restating, re-wording, and nuancing, to communicate the exact meaning he desired. Each rough draft is a jungle of crossings-out, insertions in tiny handwriting, insertions in the insertions, to the point where one wonders how any secretary could possibly make a fair copy of his labyrinthine text. The final draft, the fruit of sometimes agonizing revision, bears no trace of the cuts and the seams, but is fresh and fluid.

During the course of his studies in France, Flahiff made one or more visits to England and did some reading in the British Museum Library in London. We know he was there in March and April of 1934, for we have his book requisition slips, which he used as folders for the jottings he did on small slips of paper. This manner of note-taking became a habit in his casual reading, and it is this habit that has provided us with a collection of random thoughts, or quotes, or jokes, in various languages. Sometimes such slips of paper contain a summary of a part of a book, with the reference noted. At times, however, it is hard to know whether Flahiff the scholar is quoting directly from the book or paraphrasing or going off on his own reflections inspired by the text he is reading. Whatever the case, these myriad slips are interesting and valuable for the light they throw on his thoughts and his tastes. They are written in a tiny hand but they are always legible.

From these slips we know that he was thinking a good deal about his future teaching at the Institute in Toronto. He was reading books on the teaching of history[4] and finding ideas for his own formation. One of his notes is headed "Objectivity," and in it he is either quoting or paraphrasing one of his authors. The note reads in part: "*Method for ecclesiastical historian – objectivity … The historian's business is sim-*

ply to tell what happened; to narrate and describe facts. He must not be too
ambitious or claim too much for his subject. He is rather the provider
of material for the theologian, than the theologian. *He is not so much
the judge, as the witness.* When he deals with opinions it is *not his primary business to say whether the opinions are right or wrong* ... (Tout,
Study of Eccl. Hist. p. 9)." The note goes on, with its underlinings
here and there, to posit the respect and sympathy one should have for
the opinions of others, stating that we shall never appreciate the
views of the Albigensians or Manichaeans of the twelfth and thirteenth centuries by calling them fools. Here we have an early illustration of Flahiff's essentially irenic and generous mentality. His mind
and manner were deeply imbued with openness to and sympathy for
the opinions of others, whether in the realm of scholarship, teaching,
administration, or pastoral care. A clear effort at objectivity characterized all he said and wrote. Prejudice, intolerance, or rash judgment
were alien to his nature.

Gilson, who was monitoring Flahiff's studies as he was those of the
other young Basilian graduate students, had arranged for him to get
in touch with Professor (later Sir) Frederick Maurice Powicke, then
Regius Professor of History at Oxford University, and a leading
British scholar of the Middle Ages at that time. We do not know the
exact nature of his association with the eminent professor, whether it
was in conversations or in written submissions or seminars, nor the
frequency of their meetings. Nevertheless, Flahiff seems to have received a good deal from Powicke, whose "main efforts, and nearly all
his influence, lay in the congenial work of inspiring and guiding
young medieval historians. For this he had an exceptional gift which
arose mainly from his power of conveying a tremulous [*sic*] sense of
the significance and manifold ramifications of often quite obscure
events ... His foremost quality was insight: he illuminated rather
than explained; suggested rather than resolved ... Powicke encouraged pupils on to their own course in their own way, while remaining
himself the most important single influence in their work."[5] This description could be that of Flahiff the teacher in the years to follow. He
certainly found in the great British scholar a kindred spirit. What was
important to both men in education was the person. An admirable
personalism was consistently operative in Flahiff's teaching, writing,
and administration throughout his life.

As was expected of him as a student of art and history, Flahiff did
some travelling within France, chiefly to study architecture. We have
an account of only of these trips, which he took alone in central
France, and of which he wrote a short diary of three days. The admi-

rable transportation system in France made it possible for Flahiff to move quickly and to see more than one town in one day. He set out southward from Paris, beginning his account at Bourges, where his chief interest was the cathedral which he found "extremely interesting," then commented: "No use trying to describe it: there are books for that. The stained glass is a real museum of the art (13th c. & 15th c. especially). The sculpture is also fine, the 2 side portals presenting splendid examples of Romanesque sculpture. The crypt is large & airy except for the old part dating back to the 9th c. (caveau des archevêques.) One of the capitals of the 12th c. crypt is quite unique: a rear view I have never before seen in iconography." Then he visited Charité-sur-Loire and Nevers, where he spent more time and made more commentary. He went on to Moulins and Vichy (only to see the famous resort), to Riom, and finally to Clermond-Ferrand where the brief account ends. In each place it is chiefly the architecture of the houses and churches that interests him. In Riom, a town just outside Clermont, he gives us a glimpse of his talent for observation and description: "For some time I stood and gazed at the statue of Our Lady before the 'Eglise du Marthuret' – one of the most pleasing I know with the Infant Jesus playing with a bird and the mother regarding him with tenderness and a certain tolerance. A slow smile plays on her face at certain angles. The child's expression is curious: satisfaction, glee, etc. As you pass from one side to another, as you advance or retreat, the expression on the two faces & their relations to one another seem to vary. – I find in this statue all the charm & the variety of a Mona Lisa."[6]

This visit to a few towns in central France took place in March of 1935. We can see from his reactions and terminology that Flahiff had acquired a good deal of knowledge and appreciation of art. He was laying the groundwork for the inspiring classes in art which he would give in his professorial years. All his life art was a source of great interest and joy to him; he was ever alert to beauty in the world around him, in buildings, streets, clothing, people, or the sound of a voice. Sister Irene McDonald, who tended Cardinal Flahiff in the final months of his life, recalls how when she took him out in the wheelchair around the university area in Toronto of an afternoon or evening, he would draw her attention to various features of the houses and university buildings. He always spoke self-deprecatingly when it came to criticism of art, considering himself but an amateur. This indeed he was in the root sense of the word, because he loved his subject, and his love took him beyond the rigidity of professionalism to great freedom in his enjoyment of the world.

His travels were not limited to England and France. In the course of his time in Europe he visited Germany, Italy, and probably Spain as well, though concrete evidence for this last is lacking. It was the desire of his Basilian superiors that he visit these places, for research in his particular fields of study, and for general enrichment. From time to time, there were gatherings of the Basilian graduate students in Rome, and there were visits by Basilians, one to another, in their various places of study in Europe. David Tough, one of Flahiff's boyhood friends, visited him at least twice, once in Paris, and once in Munich. What impressed Tough was the poverty of Flahiff's surroundings. The Basilian students lived frugally, in the spirit of religious poverty which they had vowed. Moreover, there was little money for their support in the economically depressed years of the early 1930s.

Flahiff finished his studies brilliantly at the École des Chartes, being awarded the rare and difficult "Diplôme d'archiviste-paléographe" by that institution. He kept in contact with the professors and staff of the École; in later years they would refer to him as "Our Cardinal." France had marked him deeply and for life. He came away with a great respect and abiding love for France, and he always enjoyed returning there. He appreciated the richness of French history, the contribution of France to the Church and to the civilization of Europe, and the profundity and precision of French thought. He studied French spiritual authors in preference to others, and much of his spiritual direction was inspired by French spirituality. He also became a connoisseur of French cuisine and French wines. Someone once remarked that the spirit of France and the spirits of France found a happy harmony in George Flahiff.

One day, as he enjoyed recounting in later years, Flahiff, the young student-priest from Canada, found himself at a gathering of people from the academic world in Paris. A certain woman asked the young foreigner where he was born. "I was born, Madame, in Paris ... Ontario." The woman, intrigued at the possibility of another Paris in the world, asked what the population was of Paris, Ontario. When Flahiff replied, "About 4,500," she exclaimed, "Quelle présomption!" What presumption, indeed, to give so prestigious a name to so insignificant a town. The woman might have been even more indignant had she known that Paris, Ontario, was not named for the City of Light, but for the deposits of gypsum found there which produced plaster of Paris and supported the town. Far from taking any offence, the small-town Ontario boy was delighted with the coincidence, as well as with the reaction of *la française*. If one Paris had made the boy, the other had made the man. He knew what he owed to each, and he was at home in both.

CHAPTER FOUR

Professor and Pastor

The University of Toronto, to which George Flahiff returned in the summer of 1935, was a much smaller and more closely knit institution than the one we know today. In that year it enrolled some 7,984 students in its classes, libraries, colleges, and laboratories, that is to say, slightly less than one-fifth of the number it now has on the St George campus.[1] In 1935 it was much easier to know the whole institution and to know the professors, even of departments and colleges widely different from one's own field of study or teaching. The word "specialization" characterizes contemporary learning, the necessary consequence of the knowledge explosion of our times. "Generalization" prevailed in the thinking of previous generations, and both students and teachers benefited from the easy inter-disciplinary atmosphere of the university. The fact that the university was so small favoured this familial or club-like atmosphere, which respected the specialist but cherished the values of broad culture as essential to the educated person. Flahiff was a graduate of one of the best examples of a general culture course: "English and History." That program not only formed a student in several disciplines but brought the student into different parts of the campus and into contact with professors in a number of colleges.

The Institute of Mediaeval Studies on the campus of St Michael's College, where Flahiff was to spend the next nineteen years of his life as professor and administrator, had been received into the ambit of the University of Toronto in 1929. It was seen as a centre of research and instruction which would enrich this larger university complex, even though it specialized in the investigation of but one area of study, the Middle Ages. It was another component of the system of federated colleges, pioneered in Toronto, which had successfully fostered cooperation and mutual benefit among institutions of higher learning of various persuasions. Though the institute was not another federated college – there are only three of these – it was born of the same spirit of enrichment by diversity. This was very much the thinking of Gilson and Carr, and of the young professors who formed that first teaching body in 1935.

Flahiff was twenty-nine, in excellent health, highly qualified as a professor with a diploma from the École des Chartes – a qualification which few in Canada possessed at the time. He was pleased to be back in the familiar surroundings of the University of Toronto, with an interesting and challenging career ahead of him. He brought to the campus good teaching, the charm of his appearance and manner, his interest in people, in sports, and in the life of the university, generosity with his time, and deep spirituality. If there were ever a man fitted to his environment, it was he. Colleagues in the university were pleased and even honoured to have him at meetings, not only for his balanced opinions, but also for his friendly and unpretentious manner. He was, of course, one of theirs, a product of the University of Toronto itself, and one whose reputation as a splendid athlete was still alive.

He plunged into a busy schedule. He knew the high standards upon which the institute insisted, and he was an ardent supporter of them. Although he was fresh from his courses in history and art, there was still the important work of organizing his material for presentation to his students. Flahiff had an absolute horror of being unprepared for a lecture, a talk, indeed for an event of any kind. This passion for preparedness was to cause him some annoyance later on when dealing with the Roman Curia, or with persons who had invited him for a lecture or a liturgical event, and who were casual or remiss in sending him the information which he considered necessary and which they had promised. Flahiff could acquit himself very well with an impromptu homily or talk if necessary, but when possible he would always prepare his class or his talk with care, and he reworked speeches or articles for weeks before he thought them satisfactory. So too with meetings he was to attend: he insisted on having the material of the agenda well ahead of time for his careful perusal.

In addition to the demands of lectures and meetings, a great deal of his time was given to students. Flahiff kept his office door open and received all comers. If he were writing when someone knocked, he would finish the sentence before he raised his eyes. Then, however, the person received his full attention, and he gave all the time needed. He would not be the one to put an end to the visit. Nor was his time given only to his own students. Two young Basilians, just beginning their university courses in the late 1940s, tell how, after their first taste of a history lec-

Professor George Flahiff, Pontifical Institute of Mediaeval
Studies, Toronto, 1945. (Basilian Archives, Toronto)

ture at the university, they were sharing their confusion and dismay as
they returned across Queen's Park, wondering whether they would be
able to follow the professor, to meet his standards – in a word, whether
they would be able to "make it." One said that he had heard that there
was a priest at the Institute of Mediaeval Studies who was very good in
history. They did not even know his name but they went in and asked
for "the history professor." Flahiff received them, diagnosed in a very
short time the common problem of freshman jitters, and chatted with
them for a full hour. He gave them a good general outline of their
course, an idea of the expectations of their professor (whom Flahiff no
doubt knew personally), some hints on how to study, but most memorable of all, an experience of his kindness and interest. Finally he excused
himself, though he did not tell the reason: the ambassador of France was
outside in a limousine with a police escort, waiting to see Flahiff. The
two young Basilians left walking on air, far more impressed by the man
than by what he had said.[2] Many an example of Flahiff's universal kindness matched this one. Former students remember his particular consideration of a blind student whom he assisted with exquisite tact.

But there were extra-curricular activities as well, some of which demanded a good deal of time and effort. One of these was known as "Sunday work," going out into a parish on Saturday or Sunday to hear confessions, to say mass, and to preach. Some of the assignments were as far as two hundred miles distant, which involved taking a train on Saturday, a good deal of ministry on both Saturday evening and Sunday morning, with the return trip on Sunday afternoon. All Basilians participated in this activity. It was both a service to the diocesan clergy and a help to Basilian finances. It was of no help, however, in the preparation of lectures or in finding some leisure time on the weekends. In theory the Basilians regretted this dispersal of time and energy, especially in the case of scholars and teachers, but they found themselves compelled to continue the system for pastoral and financial reasons. Later, as superior general of the Basilians, Flahiff cautioned local superiors of houses whose members were professors to limit Sunday work as far as possible.[3] In later years, Sunday work came to be more and more restricted, partly because the demand fell off and partly through decision and effort on the part of the community authorities to defend Basilian teachers from exhaustion and consequent ill effects on classroom performance.

Another thing which took up a good deal of Flahiff's time was spiritual direction. Many people, especially women religious, sought his counsel in things spiritual. He was wise and informed, and widely read in spiritual authors, especially in contemporary French writers, who were particularly esteemed at that time. He was also keenly interested in spiritual direction, persuaded as he was of its importance for Christian life in general and for religious life in particular. Many hours of his week were given over to personal spiritual direction and counselling at the cost of his own scholarly work. He was also called upon to give retreats – to sisters, seminarians, priests, and lay people. This would involve considerable preparation and then as much as ten days of conferences and counselling. He would sometimes give four retreats of varying length in the course of a year.

Flahiff did not consider these occupations inimical either to his vocation or to his work; for him it was all of a piece. In general, his lot was not different from that of the majority of his brother Basilians who were living the same kind of life, though in Flahiff's case, calls on his time might have been greater than they were for others. He himself considered giving time to others as normal procedure for a priest and was quite willing to make the adjustments necessary to provide this sort of generosity. Others saw in these activities an intrusion into his scholarly endeavour and, while no one could say he was shirking his duty, some did think that his work as a scholar, his primary duty, was compromised by excessive pastoral preoccupations. It should be noted that this problem is not uncommon in the case of scholar-priests. There is frequently a tension between pastoral care and academic duty which in some cases has unhappy results, depending on how one sees the priorities. The problem showed up early in Flahiff's career and was never resolved during his teaching days. It found definitive resolution in his being named a bishop in 1961.

Flahiff was a conscientious and thorough teacher. His carefully ordered and very complete lecture notes bear witness to this, as do the testimonies of his students. He was also a demanding one, ever conscious of the standards to which the institute was committed and of his duty as a member of the teaching staff. One of his students recalled how serious Flahiff was in the classroom, and thought that this might have reflected the desire of the whole staff to convey the seriousness of what they were doing.[4] Habitual seriousness, however, was against his nature: Flahiff was characteristically light-hearted and ready for humour wherever it came up. One of his early students describes him in this way: "His kindness, warm friendliness and interest in the progress of his students attracted me to him. He was obviously a capable teacher who had carefully researched the material of his lectures. It was easy to trust his good judgment and the accuracy of his teaching."[5] This same early student, who went on to become a noted Basilian teacher of philosophy, goes on to say that Flahiff's scholarly approach to teaching was perhaps not what impressed his students most. He specifies other qualities: "Always a gentleman, the moral and spiritual qualities of the man came through convincingly as signs of an inner strength of character. His usual affability, too, seemed to flow from the very goodness of the man. Persons who came to know him quickly recognized the traits of saintliness in his willingness to listen and be of help in the problems of others. Religious sisters who frequented his office for advice and spiritual direction took advantage of his availability to be of service to others. I have at times speculated whether the time he spent helping others may not have prevented him from publishing more than he did." The same student also remembers being annoyed by Flahiff's habit of keeping the class five or ten minutes overtime in his zeal to cover all the work.

Flahiff possessed those qualities of imagination and enthusiasm that make a good teacher. He did not do stunts, and was nothing of a showman, but he found interesting ways to enhance and vivify what he said. One day he constructed in front of his class in art and architecture a miniature gothic vault made of small wooden blocks. One student who witnessed this remembers especially the quasi-triumph of the moment when he dropped the tiny keystone into place, and then explained the lines of force and weight.[6] On another occasion, when explaining the theology of the Blessed Virgin Mary, he took as his reference the east door of the cathedral of Chartres, and from the rich sculpture of that masterpiece, presented and explained the doctrine. Subsequently, while visiting in France, he sent a postcard of the famous door to those who had heard his talk. One who was especially impressed by the lecture stole the postcard from the bulletin board and has kept it to this day.[7] Needless to say, his courses were popular; but in many cases the medium meant more than the message.

Along with the subject matter of his lectures, two other matters preoccupied Flahiff. One was the pedagogy of history and the other was the validity of the Catholic historian. As to the first of these, we saw in the previous chapter how he had been reading on the matter of objectivity and freedom from prejudice in the historian and noting how these must characterize the good history teacher. He strove constantly to be faithful to the principles he had gleaned from reading E.J. Tout's *The Study of Ecclesiastical History* and from personal contact with the famous Professor F.M. Powicke. Nor was his objectivity confined to his teaching. As an administrator later on objectivity, fairness and deliberateness were his watchwords.

With regard to the second of these preoccupations, that is, the validity of the Catholic historian, Flahiff wrote at some length and cogently on the matter, and his thinking will be presented in a later chapter in the context of a resumé of his whole understanding of history. Suffice it to say here that he firmly believed that an historian's Catholic faith was no hindrance to his being an objective and honest historian. Faith for Flahiff was not a restricting nor perverting force but rather the agent of a wider vision.

In 1943 Flahiff was named secretary of the Pontifical Institute of Mediaeval Studies ("Pontifical" having been added since the awarding of a papal charter in 1939), an office which corresponded to that of registrar. He would interview prospective students, consider their credentials, lay out the requirements, discern the students' aptitudes and aspirations, counsel them and then, in consultation with the other professors, accept or reject them. He would go to considerable lengths to accommodate the candidates, but he would not compromise on the standards of the institute any more than he would tolerate mediocre performance or slipshod work on the part of his students. This responsibility added to his already heavy schedule. It was, however, congenial to him since he had a special affection for students. He maintained the responsibility of secretary until his election as superior general of the Basilian Fathers in 1954. During the last three years of his time at the institute, Flahiff was also superior of the Basilian community there.

Two other responsibilities fell upon Flahiff's shoulders during this period. The first of these, something which would involve greater contact with the university, was a cross-appointment in 1940 to the Department of History in the School of Graduate Studies of the University of Toronto. This meant obligations to attend meetings and to supervise some theses; it did not mean more lectures than those he was already giving at the institute. This appointment was of benefit to both sides: the department enjoyed his counsel and his sharing of thesis reading; he and the institute enjoyed the contact with colleagues across the campus.

The second of these added responsibilities, and one which was destined to change his whole life, was his election in 1948 to the General Council of the Basilian Fathers. A councillor not only deliberated with and advised the superior general in the overall government of the Basilian Fathers, but also carried out a number of official visits to the various houses of the congregation from time to time. Thus the hours of the priest-professor-scholar became yet more crowded. But he still managed to go to the odd football game, to play some tennis, to spend time at Strawberry Island (the summer home of the Basilian Fathers), and to see something of his family and friends. Nor did he miss a play, a concert, a movie, or a party, when one of these came his way.

As a member of the institute staff, Flahiff was expected to publish scholarly articles and books. The institute inaugurated its annual scholarly journal, *Mediaeval Studies*, in 1939, the same year in which it received its charter from the Holy See. To the second issue of the journal, and to four other numbers, Flahiff contributed a scholarly article in his field of mediaeval history. Before he left the institute in 1954, he published six other articles, though not in *Mediaeval Studies* and not of the calibre or depth of his five institute articles. Three of these outside articles have to do with history and three with art. He also did seven book reviews for *Liturgical Arts*, whose editor was a good friend of his.

The five scholarly articles written for *Mediaeval Studies* between the years 1940 and 1947 are splendid examples of Flahiff's ability as thinker, researcher, and writer. They treat of English history in the

twelfth century, and particularly of the work of Ralph Niger (*c.* 1140–
c. 1199),[8] a subject which offered an open field for original work.
These articles are thoroughly researched and remarkably readable, in
spite of their highly specialized subject matter. They represent painstaking research and careful organization; one could not ask for more
from a scholarly point of view. The fourth of these, "The Writ of Pro-
hibition to Court Christian in the Thirteenth Century,"[9] which is the
longest, the best, and probably his most valuable scholarly contribution, appeared in two parts in successive years. A third part was
promised but never appeared. The last of the five *Mediaeval Studies* articles, wittily entitled *"Deus Non Vult,"* ("God Does Not Will It")[10]
published in 1947 and perhaps the most interesting, is an account of
Ralph Niger's objections to the Third Crusade, which bishops and
popes were proclaiming and encouraging in the twelfth century. It
marks the end of Flahiff's writing as a professional scholar, though
the scholarly habits of mind, his imaginativeness, and his admirable
perceptiveness, would remain and would serve him in good stead.

In 1954 Flahiff gave a paper at the annual meeting of the Canadian
Historical Association, entitled "Twelfth Century Critics and Humanists." If one wishes to get an impression of the man as teacher, this is
the text to read. We find careful distinctions being made with regard
to "humanism" and "renaissance," and we observe his openness, his
scholarly charity, his balance and irenic manner. More important still
is his vision. He too is a humanist, loving all that is human in an ordered enthusiasm for all that is good in the world. In describing these
humanists and critics of the twelfth century he betrays how he himself looks at the world: "They are men whose eyes are opened wide
on the human scene around them, and the lively account they give of
what they observe is far removed from the impersonal and uncircum-
stanced report of the annalist and chronicler. Nor do they stop with
merely reporting in detail; they reflect, react, judge and criticize …
They run the whole gamut of human life and conduct. By their fluent
criticism which becomes at times polished satire, they are far more
akin to a Valla and an Erasmus than to their predecessors or to a great
many of their own contemporaries." [11]

Flahiff's writing on art during his years at the Pontifical Institute –
three articles and seven book reviews – is not of the same scholarly
quality as his historical work. It is, however, related to his teaching,
and it is interesting as far as it goes. It has been mentioned before that
Flahiff did not think of himself as an authority on art, but rather as an
historian of art. If Flahiff was not a Berenson he was certainly a
knowledgeable enthusiast. Art was a passion with him and a delight

which he loved to communicate. His reviews are perceptive and balanced, showing no hesitation to point out deficiencies or errors in the books he is reviewing.

Can Art Be Christian? (Toronto: The Basilian Press, 1952), is an elegantly printed lecture, given in Toronto in April 1952, which develops and polishes an article by Flahiff entitled "Can Modern Art Be Christian?" (*The Catholic Art Quarterly* 16, 1952), published a month earlier. The problem treated in this essay is not that of prejudice in the production, but rather whether production of a certain kind is even possible. Can we validly speak of Christian art? He makes it very clear that merely a religious theme or detail does not make Christian art. He is categoric in his holding that the thing made must be truly art, that is, beautiful, true, and moving. Much of what is commonly called Christian art, he says, especially in recent centuries, is bad art. An example of this would be what is commonly referred to as *l'art de Saint Sulpice.*[12]

His argument concentrates on the artist, on his ability, his mentality, his goodness, and his belief. The Christian artist will produce Christian art, and the great Christian artist will produce great Christian art. Subject and theme are secondary to the person and skill of the artist. Flahiff shows himself in this lecture familiar and very much at ease with artists throughout history and even with contemporary artists. As is usual with his writing and with his lectures, one has a sense of rich background, of long reflection, and of personal conviction. "Let the artist," he wrote, "who is also a man, and, by God's grace, a Christian, become more Christian ... His view of reality will then become likewise more Christ-like. Picasso spoke a great truth – greater, I suspect, than he knew – when he said paint only what you love. If the Christian painter truly loves God and loves with the love of God that which he depicts, he will inevitably paint what he should and as he should whenever he paints freely and without preoccupation."[13]

Reading the work of Flahiff during his professorate at the institute, one cannot help sharing the sentiments of those who regretted his passage from the academic world. It must be recognized, however, that good as this work was, his record of scholarly writing over nineteen years is meagre. One can see how his academic and religious superiors might have been disappointed in his work as a scholar, especially when one observes the attention he gave to lighter writing in the form of book reviews. The record does not reveal so much a lack of diligence – no one would or could accuse him of that – as it does a lack of concentration. Clearly his interests were multiple; he would have been following his own instincts of integration of various aspects of the life in which he found himself. Edmund McCorkell, however, Flahiff's superior general, was disappointed in the scholarly achievement of a man he considered potentially a great scholar.[14] But not many others would have agreed. The reputation of Father Flahiff around the campus of the University of Toronto was that of a splendid teacher, a brilliant scholar, an affable colleague, and a deeply spiritual man.

Though Flahiff's scholarly output was thin, his teaching was memorable, as were his availability and friendly manner. Consciously or unconsciously, he was choosing a more pastoral than academic role, in the conviction that his direct work with people was more important. Moreover, his religious superiors were not entirely blameless in the matter of his limited output. McCorkell himself did not hesitate to call upon Flahiff for the preaching of retreats. His religious superiors, for all their lofty vision of the Pontifical Institute and their recognition of the demands of scholarship, were not to make the sacrifices for the scholars they had trained when it came to the stern realities of the apostolate and financial necessity. Perhaps Gilson was too respectful of religious life and the directors of it to point out that scholarship demanded more concentration than the Basilians were allowing. In any case, there remains some unquiet thought that Flahiff was not sufficiently channelled, and that, obedient as he was, he might have been more firmly directed in his scholarship. But it was the Basilians themselves who took him out of scholarship and writing and teaching by electing him superior general in the Basilian General Chapter of 1954.

All through his life, Flahiff carried with him a nostalgia for the Pontifical Institute. He kept in touch with developments there, and was frequently in contact with various members of the institute, especially with Father Laurence Shook. In the much agitated life of an archbishop and cardinal, he hankered for the life of study, the academic atmosphere, the contact with students, and the pleasure of community life. When preparing for retirement he hoped unrealistically that there would be some place for him as a teacher or supervisor of theses, or something of that kind, not realizing that his twenty-eight-year absence from the academic world was an insuperable obstacle to his return, not to mention his deteriorating health at the time of his retirement. The institute, for its part, has never forgotten the contribution made by George Flahiff, and rightly considers him one of their *illustrissimi*.[15]

CHAPTER FIVE

The Light Within and Without

What was animating and enlightening the popular professor of history who seemed to be so in harmony with life? Perceived to be a man of prayer, Flahiff had based his life on faith, finding in it the wellspring of all he did. His faith had come to him through the circumstances of his birth and had been fostered by his family. It seems never to have wavered or dimmed, but rather grew constantly by his own openness to the life of the spirit and by study and prayer. By the time he had become familiar and confident in his life as professor, Flahiff's spirituality was luminously centred on the truth of the Incarnation, the belief that God became human in Jesus Christ. This belief conditioned him in his whole person, in his view of the world, in his relationship with every other person, and in his teaching. If it is true that great thinkers and writers ring the changes on one basic and important truth, then Flahiff is an example. The Incarnation obsessed him.

It was not only the stupendous truth that God took on humanity that inspired Flahiff. The wondrous result of this truth was that human beings took on divinity, and that human life and the world itself were made holy in all aspects. Thus he saw life, the world, events, and especially persons as fundamentally good. Life had meaning, even great meaning. Hence his optimism, his patience, and the impression he gave of being at home in the world. "There is an enormous truth to be realized," he wrote in 1944, "that everything we do or endure, say or think is of *no* value supernaturally except in so far as it is united with Our Lord's. Everything is per Dominum nostrum Jesus Christum (through Jesus Christ our Lord)."[1] And in the same vein two years later, "The fact of the Incarnation, and its stark reality, – I mean all the ordinary every-day things that God did in his human life – gives meaning and even a divine quality to the commonest things in our life."[2] In speaking to seminarians from across Canada in 1950, he said, "Our life on earth has no meaning and no purpose but, through and in Christ, to live as the sons of God that we are, amid all the circumstances and all the activities of human existence in time and in a material universe. This is precisely what the Only-begotten Son of God, our Head, did in his physical members." And in a conference to the Loretto Sisters in December of the same year, he said: "The Word that was made Flesh must continue His Work, dwelling amongst us, dwelling *in* each one of us."[3]

Flahiff's vehicle for presenting his incarnational theology was the doctrine of the Church as the Mystical Body of Christ, which had been receiving attention among theologians in the early part of the twentieth century, reaching a culmination in the encyclical letter of Pope Pius XII in 1943, *Mystici Corporis* ("The Mystical Body of Christ"). Before the pope published his study of the doctrine, Flahiff was familiar with theological works on the Mystical Body and was presenting the teaching in his retreat conferences and to those who were receiving his spiritual direction.[4] The pope's encyclical gave him impetus and confidence. He studied it thoroughly, referred to it constantly and popularized it in his scope of influence. His personal copy of the encyclical, now in the Basilian Archives, bears witness by its well-used look and by its myriad markings and annotations to the attention he gave it.

One can readily appreciate how Flahiff would find expression in this doctrine. He realized the teaching potential of the analogy – as is the head to the body, so is Christ to the Church – to express our union with Christ, the fact that we live by his life, and that every member has a function in the harmony of the whole.[5] There is not a conference or letter of spiritual direction in the Flahiff collection from the 1940s up to the time of the Vatican Council which does not contain a reference to the Mystical Body of Christ.

His understanding and appreciation of the doctrine is touchingly summarized in a beautiful typewritten copy of his conferences given to sisters, now in the Basilian Archives. This booklet bears the hand-painted title, "As He, So We," surmounted by an elegant chi-rho monogram and, at the bottom of the title page, "Toronto, 1946." On the next page is the inscription, "The following series of conferences given by her brother, George B. Flahiff C.S.B., is lovingly offered to Sister Thérèse Carmel on the occasion of her Final Profession – August 15, 1946." This work, which Margaret treasured all her life, says more than the words it contains. It tells of the author: his love of the doctrine of the Mystical Body of Christ, his integrated view of art and devotion, and his touching regard for his sister who shared with him the grace of religious life.

The doctrine of the Incarnation, then, and its expression in the Mystical Body of Christ, are the basis of Flahiff's spiritual direction. He himself had sought spiritual direction from Louis Bondy, his former superior in the seminary and a man eleven years his senior. It was an interesting relationship, for there could not have been two men among the Basilians more different in their approach to the spiritual life than Bondy and Flahiff. The former was of French-Canadian family and background. He held a doctorate in French literature from Johns Hopkins University and was a life-long student of Thomas Aquinas and John of the Cross, as he was of French spiritual writers, both classical and contemporary. Bondy's approach to spiritual direction was rather authoritarian and rigid. He always referred to Jesus Christ as "the Master." He was more inclined to talk to his directee than to listen. He counselled strict adherence to the commandments of God and to the rules of religious life. But he was also a man of prudence and charity, who knew how to temper the wind to the shorn lamb. He was much sought after as a spiritual director and preacher of retreats. Bondy's influence on the spirituality of the Basilian community has yet to be studied and chronicled, but it is recognized as significant by the many Basilians who experienced his spiritual guidance.

Flahiff took from Bondy none of his rigidity but much of his insight and ardour. He was a disciple, but very much his own man, following his own instincts of gentleness and discretion in his work of spiritual direction. While he had great respect and affection for Bondy, whom he always addressed as "Father," even after he himself had risen to the rank of cardinal, he exercised independence of mind and manner which Bondy fully respected.

On a CBC nation-wide radio program with Peter Gzowski on 28 January 1974, Father Arthur Gibson[6] gave a highly amusing and wonderfully apt example of the difference between Bondy and Flahiff as spiritual directors. The subject of the program was Cardinal Flahiff, who was to be interviewed the next day, but who was not present in the first interview. With Gibson was a panel of four other persons: Monsignor Norman Chartrand, chancellor of the Archdiocese of Winnipeg; Sister Margaret Flahiff; Viola Specht, the cardinal's secretary; and Father Bondy. Gibson related that when he came into the Catholic Church in the late forties, he was seeking a spiritual director to help him in his new-found faith. He approached Father Bondy and asked if he would be so kind as to accept him as his spiritual directee. In consenting, Father Bondy said to him: "Now, Arthur, there is one thing about which we should be very clear. If I am to be your director, you will have no will of your own. And as for the will of God, it will be whatever I say." Gibson swallowed hard and accepted, but found after two weeks that the relationship was intolerable. He appealed to his friends to suggest another person to whom he might go for direction. They suggested Father Flahiff. In accepting the task, Flahiff said to Gibson: "Now, Arthur, there is one thing about which we should be perfectly clear ..." "Here it comes again!" thought Arthur, and then was pleasantly surprised to hear Flahiff say: "The task of the spiritual director is to keep out of the way of the Holy Spirit." The story not only sums up the difference between Bondy and Flahiff as directors; it also shows the magnanimity of Father Bondy, who, it seems, enjoyed the joke as much as did the listeners who knew both men.

Flahiff gave a good deal of time to the work of spiritual direction, as we saw in the previous chapter. One of his directees has provided an exceptionally good illustration of Flahiff as spiritual director, from the letters she received from him. Helene Marie Darte[7] first came to know Flahiff while at the University of Toronto in 1935. Having completed her MA in 1937, she enrolled in the Institute of Mediaeval Studies, one of the first two women students to be accepted there. Two years later, following her friend Margaret Flahiff, Darte entered the Sisters of Charity of Halifax and was professed on 24 January 1941. Seeking spiritual direction in the first year of her religious life, Darte began a correspondence with Flahiff which continued for over forty years, the last communication from him being dated September 1988, a few months before he became incapacitated. She has kept some sixty letters and about forty cards from Flahiff, who replied to her letters very much as an interested friend, eager to share insights into the workings of the Spirit and ready to encourage her at every turn.[8]

The first thing one notices about the letters is a certain formality, typical of pre-Vatican II manners in correspondence between religious. She writes "Dear Father," and he, "Dear Sister," although sometimes in the body of the letter he uses her first name. This continues into the early 1970s, when the salutation becomes "Dear Helene." The tone of Flahiff's letters, however, is friendly and personal. He writes at length and in longhand, as was his custom in his correspondence with friends. He neglects no point that has been raised in any of her letters and he takes pains to comment on it as fully as he can. There is no commanding, no dominance, but rather a pervading respect for the person to whom he is writing. His advice is never merely rote, but thoughtful and personal. One has the impression not so much that he is directing as accompanying, that he is less a mentor than a companion. His method is that of suggestion rather than obligation. He seems to be sharing ideas, readings, problems and decisions, not concluding them. He does indeed seem to be standing aside to let the Holy Spirit work. His respect for the person he was directing also implied responsibility on the part of that person. Flahiff called directees to maturity by reminding them that ultimately the decisions were not to come from him but from them. If his manner was gracious and friendly, his direction was challenging, uncompromising, and profoundly theological.

While he assumes, and at times makes explicit, the importance of the Incarnation to his directee, Flahiff counsels abandonment to the will of God, a way of spiritual advancement he was much taken with during the 1940s, after reading the spiritual classic, *Abandon à la Providence divine* ("Abandonment to Divine Providence") by the French Jesuit, Jean-Pierre de Caussade (1675–1751), first published in 1861.[9] As the title indicates, the book is a treatise on a spirituality of peaceful and willing resignation to God's providence. It is not a book of quietism, for the soul is actively engaged in seeking the will of God and in accepting and fulfilling his will at every moment. This doctrine appealed strongly to Flahiff, though it would come home to roost when he himself was called to change his life so drastically to follow the will of God, as manifested in his election as superior general of the Basilians and later in his being named Archbishop of Winnipeg. There is an interesting parallel in his use of Caussade's book for the direction of his own life and that of others. The book came out of letters and conferences which Caussade sent or gave to a community of nuns at Nancy in France in the early eighteenth century. *Abandon* proposes and develops a spirituality especially for women religious, persons to whom Flahiff gave much attention. His manner and his doctrine were adapted to sisters and to the living of consecrated virginity. In his letters to Helene, abandonment to the will of God is a recurring, underlying theme; he sent her a copy of the book.

Closely related to the doctrine of abandonment to the will of God, and concomitantly developed in Caussade's book, is the teaching on the value of the present moment, or what is sometimes called the "sacrament of the present moment." This was also an extremely important notion for Flahiff in his spiritual direction. "His Divine Life can come to us," he wrote, "only at those successive points at which we touch eternity, namely the successive present moments" (8 January 1945); and again: "Do not think of your life and your existence as a sort of road or ribbon stretching out behind you in one direction and far ahead of you in the other. The truest notion of our existence is just a NOW that should be 'YES!' It is *all* that we have. We do not go along trailing clouds of glory (or of ignominy); there is no trail stretched out behind; there is just what we *are* NOW! Past experiences have, of course, affected us; but they are over and done with; their only value now is in the effects in us *now*" (11 July 1946). This latter quotation suggests another quality of Flahiff's direction and advice: it was always very much related to the actual condition of the person he was addressing. He was practical and realistic, taking into account the circumstances of a person's life.

As one might expect, prayer – its manner, frequency, fervour, and consistency – was a pivotal matter for Flahiff in his direction of souls. He was conversant with the teaching of the masters, such as Augustine, Thomas Aquinas, Ignatius of Loyola, Pascal, and Bossuet, as well as with the writing of contemporary ones, such as Paul Claudel (1868–1955), Dom John Chapman (1865–1933), Caryll Houselander (1901–54), Edward Leen (1885–1944), Abbot Columba Marmion (1858–1923), and others. But he did not counsel, much less dictate, adherence to any one exclusively. He drew from them all, adapting to the person and the circumstances. Some counsels Flahiff stated repeatedly, such as "Pray in the way you can, not in the way you can't," which he learned from Dom Chapman; and, "It is not our task to cause truth to triumph but to struggle for its triumph," which he took from Pascal. But his own words can be equally striking and pithy, and warmer for being so personal. For example, "He has told us to pray and He has even let us in on the big secret that it is His own Spirit that prays in us" (28 January 1953); or, "All I would urge, as I have done before, is to *desire* ever more and more of God, closer and closer union – whether you are conscious of it or not" (29 September 1953); or again, "But we must keep remembering that as long as our will is that it should be so – I mean that we *want* to get through to Him – then we do. Our realizing it is little more than the recording of a phenomenon; the recording has nothing to do with its taking place" (22 March 1951).

Flahiff's spiritual direction was anything but dull. It sprang from friendship and an enthusiasm for the life of the spirit, and it benefited from his talent for expression. "But sanctity and love" he counselled, "consist neither in storms nor in calms but solely in clinging to God's will" (6 January 1944). In the same letter he wrote, "The realization of what we are and what we are for is the work of a lifetime." He evinced a certain enjoyment and informality as parts of spiritual direction: "In a way, it seems a pity that we all are so shy of talking about the things that really matter. It is wonderfully satisfying just to chat about them. That is possible with you" (30 May 1944). The letters to Helene Darte have indeed a chatty quality, as do many of Flahiff's letters. As time went on, the letters became much less directive and more conversational, concerned largely about the life and activities of both persons.

The impression of Flahiff which one forms from the letters to Helene Darte is that of a man who was balanced, widely read, encouraging, and very respectful in his dealing with a person's spiritual life. The friendly tone of the letters did not preclude a certain firmness of manner. On one occasion, when Darte had brought up the matter of wanting to be sure she was doing God's will, he said: "There is a 'bourgeois mind' in the spiritual life, too, you know, the surest sign of which is that desire for a sense of security regarding the future – the comfortable feeling one gets from an adequate fixed income, whereas in reality we must learn to live from moment to moment on the unfailing alms of God" (9 November 1944). As a young priest, I remember being reprimanded by Flahiff, who was at that time my spiritual director, for calling him on the phone to ask for an appointment during a time when the rule called for silence. The gentle but clear reprimand was given not at the time but at the next meeting. Another young Basilian, who went to him with a problem of conscience, being worried that the place in which he was working was a source of temptation, and thinking that Flahiff, then superior general, might readily change his assignment, was surprised to hear him say simply, "I think you can handle it." He was always accessible and one looked forward to a session with him. But he never offered pablum.

In a recent letter to the author, Sister Helene Darte wrote what might serve as a summary of Flahiff's method and manner of spiritual direction:

Perhaps knowing me as well as he did and my desire for a clear cut, organized plan, he felt he had to remind me (as he did more than once) that God writes straight with crooked lines: a saying of Claudel that really was a help as I tried to understand some of the seeming contradictions I found in religious life. (I was almost twenty-six when I entered and couldn't help seeing things that the younger Sisters missed.) But he never imposed his ideas on me. It would be: "Perhaps … God is keeping the cross for later in your life" or "I think, maybe …" Never "*this* is what God wants" or "this is what you should do." In other words he left you free to find God's will yourself.

All his work of spiritual direction was curtailed when he became a bishop and gradually it ceased altogether. Perhaps it is truer to say that what he did in spiritual direction and in retreats not so much ceased as took other forms, notably those of talks, homilies, speeches, and participation in conferences of various kinds. He moved on to a wider stage which called for other methods. But no advance in status, no increased dignity, no growing fame diminished in him his ardour for the spiritual life or his love for quiet conversation about the things of God.

It is true of his spiritual direction, as it is true in so many aspects of Flahiff's life, that what people remembered, what people were touched by, what people appreciated most was not what he said, but what he was. The dictum, "What you are speaks so loud I can't hear what you are saying ," applies eminently to Flahiff. In listening to persons who knew him and sought his spiritual direction, one hears almost invariably the reflection: "Father Flahiff made God present."

CHAPTER SIX

As One Who Serves

At the General Chapter held at St Michael's College in Toronto in July 1954, Flahiff was elected superior general of the Basilian Fathers. His election was not a surprise for he had been spoken of as a candidate for the office from the time six years previously when he had been elected to the General Council. During this time he became familiar with the government of the congregation as he fulfilled his duties as councillor. The election was neither difficult nor close: Flahiff received 71 per cent of the vote on the first ballot. There was general satisfaction throughout the congregation, though dismay on the part of some at the loss of a good scholar to administration, a man in whom much had been invested and who had proven his ability as a teacher and researcher.

Why would the Basilian Fathers have elected Flahiff to be their leader? Did they not consider the advantage of leaving him to his teaching and studies in the Pontifical Institute? There were other candidates, of course, and the electors were quite aware of Flahiff's value as a scholar and teacher. Finding the right person to be leader of the congregation, however, took priority over all other considerations, and the Basilians found in Flahiff the qualities of intelligence, goodness, deep spirituality, and humanity that were desirable in the person who was to hold the most important position among them. He himself was deeply dismayed at his being chosen, for, despite what some said about his ambition for the office,[1] being superior general was not his preference. But he accepted the office, in looking upon his election as the will of God, he followed the advice he had given to many others.

Flahiff was the fourth superior general of the North American Basilians since their separation from the French Basilians in 1922. His predecessors in the office, Francis Forster (1922–29), Henry Carr (1930–42), and Edmund McCorkell (1942–54), while quite different one from another, were all men of vision with talents for organization and leadership. Flahiff received from them a congregation which was united, vital, growing, well organized, and confident. In 1954, there were 312 priests, 196 scholastics (young men preparing for the priesthood), and twenty-three novices.[2] There were some twenty-nine Basilian houses in Canada and the United States. The average age was somewhere in the forties; the problem of care of the aged had not yet arisen. Financially, the congregation was solvent. The new superior general knew all the Basilians, most of them very well. They had confidence in him; they knew him to be approachable and ready to listen to them.

On his side, however, there was no feeling of elation. While he desired to be of service to the community in any way he could, he felt quite unsuited to the job, seeing himself in no way as apt or capable as his predecessors. The prospect of leaving the Pontifical Institute and his teaching weighed heavily upon him.[3] And what weighed even more heavily upon him was the thought of having to deal with his confreres in any kind of disciplinary way. This aversion for disagreeable relationships was his Achilles heel and would plague him both as superior general and later as archbishop.[4] His talents and propensities all inclined him to the fostering of friendship, but he knew very well that his new position would mean at times refusals, corrections, disciplining, and appointing persons to positions or places possibly against their preference.

Among the congratulatory letters he received was one from Professor Gilson, who wrote from France: "May I join your friends in extending my felicitations for your election? I do it the more sincerely as I have known you long enough to understand the reasons for such a choice. I pray God, with all my heart, to make your burden as light as possible." In replying at some length to this letter, Flahiff gave a glimpse of his interior state. After thanking Gilson and saying how much he was touched by the letter, he wrote: "Doubtless I need not tell you that it is with considerable personal regret that I accepted the office. There are many reasons for questioning the wisdom of the capitulants, but they are now beside the point; the result must be, as I say, God's will, in some way and I accept it as such for better or worse. However, this does not exclude very real heartaches, and chief among these is the quasi-separation from the work of the Institute ... My heart shall always be in the Institute." He then recalled his debt to Gilson for his support and his example, saying, "We have *seen* [in

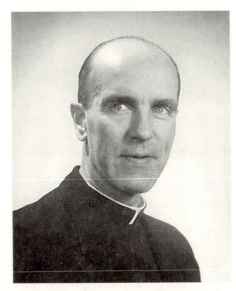

George Flahiff, Superior General of the Basilian Fathers, 1956.
(Photo: Michael Burns, Toronto)

you] what it is to love God in a life of scholarship."[5] The nostalgia of the letter ran deep. Flahiff would dream about a return to the institute and to teaching. He could not know at the time of his election in 1954 that this would never come about.

In a somewhat lighter vein came a telegram from his sister Catherine in New York. At that time there was a well-known advertisement for Premium Ham seen on bill boards and in the press, which featured a little pig looking soulfully at a tin of Premium Ham with the caption, "Alas, my poor brother." Catherine sent a telegram to her brother with only these words. Father Bondy read the telegram to the assembled Chapter, with Flahiff's permission, to general amusement and relief.

In his first letter to the whole congregation, published in the *Basilian Annals* of October 1954, the new superior general sounded what would be the theme of his administration in calling every Basilian to fidelity in the pursuit of perfection in religious life. He commented on the recent visit of Cardinal Valeri, prefect of the Sacred Congregation of Religious in Rome, which had taken place in September 1954 at St Michael's College. He recalled the encouraging words of the cardinal and his generous compliments on the work of the Basilian Fathers. But then Flahiff took a more urgent tone as he reminded his confreres that withdrawals of scholastics and novices in the current year had been the highest on record. "There is little doubt," he wrote, "that in certain cases these young men, some of whom gave great promise, simply did not find flourishing among us that noble ideal of religious life that they had conceived."

He then called upon the Basilians to heed the words of Pope Pius XII spoken at the First International Congress on the States of Perfection held in Rome in 1950: "The purpose which [the pope] had chiefly in mind, and which he voiced time and again was to enjoin upon religious yet more urgently than ever the obligation to which they have bound themselves by vow of seeking perfection." He quoted the Holy Father on the importance of obedience as the foundation of sanctity and of apostolic work. Then he asked whether, given the progress of the community in various academic and social areas and its spirit of adaptation to the circumstances of the times, there has gone along with this progress a corresponding "increase in sanctity" and a "proportionate deepening of the religious spirit?"[6]

Two things are important to notice in Flahiff's letter in order to understand and evaluate his administration of the Basilians: first, his attention to the voice of the Church, an attention constant and salient throughout his years as superior general; and secondly, his preoccupation with spiritual leadership of the congregation. He would do some founding and some building, and he would foster growth in the community during his time as superior general. But his more important accomplishment was in calling the community to diligent and generous practice of authentic religious life.

One of the most notable events of Flahiff's generalship, and one which was a great personal joy to him, occurred soon after his election. The same General Chapter which had elected him also approved the reunion of the French branch of the Basilians with the branch in North America.[7] In 1922, for various reasons, the French Basilians had petitioned Rome for a separation of the two communities. Accordingly Rome set up two distinct congregations: the Basilian Fathers of Toronto and the Basilian Fathers of the Diocese of Viviers in France. Communication between the two branches had been limited since the separation, though not through ill will. The French Basilians had suffered a good deal during the intervening years, especially during the Second World War, some of them having been taken for forced labour by the Germans, and all of them having known hunger and insecurity. In 1954 they numbered only fourteen priests, two aspirants, and nine juniors.

Though the reunion with France had been planned and negotiated by his predecessor, it fell to Flahiff to effect the actual rejoining of the two communities. Thus, to prepare for the event, he sent two young Basilians, Kevin Kirley and myself, in September of 1954, to join the

French community at Annonay, France, and to begin studies at the Université de Lyon, with a view to qualifying as teachers at the college at Annonay. A decree from Rome was duly received, dated 14 June 1955, the Feast of St Basil, officially reuniting the two communities and delegating the superior general to implement the decree. The date chosen for the act of reunion was 29 September 1955.

Flahiff was deeply affected by the occasion. He loved France; he loved the Basilian community; and being an historian he was keenly aware of the importance of the event for the Congregation of St Basil. What pleased him most, however, was the fact that this event represented a reconciliation between two communities which had been divided by misunderstanding and by seeming incompatibility for thirty-three years. The reunion was a healing of the wounds of history, and a very clear testimony to goodwill overcoming any lingering resentment there might have been on either side of the Atlantic. Flahiff was certainly the man for the moment. It was his first visit to Annonay. His fluent French and his natural charm were but incidental to the depth of feeling he evinced by his manner and his words as he read the decree of reunion in the tiny chapel of the Maison Saint-Joseph, and as he received the vows of the French Basilians. Father Charles Roume[8] was the superior at Annonay at the time. It was he who had conceived the idea of the reunion, promoted it in the French community, and formally petitioned the Basilians in North America for reunion with them. He was as affected as Flahiff and as deeply conscious of the significance of what was taking place.

Before leaving Annonay, Flahiff addressed a letter to the whole congregation, dated 4 October 1955, the feast of St Francis of Assisi. He described some of the events of the reunion, mentioning especially his visit to the tomb of the founders of the Basilians in the tiny cemetery down in one corner of the garden, as well as to the graves of some confreres, such as Patrick Molony, the first Basilian to go to Canada, and that of Mathieu Soulerin, the founder of St Michael's College in Toronto.[9] Flahiff wanted to bring home to the community the opportuneness of the reunion as a moment to recall Basilian roots, and to be inspired anew by those men who had made great sacrifices, both in France and in America. He hoped also that the reunion would "broaden the outlook of confreres on both sides of the ocean" and that the perspective of the community in general would be thenceforth "more truly catholic." The letter ended with an exhortation to learn from the confreres in France the value of a simpler life-style inspired by the example of St Francis of Assisi, who had been a patron of the Basilians from the beginning.[10]

Flahiff spent nine days with the Basilians at Annonay, getting to know them and some of the family and friends of the community there. Then, after paying his respects to the bishop of the diocese of Viviers, and accompanied by Roume and myself, he set out by car for Rome by way of the French Riviera. It was a beautiful time of year. The vivid autumn colours had come to the vineyards in the Rhône valley as the grape-gathering progressed, adding spectacle to the charming countryside. We stopped for one night at the Basilian vacation house at St-Alban-sous-Sampson, a spot particularly dear to Roume. Flahiff, of course, enjoyed every moment of the trip. His affection for France and things French was being revived by the hour. His interest in art prompted a desire to visit the Matisse chapel at St-Paul-de-Vence, not far from Nice. The chapel is quite small. Filling the south wall, and receiving the full benefit of the Mediterranean sun, is a row of stained-glass windows in bright yellow and deep blue, with a very simple design. Flahiff stood as though enchanted by the sight. He seemed childlike in his delight as he exclaimed, gesturing with his hands, "The light! The extraordinary light! You can almost feel it." He was highly pleased with the whole chapel, though Roume was not. He too was a lover of art and also a connoisseur, but Matisse was not one of his favourites. He was polite though undemonstrative and, being French, he could dislike Matisse, while a non-Frenchman might enthuse. We drove on to Nice where Flahiff took the train for Rome, rather exhausted from the events, the visits, and the general excitement of the reunion, as he reported in a letter to Robert Scollard, secretary general of the Basilians in Toronto.[11]

As superior general, the highest ranking person in the Congregation of St Basil, and one to whom more than five hundred men owed respect and obedience, Flahiff maintained his customary courtesy and friendliness towards all. Attitudes or gestures of superiority had no part in him, though he was conscious of his position and always commanded respect. He in turn respected his confreres from the youngest to the oldest. He knew everyone's first name, and used it, except in the case of a few older priests whom he continued to address as Father. One felt rather honoured to be spoken to by him, though all were at ease, or immediately made so, in his company. When he spoke formally, he was listened to. When he offended, or thought he had offended, he apologized immediately. Most often the so-called offended party was unconscious of any breach of courtesy.

Flahiff was much more comfortable in his role of spiritual leader of the community than in that of director or, from time to time, corrector. He wrote regularly to the community, encouraging the members to zeal, to exact observance of the rule, to generosity, and to prayer. He was careful to direct the attention of the community to papal documents, and he would use these as the basis for his own advice to the confreres.[12] His own example of a fervent and authentic spiritual life was an even stronger teacher than his words.

Assigning Basilians under his jurisdiction to various posts and works in the different apostolates of the congregation was one of his chief duties and one of his heaviest crosses. He disliked asking a person to take a position lest he impose on him. In his time, appointments – the term used to designate the annual obediences within the community – were made with little or no consultation. In one way this relieved Flahiff of lengthy, frequent, and possibly difficult, interviews or confrontations. In another way it put him in danger of unintentional offence. He laboured and agonized over appointments; he never failed to hear objections from those who were not pleased; nor did he fail to point out to someone the merit of obedience and of self-sacrifice in accepting an appointment. This lack of consultation should be seen as not so brutal as it might appear from today's perspective. Religious generally accepted the practice and found merit in doing so. Exercised by a person such as George Flahiff, the custom did not lack humanity.

Like any person in high place, he could and did make mistakes. On one occasion, for example, when he had to make an appointment at an odd time, he travelled to the city where the confrere concerned was teaching, in order to speak to him personally. The priest was conducting his class at the moment of Flahiff's arrival. Pressed for time, he asked the local superior to call him from class. Together they went to the classroom door, where the local superior called the confrere and spoke to him at the door, asking him to dismiss his class because Father Flahiff was there to see him. The Basilian in question did not know that Flahiff was standing a few feet away. When the confrere left the door to excuse himself to his class, the wind from an open window caught the door and slammed it. Not realizing that the slamming was accidental, Flahiff took this as a display of temper on the part of the young Basilian. When the man emerged from his class, Flahiff upbraided him roundly and refused to accept his explanation.[13] With all his exquisite courtesy, Flahiff had a stubborn streak which came into play when he was convinced of something. This quality sometimes served him well, but not always. He was also capable of moments of anger, though these were so rare as to be very surprising and extremely effective.

On another occasion Flahiff appointed a confrere to Texas, and then had to change the appointment to Rochester. The man, who had prepared his move to Texas, dutifully packed his books and personal belongings and prepared to go to Rochester to take up residence. Then it became possible and desirable that he go to Texas after all, according to the original appointment. Flahiff was chagrined by the trouble he had caused and the further trouble he was about to impose. He did what he thought best: he sought out the confrere to explain personally the reasons for the change and to apologize for the whole situation. The Basilian in question was edified by the sensitivity of his superior general and never forgot this signal mark of courtesy.[14]

One may be inclined to imagine that Flahiff was not firm in his leadership, so numerous are the examples of his exquisite courtesy and sensitivity to all categories of persons. Though firmness is not the first thing that comes to mind when one thinks of Flahiff's record, it was certainly not lacking in his character. Nor was courage. In 1955, just after his return from France and Rome, he wrote to one of the young priests who had repeatedly failed his junior priest exams, which at that time were obligatory for all during the first five years of priesthood. He addressed the person in question as Father, which was unusual and indicative of his mood: "I regret to inform you that the results obtained by you at the Junior Priests' Examination last March fell far short of the passing mark. You will therefore be obliged to write the examination one more year. It is distressing to have to keep imposing this examination, but the obligation in conscience placed upon us by the Church's Law is a grave one. The one upon your conscience is equally grave and it is to be hoped that you will this year apply yourself seriously enough to satisfy the requirement. It is not ability that is lacking."[15]

An incident relating to higher authority than his own also gives us a glimpse of the firmness and courage of which Flahiff was capable. The Archbishop of Toronto, Cardinal McGuigan, had received a complaint about one of the Basilians, a man of solid and admirable reputation, who was at the time doing service in one of the parishes. The accusations against the priest were probably from a person more ready to vent his spleen than to find out the facts. It would seem that McGuigan had also neglected to check the basis of the complaints, for as it turned out, the priest in question had nothing at all to do with the case. The facts, moreover, as the cardinal related them in a very unpleasant letter to Flahiff, were quite erroneous. With his usual courtesy, but without hesitation in his duty to defend his confrere even in the face of such high authority, Flahiff set forth the true facts of the case, which he had carefully investigated. The matter seems to have ended there. Typically, some few months later, Flahiff addressed an extremely friendly and courteous letter to Cardinal McGuigan on the occasion of his silver jubilee of episcopal ordination, expressing his thanks on behalf of the whole community for the friendship and the help of the cardinal over the years.[16]

Flahiff was respectful of persons and institutions in their work, and reluctant to interfere negatively. Terence Forestell recounts that when he returned from studies in Rome in 1956 to teach sacred scripture at the Basilian Seminary, he met with some opposition from students and some criticism from older confreres, who found his teaching at odds with their notions of the Bible and with what they had learned from previous professors. There were complaints to the superior general. Flahiff never made any comment to Forestell. Two years later when a *monitum* (warning) was issued from Rome concerning a certain text which was thought dangerous for use in seminaries, Flahiff brought the *monitum* to Forestell and told him to do what he thought appropriate.[17] In other words, he deferred to the young teacher, confident that he would act for the best.

In the late 1950s the question arose at St Michael's College School as to whether Junior A and Junior B hockey should be continued. There were good reasons, both academic and moral, for suspending these teams indefinitely. At the heart of the matter were the interests and demands of professional hockey, which conflicted with the academic aims of the school. The General Council, in continuous consultation with the principal and the athletic directors of the school, considered the question at length and thoroughly over a period of two years, and ultimately listed seven factors which would support the discontinuance of the teams. The Basilian authorities in the school decided to keep the teams for the time being. Flahiff expressed his disappointment and that of the General Council, but he did not take any action.[18]

During Flahiff's term of office there were many requests from bishops for Basilian personnel either to found a school or to take charge of an existing one. These requests came principally from places in Canada and in the United States, but there were also some from as far away as Japan and Australia. It was a torture for Flahiff to refuse these requests. Each one, of course, was considered in the General Council, and in his replies he always assured the petitioner that the answer expressed the opinion of several. He replied courteously to all, and went to great lengths to explain why the request could not be granted. His discomfort in refusing is abundantly evident. To the Bishop of Nelson, British Colombia, for example, who had made a fervent plea for help, he

wrote: "This is a difficult letter to write. Doubtless that is why I have
been so slow in writing it. Your own letter of the 13th reached me more
than two weeks ago. I have reflected and prayed and I have discussed
the whole matter with the other members of the General Council ... It
is not without a great deal of thought and after careful weighing of our
resources that we find ourselves nevertheless obliged in the end to give
an answer that cannot but be disappointing to you."[19] The letter went
on for two pages with a detailed outline of the many commitments of
the Basilians and with reasons why he must refuse the request of the
bishop.

This is but one case among many. Each request received a courteous
and explanatory reply, but few were answered positively. There were
only seven new Basilian houses established during Flahiff's time as
superior general. One of these was a high school in Gary, Indiana,
which was to be very large and, exceptionally, co-educational. There
is a touch of humour typical of Flahiff in his letter of acceptance. After
stating the problem of the numerous demands on Basilian human
resources, he writes: "However, the needs of the Church are grave
and we would be lacking in both faith and generosity, if we were not
willing at this juncture to stretch our resources beyond the limit of human calculation and trust that God Himself will supply. Confreres
may have to refrain from dying during the next few years."[20] The
establishment in Gary proved successful and flourishes to this day.

One of the reasons for limiting acceptances of requests came from
Rome. Religious congregations are required to make a report to Rome
every five years on the state of the community, the work, the personnel,
vocations, and the financial situation. In replying to the 1955 report,
Rome warned the superior general not to spread community resources
too thinly – that is, not to stretch personnel and resources to limits that
would endanger the well-being of the members or the security of the
community as a whole. Flahiff often invoked this *monitum* in his letters
of refusal. For example, to a request from Brazil he replies: "Indeed,
among comments of the Holy See on our last Quinquennial Report,
was a strong recommendation that we should not think of extending
our foundations and our activities further until stability is assured in
what we are already doing."[21]

If he was chary of committing Basilians to new works, he was lav-
ish in his acceptance of requests for retreats. These were numerous,
and it can be safely said that none was refused. He did a good deal of
this work himself, as had been his custom before he became superior
general. It was time-consuming and burdensome, but at the same
time he enjoyed it. He had had plenty of practice, and many of his

conferences would need only to be adapted to the audience and revitalized. The conferences were always carefully prepared and always much appreciated. Giving retreats was probably good therapy for him, and a welcome break from administrative duties. He readily called upon his fellow Basilians to assist in this work, especially for retreats to women religious. He found willing response among them, no doubt prompted by his own example of generosity. The requests came from places in Canada and the United States. Flahiff was widely known for his spirituality and for his kindness; nor were his fine looks and exquisite manners in any way a drawback.

An organization to which Flahiff gave a good deal of time and service was the Canadian Religious Conference (CRC). At the instigation of Rome, this association of the major superiors of men's and women's religious congregations throughout Canada was founded in 1954, the year he was elected superior general. It so happened that he gave the first talk at the founding convention in July of 1954 on the states of perfection.[22] From that time on, even into the era of his episcopate when he was no longer officially a member, he participated actively in the work of the conference and gave generously of his time to meetings and to talks. He was named to the Council of the Men's Section immediately in 1954. Then two years later he became vice-president, and ultimately president in 1959. Probably no single person among the religious superiors in Canada did more to foster this conference than Flahiff. He was a faithful attendant to the various meetings several times a year, generous in the extra duties which came his way as an official, and encouraging to all by his sustained interest in the work. Once again his mere presence, physical or moral, was an example and a support to many. He was a man supremely convinced of the values and the mission of religious life and proved his conviction by word and work. His close ties with religious all over Canada was very likely one of the factors in his being made a bishop, for it was thought Flahiff would be a valuable link between religious congregations and the Conference of Bishops.

These numerous activities and obligations outside the community had their drawbacks, since they caused Flahiff to be absent frequently from his home base in Toronto. While he had capable associates in the administration who could receive calls, requests, and reports, his absences, at times for long periods, were nevertheless an inconvenience for the members of the community and for its smooth running. This was the chief criticism of Flahiff as superior general as his first mandate drew to an end. The results of his election to a second term, however, show that such criticism did not carry much weight.

Revelatory of his deep concern for the community and its work are three activities within the Basilian congregation which Flahiff fostered or initiated, and which, unfortunately, have not been continued. One of these was the annual education conference among the Basilians themselves, held during the week after Christmas, in which one specific aspect of learning and teaching was studied over a period of three days. Attendance was optional, but each house, especially one attached to a school, was expected to send one or more delegates. These conferences were popular, not only for their learning and encouraging value but also for the development of community spirit. The education conference was immediately followed by a vocations conference, which would involve another group of persons, though many from the education conference would remain in order to benefit from both.

This second conference, usually attended at least in part by Flahiff himself, bred a consciousness throughout the congregation of the importance of vocations and the urgency of actively seeking suitable members. Flahiff always insisted, however, that the main work and the one incumbent on all was that of prayer for vocations. He preached this in season and out of season, and each year brought it to a clear focus in his letter for the novena to St Joseph, held in March throughout the congregation, for the purpose of praying for vocations. Actually vocations came in good numbers during Flahiff's time as superior general, and in even greater numbers just after he left office in 1961. But there were never too many, and they were to fall off catastrophically in the middle and late 1960s.

A third and welcome initiative on the part of Flahiff was the holding of a retreat exclusively for the superiors of the various houses. He recognized the need for some kind of special attention to the needs and the formation of superiors, and he listened to the suggestions and the requests of members for some kind of help in this area. The first of these was held in July 1958, with four days being given to retreat and four days to a conference on matters touching the superior's office. It was a very successful venture, encouraging for the superiors involved, and greatly unifying for the congregation. Once again, unfortunately, such retreat-conferences did not become a regular feature of Basilian life.

Flahiff, like his predecessors, was a man of vision. He was also one who enabled others, as one of his priests in Winnipeg would later describe him. These two qualities of the man can be observed in some examples of his dealing with individual Basilians. He wanted them well educated, well prepared, and foremost in their field, and he was ready to take the measures to foster these aims wherever he could. Thus he writes to Father Scollard from France, where he has visited Donal O'Gorman, a young Basilian graduate student in Paris: "I found Don O'Gorman definitely overworked, yet not too badly off physically. His thesis will obviously be a good one and the delay in finishing is due to new things that were discovered. I finally advised him to leave the defence over until next year, to take things a bit easier right now and then see a bit of France before coming home; he has seen practically nothing after a whole year over here; for a Professor of French, that just won't do."[23]

The case of George Freemesser is particularly interesting. In the early 1950s, as a student at St John Fisher College in Rochester, New York, Freemesser had been trying without success for admission to medical school, when finally, through the good offices of some Basilians there, he was accepted at the University of Ottawa. He did well in his medical studies, ultimately finishing second in his class. But during his studies to become a doctor, the idea of combining his medical training with a priestly apostolate took hold of him. Though not particularly attracted to psychiatry, Freemesser thought that specialization in that area would be the most compatible with priestly ministry. When he presented his idea to different diocesan seminaries in his quest for acceptance in one of them, he encountered no encouragement. It was clear to him that the word psychiatry was a red flag. In his frustration, and at the suggestion of Father Russell Pendergast, a popular and dynamic Basilian professor in economics at the college, Freemesser visited Flahiff in Toronto and laid out his ideas. He had come to the right man. When Freemesser finished speaking, Flahiff said quietly: "We have been waiting for someone like you."

A year later, when Freemesser had graduated in medicine from the Univesity of Ottawa, he went back to Flahiff to ask whether he should apply for the novitiate immediately or do his internship. Flahiff was not sure. He suggested that Freemesser visit the world-famous Dr Karl Stern in Montreal and talk to him about his vision and plans. Stern found in Freemesser a man after his own heart who shared his own ideas about holistic medicine and the intimate relationship between the body and the psyche. Moreover, Stern was a man of strong religious faith and understood immediately what Freemesser had in mind and what he aspired to. He told him to finish his medicine, become qualified, then go for the priesthood. This was the beginning of the remarkable career of a priest-psychiatrist who has realized a great deal of good in his work with all categories of persons, particularly those in religious vocations. Joseph Wey, Flahiff's successor in the office of superior general, shared the vision, and gave Freemesser the opportunity to develop his talents and his dreams. There is an interesting and rather touching sequel to the story: some twenty-two years later George Flahiff and George Freemesser, "the two Georges," as they were familiarly referred to, came together in a reversal of roles, when the older, much reduced in health, was being counselled by the younger.[24]

Flahiff went into the General Chapter of 1960 quite convinced that he would not be re-elected, rather relieved at the thought, and for some reason convinced that he had done a poor job as superior general. On the first ballot he received 89 per cent of the vote. He was overcome; in fact he broke down. It was only with great difficulty and after some rather uncomfortable though sympathetic delay that he mastered his feelings and accepted. He said a rather puzzling thing, however, which possibly could only be understood by persons who were present: "May God forgive you for what you have done." What did he mean? Was this just an unguarded phrase from a man deeply distraught? Or did he wish to express in the most graphic terms his sense of unworthiness? Or was it the expression of his deepest feelings, a mixture of anger and frustration and hopelessness at the prospect of being burdened for another six years with this awesome office? Given Flahiff's scholarly background, it could also have been a slight variation on a quotation from Saint Bernard who was quite annoyed when, in 1145, one of his monks was elected to the papal office, becoming Pope Eugene iii. Bernard wrote a stinging letter to the cardinals, upbraiding them for taking a man from the life of prayer and penance and placing him in the turmoil of church government: "May God forgive you for what you have done in this regard."[25] It is impossible to know; what is evident is the intensity of his emotional reaction. Actually his tenure of office was to be sharply curtailed, as nine months later to the day, he was named Archbishop of Winnipeg by Pope John xxiii, and thus removed, albeit temporarily, from the congregation he loved so dearly and had served so well.

Father Joseph Wey, who was elected to the office of superior general in July 1961, paid tribute to his predecessor in a manner which gives a good summary of the contribution of Flahiff as leader of the Basilian Fathers:

The intense and vigorous interior life of this man of God made itself felt in the spirit of charity which he diffused throughout the Congregation and strove to instill in the heart of every confrere. His life, his manner, even his presence were a silent rebuke to any who might feel inclined to neglect the obligations of the religious vocation, and a quiet encouragement to any who were resolved to meet these obligations even in the face of great difficulty. His knowledge and experience of the spiritual life enabled and led him to guide the Congregation more and more in the paths recommended by the Holy See, and to focus the attention of confreres in an effective way on the essential purpose of the religious vocation. These are things for which the Congregation owes Archbishop Flahiff a lasting debt of gratitude. We feel that God has blessed us singularly in giving him to us as our spiritual father. It is to be hoped that his spirit will live on in the Congregation, in the men to whom he has been an inspiration, and I believe that if it does, it will be a clear sign that God wishes us to grow and bear fruit to His greater honour and glory.[26]

CHAPTER SEVEN

From Scholar to Shepherd

The announcement by Vatican Radio and the Canadian media on 15 March 1961 that Father George Flahiff had been named Archbishop of Winnipeg came as a surprise both to the Basilian community and to clerical, academic, and lay communities. It might be called "an expected surprise," somewhat like the announcement of the death of a very sick person which, though clearly foreseen, is strangely surprising when it comes. For at least a decade, Flahiff had been mentioned here and there as *episcopabile*, that is, a candidate for the episcopacy. The author remembers vividly one of the older priests of the Toronto Archdiocese saying to him, sometime in the early 1950s, before Flahiff even became superior general, "I can see a mitre hovering over the head of that man!" The possibility of his being made a bishop, however, was remote, especially considering the fact that bishops were usually chosen from the secular clergy. It was only with the vacancy of Winnipeg, caused by the transfer to Toronto of Archbishop Pocock in January 1961, that rumours heated up concerning the superior general of the Basilians, though his name was far from being the first put forward by those who were consulted. Perhaps the most intriguing comment made by one of the leading bishops in a conversation about the vacancy of Winnipeg when Flahiff's name was in the wind, a comment not without a hint of cynicism, was, "I hear they are going to appoint a bishop who prays."

How much Flahiff himself thought about the possibility of being made a bishop is hard to say. Certainly he had heard rumours, suggestions, and speculations, all of which he would have brushed off as no more than clerical chit-chat. It was not in his character to be ambitious and, in choosing religious life, he had almost surely eliminated the possibility of being made a bishop. Only one Basilian before him had become a bishop, and that was back in 1890, when Denis O'Connor (1841–1911), superior of Assumption College in Windsor, was named Bishop of London, Ontario, and in 1899, Archbishop of Toronto. He remained in office until 1908 when he resigned.

Flahiff did, however, have advance notice of the announcement, albeit of only one week. On the afternoon of 7 March 1961, just a few days after he and his Council had moved into a new Curial House on Russell Hill Road, Flahiff received a letter from the Apostolic Delegation[1] in Ottawa, informing him, in Latin, that Pope John XXIII had named him Archbishop of Winnipeg. The letter perplexed him and he doubted its validity, because the apostolic delegate's signature, with which he was familiar from other correspondence, looked very strange. He put through a call to Ottawa, only to find that the delegate, Archbishop Sebastiano Baggio, had broken his arm in a fall on the ice and had gone to Italy to recuperate. Flahiff identified himself to the secretary, Monsignor Angelo Sacchi, who had answered the telephone, and explained why he thought this letter with the curious signature must be some kind of joke. The secretary assured Flahiff that it was indeed a valid letter and an authentic, if unusual, signature. It was the last letter, he said, that the delegate had signed before leaving for Italy, explaining that two persons had to assist him, pushing the broken arm in its cast to make a signature possible. Flahiff, rather lost for words, muttered something about his surprise and his inadequacy for the office of bishop. The secretary invited him to Ottawa for a chat.

A few days later Flahiff went to Ottawa, his arguments for refusing the nomination better formulated in his mind, mostly based on his lack of experience in parochial work and his commitment to the Basilians. Sacchi said to him, "Well, I'm sure Rome has made some investigations or probably the delegate here has, and your name was proposed, and John XXIII approved it and that's that." Whether Flahiff gave his consent then and there, or whether it was after consulting his good friend, Archbishop Pocock – he was allowed to consult one person only – he did ultimately consent, concluding that this must be the will of God. He knew something about obedience and he had counselled many in the matter of accepting God's will. How could he himself renege?[2]

At Flahiff's request, it was decided that the public announcement would not be made until 25 March. This was abruptly changed when, a week later on the evening of 14 March, Flahiff was informed by phone from Ottawa that the announcement of his appointment to Winnipeg would be made public the next day. The irony was not lost on him: often in later years he referred to the fateful Ides of March, 1961.

This abrupt change in his life was traumatic. More than the sacrifice of the academic life, which he loved, and even more than the prospect of separation from the Basilian community, what haunted him was the thought of his unsuitability for the new office. He thought he had neither the experience nor the talents to make a good bishop. He was wrong in this, but his thoughts were consistent with his habits of life: to do things well, and to be well prepared for whatever he undertook. But he was also consistent in accepting what appeared to him to be the will of God, and in trusting that he would be given the grace necessary for this new charge.

The method of naming bishops with little or no consultation with the interested party has its merits, abrupt and even brutal though the practice may seem. It relieves the candidate of suspense and of soul-searching which, in the case of George Flahiff, was a great blessing. And, of course, one can always refuse; some do. The candidate, when he is asked, has the consolation of knowing that he has been carefully assessed and has been thought suitable for the job by many knowledgeable people. A good deal of consultation, among other bishops, priests, civic leaders, and the laity, usually takes place. There is no evidence that Flahiff was aware of the discussions of his candidacy going on around him, even though some of those consulted were Basilians. Even if he had heard some hints, he was hardly the man to make much of them, much less to exploit them. One can reasonably draw from the evidence we have that he was genuinely surprised and disconcerted by his nomination.

Flahiff's own state of mind is revealed in a letter he wrote the day after the announcement, in response to a cable of congratulations sent to him from the Basilians then living in Rome:

Many thanks for your cable from the Roman Basilians. It arrived this morning. I think you will appreciate how I feel at a moment like this and therefore how reassuring the prayers and moral support of the confreres is [*sic*]. While I am by no means insensible to the greatness of the honour, my feelings are, for the most part, sinking ones and there are more lumps in my throat than shouts. If God wills it, FIAT; but there is great fear and uneasiness and very considerable sadness on the human side. One of the things that hurts most is the thought of giving up confreres and associations of 35 years standing and of adopting a way of life that necessarily must be different. Moreover in the mid-fifties, one adjusts less well. Oui, ça vaut la peine d'être jeune! [It is good to be young!] What I am trying to lead up to is: please keep me in your prayers and ask the same of other confreres and friends there.[3]

The news of the appointment met with almost universal approval and rejoicing. The clergy and people of Winnipeg felt honoured to have a distinguished scholar as their archbishop. The bishops of Canada were unanimously in favour and saw in Flahiff, the historian and educator, a valuable new member of their national conference. The various religious orders, especially those of women, were delighted to know that one who had worked so closely with them through the Canadian Religious Conference, and who knew the problems and aspirations of religious, would now have a voice among the bishops. No doubt Flahiff's nation-wide connections with religious orders was one of the factors favouring his appointment. The Basilian congregation rejoiced at this high recognition of one of its members, although the joy was mitigated by the thought of losing[4] so valuable a member. Many felt delight in the imaginativeness of the appointment: neither a prominent churchman, nor a proven pastor, nor a former Roman student, but a religious and an academic, a person appreciated for his spirituality, his humility, and his charm.

But in academic circles in Toronto and elsewhere there was dismay and even anger at the appointment. Here was a man, the complaint went, who was a scholar trained at great cost, known, respected, and successful, with a growing reputation, quite able to resume his place in the academic world after serving his community as superior general, a pillar of the Pontifical Institute and one of its brightest and most promising lights, now definitely lost to scholarship and teaching. Feeling ran high among several. A Sister of Loretto, who had not heard the news on the morning of 15 March, said good morning to Father John Kelly as she entered the college to meet her class. "Good?" he said, "The air is blue around here with that news from Rome!" Flahiff's good friend Terry McLaughlin was heard to remark, "We set 'em up, and they shoot 'em down," (they being, presumably, the Roman authorities). McLaughlin, who had studied with Flahiff in Europe, knew well what went into the training of a scholar and how rare are the good ones.

The one whose chagrin was perhaps the keenest, and who expressed it clearly and at different times, was Vincent Lorne Kennedy, the liturgist, one of the group of young Basilians who had been sent by Etienne Gilson in 1930 to various universities in Europe and America. Kennedy himself had an international reputation for scholarship and believed firmly in the Pontifical Institute. Though personally not warm towards Flahiff, he recognized his ability and worth, and thought that he might have become Canada's Gilson or Maritain.[5]

Kennedy also knew the workings of the various Vatican offices. The appointment seemed to him to represent a narrow view of what was good for the Church, and the attitude that any priest would consider a bishopric a promotion. He thought Flahiff should have refused, though he recognized that Flahiff's nature and temperament would not have allowed him to do so.[6]

These negative reactions from the academic sector are understandable, for Flahiff's appointment must have seemed insensitive to those working so hard and at such cost for the cause of learning. The reactions naturally cooled with time, although they never completely died out. One still hears today, though without bitterness, the regret that Flahiff's scholarly career was cut short. The argument for the suitability of the appointment, however, can be based on the very talents some thought were being truncated – namely, his scholarliness and his ability to teach. One may well ask, what qualities are more suitable for a bishop than these? And when one adds the exceptional way Flahiff had with people, one can discern the makings of a very good pastor. If the Pontifical Institute and the Basilian Fathers lost (the word is hardly appropriate), the Archdiocese of Winnipeg and the Church in Canada gained, and that handsomely. The matter is to be seen as Flahiff himself saw it: providentially and positively. If one looks at Flahiff's appointment with the advantage of hindsight and with knowledge of his accomplishments, any regrets for what might have been pale in the light of what was.

Etienne Gilson, who might have had cause to regret Flahiff's departure from the academic scene, provides an admirable example in his manner of receiving the news of Flahiff's appointment. As founder of the institute, Gilson was proud of Flahiff's ability and work and placed great hopes in him. But just as in the case of Flahiff's election as superior general, so now when it became clear that his separation from the institute would be definitive, Gilson was serene, and wrote to him from France in terms of faith and friendship. His nostalgia moves to reassurance as the great scholar sees the appointment with a wider vision: "Dear Father Flahiff: Let me call you 'father,' as I always did. This is my last chance ... Ever since you left the Institute, I consoled myself with the thought that, sooner or later, you would come back to it. But this is not going to be, and since, after losing you to the Congregation, the Institute is losing you to the Church, how could we complain? I rather wish to look at our loss from the point of view of the immense benefit your presence in Winnipeg will be to your future diocese."[7]

The author remembers accompanying Flahiff, some ten months after his episcopal ordination, on his first visit to Gilson in Paris. Gilson came to the door of his apartment to meet the archbishop with an expression of pleasure and unmistakable reverence. He took the archbishop's hand, went down on one knee to kiss his episcopal ring, and then rose to embrace his friend. It was all done very naturally and easily, with understanding which could only come from deep friendship.

Flahiff's family was naturally pleased and proud at yet another step in the interesting career of brother George. Different members of the family wrote from their various sectors sending messages of affection and encouragement. Their words meant a great deal to him, and no doubt made even stronger the ties of family which he valued so much all through his life.

Congratulations poured in from all sides. Particularly numerous and fervent were those from individual women religious and communities of Sisters, both in Canada and in the United States. Flahiff's professors and staff of the École des Chartes sent greetings in which their pride in their former student was evident, if a bit inexact in congratulating him on being named "Archbishop of Toronto"! J. Burgon Bickersteth, warden of Hart House from 1921 to 1947, wrote a beautiful congratulatory letter from his retirement in England, recalling Flahiff's services to Hart House, both as student and professor. The familiarity and friendliness of this letter witness to Flahiff's catholicity and ecumenical spirit and to the enduring friendships he made everywhere.[8]

Flahiff always faced new situations with apprehension. This came partly from shyness and diffidence and partly from his obsession with preparedness. He was a worrier in anticipation, though seldom in retrospect. As things progressed, however, and the preparations and the problems to be faced began to take on an order and a plan, his attitude lightened and his interest grew, a pattern typical of him throughout his life. His natural propensity to be interested in whatever he was doing, whoever he was talking to and whatever he had to face, worked gradually to eliminate his apprehension and replace it with enjoyment.

Thus the preparations for episcopal consecration,[9] now set for 31 May 1961, began in apprehension but inevitably grew enjoyable, thanks to several factors. One of these was the Basilian administration: Flahiff had excellent collaborators, persons who by their kindness and efficiency soon relieved him of the burden of his duties as superior general. Then Bishop Francis Allen, Auxiliary Bishop of

Toronto and a good friend, suggested to Flahiff that he go to Rome, meet Pope John, and buy his episcopal robes and necessary parapher- nalia there, where lower prices for such articles would compensate for the price of the trip. This was an inspired suggestion, though Allen may not have realized it, for it got Flahiff out of Toronto and out of the swirl of concerns contingent on this sea change in his life.

Flahiff had loved Rome from the very first time he went there as a young student priest in the early 1930s, and he would love it to the end of his days. After being named archbishop he made many visits to the Eternal City, going there at least once, and sometimes as many as three or four times in a year, and always with pleasure. His visit in April 1961 was particularly pleasant for him. His interest in his new venture was now keen and was increasing. In Rome he found kind- ness and good wishes everywhere: at the Vatican offices, at the Cana- dian College, where he stayed, and especially in his private audience with Pope John xxiii, which was the high point of his visit. Flahiff made notes on this visit. His account is as interesting for the light it throws on the person of the pope as it is for Flahiff's reactions. The conversation took place in French, except for the pope's interjections in Italian. The following account (with some grammatical adjust- ments and the French passages translated) is what Flahiff recorded, written now in English, now in French.

"Come, come, – Bravo, bravo!" I genuflect and kiss his ring. "Now you sit here" putting me down before he sits. "Never a day since I have been Pope that I didn't see at least one Canadian. To-day you are not the first, – already one or two others. It is a country that I love; – the faith seems to be alive – a Christian country!

"Where were you born?" I told him, Paris, Canada. "Paris, Canada. – Paris! Ah! Curious! [Angelo Roncalli, Pope John xxiii, spent many years as papal nuncio to France and was a popular figure in Paris, a city for which he had great affection.] But what racial origin?" "Irish, Holy Father." "Ah, I thought so; you have the facial expression and most Irishmen I know are tall men. I have known a number ever since Msgr. Ryan was with me in Constan- tinople. He is now in the U.S.A. But you are very thin. You will have to put on some weight. How old are you?" "55 years, Holy Father." "That's fine. I was 44 when I was consecrated a bishop.

"I will tell you something. – It is all in the Pater Noster: three things: hal- lowed – kingdom – will. His will only matters. He chooses you: it is His Will. He would accomplish something through you: – His Will. Sometimes there is danger of doing our will. Some are ambitious to get their way. No – just God's Will. Eh, Bravo!

Archbishop-elect Flahiff on his visit to Pope John XXIII,
May 1961. (Basilian Archives, Toronto)

"Are you one of those to be consecrated here on Pentecost Sunday?" "No,
Holy Father." "Good. Ouf! Already there are 14! I was just seeing the M.C. to
see where we can use plural form – do it for all at once. But each head will have
to be anointed. And the Holy Father is 80! Are you to be auxiliary?" "No, Holy
Father, Cardinal McGuigan will consecrate, but for Winnipeg. I go as Ordinary,
as Archbishop. That is why I am afraid – it is new and I am inexperienced."

"That is good. We need to be a little afraid. But it is Christ who calls and
who acts in you. For me, – why should I tell the Cardinals what to do? Only
because Christ wants me to play this role. For His reasons, He put me here,
but it is He who works and acts. And for you, too, it is the same. You did not
seek; He chooses you, let Him act. He will. No, I saw the *scrutinium* [the document outlining the qualifications of the candidate for a bishopric] and we
were all pleased: you were for this post. Let Him!" I told him my motto
["Through Him, with Him, in Him" from the canon of the mass] and he
beamed. "Ah, bene, bene! That's it!"

"Ah, I must have a present for you" pulling out a drawer and rummaging.
Ah, yes – bene!"Medal of himself in silver and in case. I tried to thank Him.

[There is a short exchange here about the Basilian Fathers and Flahiff's
having been superior general. The pope was not familiar with the Basilians.]

"Come, show me where Winnipeg is." Up with great agility, leading me to
the big globe, which he first lights up; we were looking at N. and S. America;
I showed him where. He wanted to see whether Winnipeg was in the centre
of the country. I said it was so geographically, but not financially ... He was

interested in knowing what was done there. When I said "agriculture," he said "Bene – Bravo!" He was surprised at the extent of the diocese, 500 kms across. He asked how many souls, and when I told him approximately, he said, "Not too many, but enough." He pressed a button to make the globe rotate "Ah, so vast." I mentioned his care for all and burden of all upon him. "Ah, and so many don't want peace!"

Reference to Communism. "Yet," he said, "when I go around, people are wholesome – even here, where there are supposed to be many communists. The mothers hold up their babies – Ah, I like to see that!"

On the way back to the desk. "Ah, here is something for your dear ones – here, rosaries for men and women – medals!" I manage to drop a couple in trying to hold them. "Oh, just put them in your pocket."

"Ah, I will give you a word to take away. It is for you and your work as Bishop. I will give you the four F's:

FAIRE [work] – yes, you must work, there is much to be done, but

LAISSEZ-FAIRE [let others work] – others have their jobs; let them do them; don't be butting in or interfering; trust them (all together)

DONNEZ A FAIRE [assign work] – Divide it up. See that others get something to do. Work needs to be assigned to them. Proper delegation of work, etc. Finally,

FAIRE FAIRE [demand work of others] – Some sleep (gesture!) See that they do their work as they are supposed to.

And so I give you the four F's. Alors, Bravo!

[At this point, Flahiff asked if pictures could be taken. The pope readily consented and sent for the photographer and for Flahiff's companions. While waiting Flahiff told Pope John that he had offered mass for him this morning. The pope thanked him and said he would offer his mass for Flahiff the following day. Pictures were taken, and the pope had some conversation with Basilian Fathers Dwyer and Lamb, who had come with Flahiff to the audience, but who had waited outside. Flahiff's account continues.]

All the while, chatty, bubbly and bouncy. Extraordinary after a long morning … Yet he seemed relaxed and chummy and almost to enjoy himself! "When will you be consecrated?" "May 31, the feast of Our Lady, Queen of the World." He turned to me and gave me the accolade, saying: "Since I won't be at your consecration, this is to be as tho' I were." I was deeply touched and could hardly say anything. This was as we moved towards the door. I ask re giving his blessing to family, my own and my religious family. He burst out almost as though he had meant to mention this and had forgotten. "But of course, and to your diocese also when you go there. When will that be?" "June 26 [sic], Holy Father." "Bene! Adieu!"

Walking on air. A good half hour in all! All so intimate and personal – never the least nervousness. I had heard of his informality, how he puts people at ease, but I would never have believed it could quite be what it is – as though you had always known him! Childlike interest and enthusiasm.[10]

This audience, reported at length for what it reveals of both people, is interesting in the light of another comment made by Belgian Cardinal Suenens (1904–96), some years later, when he was writing about his impressions of a visit to Canada: "Next I flew from Ottawa to Winnipeg, where I had a delightful meeting with Archbishop Flahiff … He was a man overflowing with kindness and humility. He volunteered to be my driver; he wore a basque beret, and was most kind and considerate. In my notebook I find the following remark: 'Were he not so gentle, I could see him on St. Peter's throne; it would be somewhat like the days of Pope John, in a more elegant and distinguished style; essentially, he is in the same spiritual class.'"[11] Flahiff never really became a close friend of Pope John. He would see him in the course of visits to Rome in the first two years of his episcopacy, but only fleetingly. He was deeply affected when he heard of Pope John's death.

In accord with his second reason for going to Rome at this time, Flahiff visited the shop of Signore Gammarelli – "the prince of tailors, and the tailor of princes," as he was called – to be measured for his episcopal robes. "Of course, Eccelenza," said the tailor, "everything will be ready in a week, and you can take your robes back to Canada with you." And that is how it turned out. When Flahiff went for a fitting, one of the mitres he had ordered was ready. It was what is known as a precious mitre, one richly decorated and used for solemn feasts of the Church and other liturgical celebrations. It was not a squat model, but rather the very high kind and a handsome piece of work. The tailor moved to place the mitre on Flahiff's head. Immediately perceiving that he was too tall, and the tailor too short for the operation to be successful, Flahiff, in a movement as lithe as it was playful, went down on one knee so that the tailor could place the mitre on his head with ease. It was perfect; in fact, it was stunning. Not all bishops wear a mitre successfully, it being a peculiar and difficult piece of headgear. Flahiff was to the manner born. Gamarelli was ecstatic and the bystanders impressed. Flahiff was enjoying the whole thing. There was that impish smile on his face, which often characterized his humour. He might have been thinking that after all there was some fun in being a bishop.

The trip to Rome lasted some ten days. Besides seeing the pope and arranging for his robes, Flahiff took the appropriate oaths and procured the required bulls for the ceremony of consecration. Upon his return to Toronto he carried on with the business of leaving the office of superior general and with arrangements for the ceremony at the end of May. Canonically he would cease to be superior general by the act of taking possession of the See of Winnipeg, which ceremony was set for 25 June. Thus, the fact of becoming a bishop on 31 May would not immediately separate him from the Basilian community. Flahiff was pleased with this reprieve, short as it was. The separation from the community he loved cost him dearly. To be a Basilian was his whole life. He would, indeed, still be a member of the Congregation of St Basil, though his episcopal status implied a physical separation from friends, colleagues, and the particular work of the congregation, as well as the suspension of his vows of obedience and poverty.

In his years as archbishop, Flahiff remained faithful to the Basilians. He never missed a chance to call at a Basilian house, if there were one in the place he was visiting. He accepted every invitation he possibly could to ordain a Basilian candidate, sometimes at great personal inconvenience. Once he declined an invitation to say grace at a banquet given in Ottawa for Queen Elizabeth because he had promised to ordain a Basilian in Texas on that day. He was generous to a fault in being present at Basilian meetings, chapters, conferences, and celebrations. He kept in touch with many Basilians by correspondence, by telephone, or by visits. He took trouble to be informed about members, especially the sick and the young. He was always a much appreciated guest in the community, and he fitted in as though he had never left. He welcomed Basilians to Winnipeg and extended extraordinary hospitality to them.

The episcopal consecration took place at St Michael's Cathedral in Toronto in the presence of some thirty bishops, a hundred priests, and a full church of laypersons, on 31 May, the Feast of Our Lady, Queen of the World. The ordaining bishops were Cardinal James Charles McGuigan, Archbishop of Toronto; Philip Francis Pocock, Coadjutor Archbishop of Toronto and Flahiff's predecessor in Winnipeg; and Michael O'Neill, Archbishop of Regina, the neighbouring see to that of Winnipeg. O'Neill was a long-time friend of Flahiff, and a former student at St Michael's College in Toronto.

The apostolic delegate was scheduled to preach and his name actually appeared on the program. In his absence through illness Bishop John Wright,[12] Bishop of Pittsburg, who graciously stepped into the breach, gave a remarkable sermon entitled "The Loving Obedience of Free Men." Wright went from praise of the sublime gifts of freedom and learning to argue the greater value of the virtue of loving obedience. When a person, said the preacher, such as George Flahiff, who

Flahiff on the day of his consecration as archbishop outside
St Michael's Cathedral, Toronto, 31 May 1961.
(Basilian Archives, Toronto)

possesses these gifts of freedom and learning to a high degree, freely
and lovingly obeys what is seen as God's will, he is giving witness to
heroic and inspiring faith. Wright obviously understood the circumstances of Flahiff's appointment and saw clearly both the agony and
the ecstasy of the new archbishop's situation. Wright was well known
for his oratory. He came up to expectations at Flahiff's consecration,
and with all the more merit for being called upon at the eleventh hour.

The day continued in festivity with a gala clergy dinner at the King
Edward Hotel in the afternoon, and a reception in the evening for all
Basilians, some of whom had come considerable distance for the
event. Flahiff was touched by the numerous expressions of good
wishes and by the general and genuine joy with which his elevation
to the episcopacy was received. The jubilation of his consecration day
obscured for a moment the less comfortable feelings of inadequacy
for the new office and of the necessary change in his life which it implied. If there was ever a moment when his commitment to God's

will was proven, it was that morning of his consecration. The motto he had chosen for his episcopacy, a phrase that had been the lodestar of his life, would give him the strength he needed to go forward willingly into unknown territory: *"Per Ipsum, cum Ipso, in Ipso"* ("Through Him, with Him, in Him").[13] He was realizing the mystery of the Incarnation in a special way in himself, and Calvary would be much a part of it.

CHAPTER EIGHT

The Welcoming West

The new archbishop remained in Toronto for more than three weeks after his episcopal ordination, the date for taking possession of the See of Winnipeg having been set for 25 June 1961. This gave him time to recuperate from the consecration ceremony and the attendant festivities, and to write thank-you notes to various persons, a duty of first importance in Flahiff's mind. He was still canonically superior general of the Basilian Fathers, and there was Basilian business to be taken care of, although, as we have noted, he was backed by able administrators in the persons of Joseph Wey and Hubert Coughlin. It also gave him time to prepare for the retreat which he had agreed to preach to the priests of the Archdiocese of Winnipeg, now his own priests, beginning on 27 June. He looked forward to this with particular pleasure for it would give him an excellent opportunity to get to know his priests in an atmosphere of friendship and faith. If he anticipated his administrative duties as archbishop with some apprehension, he was at home and confident in the giving of a retreat. He could want for no better way to begin his new life and new duties in Winnipeg.

Archbishop Flahiff arrived in Winnipeg on the afternoon of Friday, 23 June 1961, accompanied by Basilian Fathers Terence Forestell and James Daley, both of whom had been much involved in the ceremonies and festivities in Toronto. He was met at the airport by Monsignor Norman Chartrand, chancellor of the archdiocese, who drove him to his new home in Charleswood, a suburb of Winnipeg approximately seven miles to the west. This residence had been acquired by his predecessor, Archbishop Pocock, and Flahiff would live there for the full twenty-one years of his life in Winnipeg. It was a pleasant house, though not in any way pretentious, with ample rooms, and a generous lot which was bounded on the back by the Assiniboine River. The view from the breakfast room across the back lawn to the quiet river was especially attractive. In his letters over the years there are descriptions of the grounds at various seasons, which indicate that the archbishop found a good deal of satisfaction in his residence and in the peace and beauty of its surroundings. It was the scene of social events of one kind or another, cocktail parties for clergy and friends, or dinners for as many as twelve. Cardinal Karol Wojtyla, the future John Paul II, dined there in 1973; Jules Léger, Governor General of Canada, and Madame Léger lunched there in 1975.

Flahiff had a day and a half to settle in and to get some rest before the ceremonies of his installation. The first of these was a meeting held on Sunday afternoon, 25 June 1961, at 4: 30 p.m., in the Chancery Office, "for the purposes of Archbishop Flahiff taking canonical possession of the See of Winnipeg." Those present were the vicar-capitular, Monsignor Ignatius Zielonka, who had directed the archdiocese in the interim between the old and the new archbishops; the chancellor, Monsignor Norman Chartrand; and five diocesan consultors: Monsignors Owen McInerney and Maurice Cournoyer; and Fathers Maurice Cooney, Maryn Orlinski, and Ubald Paquette. The minutes of the meeting continue: "Archbishop Flahiff presented his Bulls of Consecration and Installation to the meeting, and directed the Chancellor to read the Bull of Installation [in Latin and then in English]. Following the reading of the Bull, Archbishop Flahiff confirmed the Diocesan Consultors in office, and reappointed Right Reverend I.E. Zielonka vicar-general of the Archdiocese of Winnipeg; Very Reverend N.J. Chartrand, chancellor; Very Reverend J.K. Warczak, *Officialis* [Head of the Marriage Tribunal]; and Reverend C.A. Halpin, vice-chancellor."[1] Thus Flahiff ceased to be superior general of the Basilian Fathers and became officially Archbishop of Winnipeg. The meeting lasted twenty minutes; the members adjourned for refreshments and a light supper. The more interesting event, the actual installation, was to follow in the evening.

Though not as numerous as they had been at the consecration ceremony three weeks previously in Toronto, the Canadian bishops, especially those of the western dioceses, were well represented in St Mary's Cathedral that evening. Chief among those present was Maurice Roy, Archbishop of Quebec and Primate of Canada, to whom fell the honour of installing the new archbishop. The Lieutenant Governor of Manitoba, the Honourable Errick French Willis, and other civic dignitaries were present, as well as leaders of various religious denominations. St Mary's, though not a particularly large church – it had not been built as a cathedral, but had been adapted thereto – held a good crowd and was packed to capacity. Flahiff cut a fine figure as he processed up the aisle in front of the primate. He was touched by the reverence of the people and by their obvious enthusiasm for his coming among them. One wonders what other thoughts were his at that moment, in a new and unknown place, among new colleagues. In many ways he was entering a much more public and controlled world, and one which set him apart from others. But it would never separate him from people: rather, the dignity of archbishop would be for him simply a means to move in a wider world of friendship.

The ceremony was simple and short. With the primate seated on the episcopal throne, and Flahiff to one side on a humbler chair, the papal Bull of Installation was read. Then the primate rose, went to where Flahiff was seated, took him by the hand, and accompanied him to the throne which Flahiff then occupied for the rest of the ceremony. The primate spoke briefly in English and French, and then Flahiff spoke, also in the two languages, thanking the primate, his fellow bishops, the various dignitaries, and the people for receiving him as their archbishop. He pledged his devotion to them and asked their prayers for himself in his new office. Prayers for the pope, the queen, the country, and the province followed, with appropriate hymns rendered beautifully by the cathedral choir. A reception for the dignitaries and the bishops followed in the Cathedral Parish Hall.

The following morning Flahiff, surrounded by a number of his fellow bishops and in the company of the priests and faithful of his archdiocese, celebrated a Solemn Pontifical Mass in the cathedral. Once again, religious leaders of various denominations, members of local government, representatives of the judiciary, and business and professional leaders were present. The new archbishop preached the sermon in which he again pledged himself to serve the faithful of the archdiocese to the best of his ability, asking for their prayers to accompany him. And well he might, for the task ahead of him was formidable and his knowledge of the terrain very limited. He certainly felt welcome among the people of Winnipeg who were genuinely happy with the appointment of their new archbishop. On the other hand he felt inexperienced for the work he was undertaking. After a gala clergy dinner at the hotel which went late into the afternoon, he said an emotional goodbye to the Basilians who had come for the occasion. His confreres knew what this new venture was costing him.

What was the condition of the Archdiocese of Winnipeg when Flahiff took office? As an archdiocese, Winnipeg was relatively young, having been cut off from the Archdiocese of St Boniface in

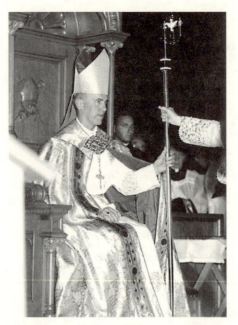

Installation as Archbishop of Winnipeg, 25 June 1961:
the new archbishop receives the crozier from the Primate
of Canada, Archbishop Roy of Quebec.
(Photo: Napoleon Studios, Winnipeg)

1915, amidst a good deal of rivalry and politicking among French and Irish elements in the West.[2] Flahiff was only the third Archbishop of Winnipeg, being the successor to Alfred Arthur Sinnott (1916–52) and Philip Francis Pocock (1952–61). During the last seven and a half years of his episcopacy, Sinnott had a coadjutor-archbishop, and ultimately apostolic administrator, in the person of the humble and saintly Redemptorist, Gerald Murray. This man never held the title "Archbishop of Winnipeg," even though he possessed and exercised, not without difficulty, full canonical jurisdiction. Pocock, who was named apostolic administrator and then coadjutor-archbishop in June 1951 and succeeded to the office and title of Archbishop of Winnipeg in February 1952, was a man of courtesy and affability and an able administrator. He was much beloved of the people of Winnipeg. He left to Flahiff a legacy of goodwill and cooperation among the various elements, both Catholic and non-Catholic, of the archdiocese he had served so well for nearly a decade.

The Archdiocese of Winnipeg had been established primarily to accommodate the growing English-speaking population of the Archdiocese of St Boniface.[3] By 1915 Winnipeg was a vibrant city, destined to absorb the municipality of St Boniface, which it has now done. The establishment of the new archdiocese, with no suffragan sees and no metropolitan area, set up the anomalous situation of two archdiocesan centres within the same city, each having a cathedral, although with distinct diocesan territories and boundaries. Complicating the situation was the eastern rite ordinariate, established in 1912, and also centred in the city of Winnipeg, for the numerous and increasing population of Ukrainians in the area. The ordinariate developed into an archeparchy, which it is today. Winnipeg thus has been a city of archbishops, having had at one time, with ordinaries and coadjutors, as many as six.[4] Numerous, however, did not mean inimical. There had been, on the whole, a peaceful relationship among the various jurisdictions, a relationship which Flahiff was to enjoy and foster during his time in Winnipeg.

When he arrived, his own archdiocese counted some 95,000 Catholics in seventy-four parishes and ninety-one missions, served by seventy-five diocesan (or secular) priests and 101 religious priests – that is, those belonging to a religious community. There were ten religious orders of men and eighteen of women, with some 537 sisters.[5] Two secular institutes had houses in the archdiocese. There was one Catholic college, affiliated with the University of Manitoba, and seventeen secondary and thirty-two primary schools which were either parochial or public, under the direction of religious. There was a diocesan newspaper, the *Sunday Herald*, published weekly. The Oblate Fathers published a French-language weekly, two mission periodicals, and a *Catholic Year Book and Ecclesiastical Directory*. Societies active in the archdiocese included the Propagation of the Faith, Holy Childhood, Sodality of Our Lady, Eucharistic Crusade, Apostleship of Prayer, Christian Family Movement, the Serrans, Catholic Youth Organization, and the Knights of Columbus.[6] The Archdiocese of Winnipeg has never had a diocesan seminary of its own. Candidates have been sent to seminaries in other parts of Canada and the United States, or to Rome. This may account in part for the perennial shortage of priests from which Winnipeg has suffered and which was a matter of concern to Flahiff, as it has been to the other ordinaries of Winnipeg.

Flahiff's predecessor had left him a well-organized and smooth-running curial office. He also bequeathed him some capable administrators whom the new archbishop confirmed in office. The chancellor, Norman Chartrand, was thirty-six years of age, with eleven years of priesthood. Chartrand was a native of Portage la Prairie, Manitoba, and had done his studies for the priesthood at St Paul's Seminary in Ottawa. He was ordained in 1950 by Archbishop Murray and following his ordination did parish work for six years, five of them at the Cathedral parish in Winnipeg. In 1956 Archbishop Pocock named him chancellor, a position he was to hold for the following twenty-six years. Chartrand was a capable administrator, with the kind of intelligence, efficiency, and experience Flahiff needed in a person in this crucial position. Chartrand had been living with Pocock in Charleswood, and Flahiff invited his chancellor to continue living in the house. He became very dependent on his chancellor, placing full trust in him, and being guided by him in the many matters with which he himself was unfamiliar. He named him monsignor in December of 1961 and invested him with the honour the following January. Chartrand was a faithful and devoted collaborator whom Flahiff appreciated greatly, in spite of some problems which arose at various times – problems due in part to Flahiff's frequent absences and reluctance to face unpleasantness.

A second valuable colleague whom Flahiff inherited from his predecessor was Charles Halpin, a man five years younger than Chartrand. Halpin was born in St Eustache, a small town to the west of Winnipeg, did his studies for the priesthood in St Boniface, and was ordained in 1956. After ordination he took a degree in canon law in Rome, returning to Winnipeg in the late 1950s and serving briefly in a parish until Pocock brought him into the chancery office in 1960. Halpin, or as everyone called him, Charlie, was a man of a most affable and warm disposition. He and Flahiff were kindred spirits and became close friends. He often accompanied the archbishop on confirmation tours and provided the opportunity for confidential conversation which Flahiff needed. To Flahiff's great regret, though on his recommendation, Charles Halpin was named Archbishop of Regina in the fall of 1973, and was installed there on 12 December of that year. It was a blow for Flahiff who regretted having "let him slip through [his] fingers," for he might have had him for his auxiliary bishop.[7]

In these two men Flahiff could hardly have found better collaborators. They served him generously and faithfully. An archbishop who was away from his archdiocese fully half the time needed good men to replace him. This they did, and did well. In fact, it was said that the archdiocese ran better when the archbishop was away than when he was home. It had its negative side, however. Naturally enough, some of the priests resented the fact that appointments were being made, not by the archbishop, but by his assistants. Some were also put off by the fact that their problems had to pass through levels lower than that of the archbishop, when they knew Flahiff to be a wise counsellor and a sympathetic listener, if only he were available.

The problems and challenges facing Flahiff were, in general, those of any bishop in North America in the turbulent 1960s: changes in the Church as a result of Vatican II, theological turmoil, defections of priests and religious, shortage of vocations both to the priesthood and religious life, the engulfing of society by consumerism and secularism, and the abandoning of Christian values, even by those who were once staunch and faithful. Also Winnipeg offered its own particular problems and challenges. One of the latter, and perhaps the most important, was the extraordinary ethnic diversity of the province, and so of the archdiocese. There were parishes or groups of French, German, Portugese, Italian, Slovenian, Hungarian, Lithuanian, Croatian, Slovakian, Métis, and First Nation peoples, whose various problems and customs had to be taken into account by the administration. Racial diversity such as this is not uncommon in a large archdiocese in Canada; what was peculiar to the situation in Winnipeg was the short time within which some of these groups had come to the archdiocese and the consequent lack of adaptation. Flahiff made every effort to see to the needs and welfare of all.

He took to his archdiocese wholeheartedly, as an adventure, and with great interest. Its vastness – about equivalent to the size of Ireland – and the location of the episcopal see on the extreme east side meant there would be long trips to visit the outposts of his jurisdiction. This pleased him, and it proved to be a boon. Every foray would mean enjoying the countryside, meeting different groups of people, and sharing hours of conversation with one of his chancellors as travelling companion.

There would be a certain joy of discovery as he went about the work of being archbishop: "Charlie Halpin and I drove to St. Lazare on Saturday," he would write. "It is about 225 miles west and north, right near the Saskatchewan border: one of the loveliest sights in the diocese. Believe it or not, there are *hills*, two deep river valleys, indescribably beautiful foliage and brilliant sunshine to make it all a beautiful sight as well. We had Confirmation there on Saturday night."[8]

Of another part of the archdiocese, this time in the southwest corner, he would write delightedly and with a hint of ownership: "The week-end trip was really enjoyable. That part of the province has a rolling quality to it with a few very picturesque valleys. Just south of Boissevain, straddling the American border (some 12 miles away) is Turtle *Mountain*, even if only some 2000 feet. Beautiful autumn weather throughout the two days! While most of our leaves are now gone, there were a few to add golden tones. The farmland is particularly good out there and the farmers quite prosperous."⁹

The winter he would find fascinating. Its severity roused his sense of wonder; its astonishing visual effects, his sense of beauty. He would comment frequently on the temperature and seem positively gleeful as it reached extremely low degrees. On one occasion he went out for a walk of fifteen minutes when the temperature was −40 Fahrenheit and Celsius, just to be able to say he had experienced the cold where the two scales coincide![10]

After more than a dozen years of living in the West he would still write about the weather with great interest and sensitivity:

The New Year began with a reading of 43 degrees [Fahrenheit] below zero around 2.00 A.M. on Jan. 1st ... The extreme cold means, of course, a HIGH and therefore very clear air, – as to-day, for instance. That is why they are such beautiful days – and nights. The moon that began as a slim crescent ten days ago or so and is now waxing to full has been magnificent ... The early evenings are particularly outstanding when the afterglow of the sun gives an extraordinary luminosity to the still blue skies. On the Thursday after Christmas, against that type of sky, we had that very delicate crescent in the S.W. and, right within reach, a brilliant Venus and a very clear Mercury. Really quite a display! Further east, Mars and Saturn were also on hand; we don't usually see four planets at the same time, I'm told."[11]

He would also experience the hazards of winter when his car would slide into a snow bank and he would shovel in vain for half an hour (at sixty-nine years of age!) before calling a tow truck,[12] as well as the depression produced by the length of winter, when there would be snow in May. When writing about this he would actually use the words "depression" and "discouragement," words not usual with him but certainly understandable in the circumstances.

But most of his weather reporting and descriptions came from his talent for observing and his delight in commenting on the beauty of each season. Writing in mid-September of 1979 he described the season lyrically, even though the moment was heralding winter again:

There has been frost already in some of the rural areas, but not in the city. As a result, leaves are almost completely intact and, for the most part, still solidly green. I say "for the most part," because there is an occasional strain of bright yellow and gold, – even of rare russet of which we see so little. Everything is really delightful. I drive home regularly through the park and stop on a hill over the river to truly enjoy it all. Yesterday, I had the advantage of going out to Petersfield, a tiny village some 25 miles N. of Winnipeg on the West shore of Lake Winnipeg. The completely rural setting added a touch of its own to a particularly beautiful day."[13]

In his new life Flahiff developed an attitude of belonging and even of ownership to the place and the people. If he suffered nostalgic moments, as doubtless he did, he never seems to have made this known. A papal decree had made him Archbishop of Winnipeg in law, but it was his own love and desire to serve which made him such in heart.

CHAPTER NINE

Rendezvous with History

Flahiff's appointment as Archbishop of Winnipeg came at a time that was both crucial and propitious. Two years previously, in January 1959, Pope John XXIII had announced the Second Vatican Council, which was to be the most significant event in Flahiff's life, next to that of being made a bishop. The council would change his thinking and his outlook, as it did for many. He was to have the privilege of participating in it actively. He was a person whose background in history and theology made him particularly apt to be a moving force in the council. He became what one might call a herald of the council to the world, proclaiming the teaching and the message in almost every one of his public speeches during his episcopacy. It must have stirred him to think that he would be an integral part of a great moment in the history of the Church in the modern world.

Like so many Catholics and other Christians, Flahiff was looking forward to the council from the time it had been convoked. Pope John had electrified the world by his announcement, and raised hopes by his call to *aggiornamento,* to "up-date" the Church. In his letter to the community that same year, Flahiff, as superior general, called upon the Basilians to heed the appeal of the Holy Father and to pray for the success of the council. Looking back, one can perceive a touch of irony as Flahiff begins his appeal with the words, "I doubt if we the Basilians will be called upon to play any great role therein." Little did he suspect that he would be participating in an official manner. By his letter he wished to involve the Basilians in the great campaign of prayer for the success of the council which the pope had launched. "I am confident," he wrote, "that Basilians individually have heeded the Holy Father's request. It is the purpose of the present letter, nevertheless, to make sure that all are aware of their responsibility in this regard."[1]

During the year between going to Winnipeg and the opening of the council, Flahiff was able to get his sea legs in a new city and a new position. His preoccupation, however, was much with the impending extraordinary event. Just as going to Winnipeg had something in it of adventure and of challenge admirably met, where his talents for friendship and his zest for life found scope, so going to the council bred an excitement in him far beyond a mere sense of duty. He was going to be not just a spectator but an agent in the renewal of the Roman Catholic Church. The council organizers were not long in fingering the new archbishop to help in the preparation: in January of 1962, the year in which the council was to open, and just six months into his episcopacy, he was named to the Preparatory Commission on Religious Life. After the council began and the preparatory commissions were dissolved, Flahiff was named to the Council Commission on Religious Life which ultimately produced *Perfectae Caritatis*, the manifesto on religious life for the renewed Church, promulgated in November 1965.

Flahiff wrote long letters – he rarely wrote a short one – describing the council to three groups in particular: the Basilians, the priests and people of his archdiocese, and his family. These letters provide not only an interesting and honest presentation of many aspects of the council, but also a fascinating insight into his own mind, his reactions to things and events, and his gentle, whimsical, and wondering view of life. He is awed by the event; he is conscious of its historical importance; but he does not miss the moments of humour nor the humanity of the situation. His talent for description finds scope, as does his historical habit of mind which enabled him to see Vatican II in the context of twenty other ecumenical councils over twenty centuries. He could appreciate what was taking place, both intellectually and sensitively. With a mixture of the wonder of a young mind and the knowledge of a seasoned one, he could see the events before him as new and yet as the fruit of centuries past.

Presuming that his readers had viewed the pomp and circumstance of the opening ceremonies on television, he began a long letter to Basilian confreres with a detailed description of the aula, the space in which the council sessions were to be held. St Peter's basilica had been transformed with a papal throne (usually kept vacant and placed more for symbol than for service) built over the tomb of St Peter and with long lines of bleacher-like seats for the "Fathers of the Council." The first blocks of seats on the right were for the cardinals, and opposite them, the seats for the non-Catholic observers and guests of honour. The rows of seats were so arranged that anyone who wished to speak needed to pass in front of no more than three persons and go down two or three steps to a microphone. The acoustics were perfect; there was no echo or resonance of any kind. "The artistic use of rich red drapes with gold fringes and of magnificent tapestries to span the space between the pillars and close in the 'hall' makes the present arrangement of St Peter's something of real beauty," he wrote. "Many feared that the set-up would mar the appearance of the basilica, but the general consensus of opinion is that it enhances it ... The lighting is superb: unobtrusive, yet providing very clear visibility at all times for reading and writing."[2]

Flahiff seemed to relish giving descriptions and details to his correspondents, with an obvious desire to involve them so that they might enjoy it with him. He wrote with an eye for the interesting and the meaningful and, beyond this, with insight and reflection on the significance of what he was experiencing. What came over him strongly was a new sense of the Church, its universality, its unity in diversity, and its freedom. "No need to say that the Council is a thrilling experience," he wrote, "The impression of universality combined with unity, which was so strong [at the Solemn Opening], continues still. What has been added is an underlining of the reality and value of the *individuals* who make up that universality. If there is unity, it is a unity of free and intelligent human beings who are free to express their views and make their wishes known. There is nothing monolithic about it."[3]

Every bishop who wished to speak was given his chance. The time for each was limited to ten minutes; no one, no matter how tedious or repetitious, was cut off before his time was up. Flahiff did not hesitate to say that not a few were difficult to listen to. "The human element in the speakers is evident," he wrote. "Some are repetitive. Some tend to go overtime. Some are highly personal in what they have to say. Some, God bless them, manage to inject a real touch of humour, even in Latin; it may be conscious or it may be unconscious. Even the checking by the chairman of someone who has gone overtime or is wandering from the subject is not without its humorous side at times."[4]

But he was delighted by the respect shown each speaker. One of these gave up his chance to speak because what he had to say had been said by another. The same person then asked that others be limited if they were obviously repeating points already made. The presider refused, saying *"Non possumus"* ("we cannot"). Flahiff commented: "It was rather thrilling to have that public and official witness to the fact that no one would be prevented from speaking who wished to do so."[5] One wonders how many of the council fathers were repeatedly as thrilled as Flahiff was by the council events as they unfolded.

Like many of his fellow bishops, Flahiff experienced a broadening of his own views and a deepening respect for the opinions of others. By nature he was disposed to openness of mind and to learning. The council made him even more truly catholic. He wrote:

You cannot but be impressed by the zeal, the deep seriousness and complete frankness with which bishops from all parts of the world present their opinions on these and many other detailed matters. Those from China and Japan, Indonesia and Viet Nam, India, Ceylon and the Near East, Africa and Madagascar, South and Central America, as well as those from Australia and Europe, come up often enough with a point of view that you simply had not thought of. You begin to realize how insular and sometimes narrow we can be, and you begin to appreciate something of the universality of the Church. And I think you begin to grasp that its essential unity is not impaired or even endangered by healthy, loyal differences in externals, and in the application of laws and principles in so far as local needs require. I know that I am beginning to realize just how far some conditions are removed from what we take to be normal in our parishes and religious houses.[6]

Flahiff realized that the experience of the council was a singular grace for him at the beginning of his episcopacy. It marked him deeply and doubtless made him an even better pastor than he would have been without it. And while he writes these serious reflections, he is not oblivious to the lighter side of things. He enjoyed the coffee stations that had been set up just off the council hall, where one could find not only the usual cappuccino and espresso but Coca-Cola and plenty of conversation. In fact, apropos of the council president's admonition not to spend too much time in "Bar-Jona," as one coffee station was playfully referred to, Flahiff remarked sapiently that perhaps the president did not realize how much council business was transacted over coffee.[7]

His rich academic background enhanced Flahiff's experience of the council. "To one interested in history," he wrote to his fellow Basilians, "the Council is of absorbing interest for the light it throws on the councils of the past. You begin to appreciate why certain things happened as they did. Above all, you come to realize the extent to which the texts that we cite glibly from councils of the Church as arguments from tradition have been hammered out in very human fashion by

Archbishop Flahiff with Cardinal McGuigan at the Vatican Council,
St Peter's Basilica, Rome, October 1962. (Photo: Barontini and Juliani, Rome)

ordinary members of the Mystical Body of Christ, whose Spirit nevertheless was guiding them all the while."

He was then led into a reflection on the Church itself, in a passage
which must be among the most beautiful and heartfelt he ever wrote:

Not only the history, but the very nature of the Church takes on new light and
new depth. The apparent paradoxes that characterize it are seen as a true enrichment: wide diversity, on the one hand, and essential unity, on the other;
real liberty, on the one hand, yet under authority, on the other; a human element that is so obvious, on the one hand, yet an ever-present divine life and
divine guidance, on the other. Nor would one ever have the same opportunity as at a Council to witness the beauty and the variety of the Church's liturgy. As we assist daily at ceremonies, both simple and solemn, of the many
rites in the Church, we are grateful that uniformity is not required here.[8]

The first session of the council settled quickly into a rhythm of
work and went smoothly for the most part into early December 1962
when it was suspended until the following year. Through the session
Pope John xxiii rarely intervened and was never present, though he

watched the proceedings on closed-circuit television, and presided at various liturgies. But he was present by his benevolent spirit, so to speak, carrying on other church business, receiving visitors, and holding his weekly audiences for the public. The council fathers knew he was there and knew he was watching. What they did not know was that he was dying and that he would not see the completion, let alone the fruition, of the council he had called. News of his failing health became more widespread in the new year. "Good Pope John" died on 3 June 1963, mourned by the world. The question immediately arose, what of the council? It was answered before the month was out, for one of the first pronouncements of Giovanni Battista Montini, who became Pope Paul VI on 29 June, was that the council would continue, with just three weeks delay from the scheduled 8 September date for the second session.

Between sessions council work continued, especially among those who were members of various commissions. Flahiff made a trip to Rome in late February 1963 for a meeting of the Commission on Religious Life. He did not return to Rome for Pope John's funeral, nor for the coronation of the new pope. He did, however, arrive in Rome a week before the beginning of the second session in late September, making visits on the way to the Basilians in Paris and in Annonay, and stopping long enough in Nice for a stroll along the beach. His early arrival was once again for a meeting of his commission. He wrote light-heartedly about his return to Rome, remarking on the warmth of the reception at the hotel where he and a number of the Canadian bishops had stayed during the first session:

I must say that I was surprised at the warmth of the reception that each one of us received. I really do not think that our tips of last year were that big; they are just nice people ... I walked a good deal on the first day, just to absorb Roman atmosphere, managing to be in St. Peter's Square at noon to get the new Holy Father's blessing for the first time. Work began next day, September 23rd, with a meeting of the Committee, or Commission, for Religious ... We met every afternoon for some three hours. There was a certain amount of "homework" but I still had time for a bit of walking in the favourite parts of Rome.[9]

The second session began on 29 September 1963 with ceremonies which were much more subdued than those of the previous year. The new pope wanted to give the impression, not of beginning something new, but rather of continuing something already under way. Flahiff reported: "The procession did not go out into St Peter's Square but entered the basilica by the inside passage. Once the Mass started, however, it was truly glorious. The Holy Father's address was excellent, reflecting many of the ideas of Pope John XXIII but adding details characteristic of the new Holy Father. The non-Catholic observers were deeply impressed as were all of us. The diplomatic corps were present and a number (limited) of others who were fortunate enough to get invitations. All in all, it was a colourful event." [10] The work sessions of the council began the next day, almost as though there had been an interruption of only a weekend.

Flahiff appreciated the camaraderie of the returning bishops: "At first it was like 'old home week,'" he wrote, "or like going back to school in the Fall; you were shouting greetings to bishops you had got to know during the first session and who had spent the intervening months in all parts of the world. It was a moving and heartwarming scene that recalled the unity of the Church in an effective, if unofficial way." He also reported on the seating arrangements at the new session:

The view I have is as good as ever; the only inconvenience is that I am not on the aisle and so have more difficulty getting out for coffee! A few of my neighbours are the same as last year, but the shift has brought some new faces. What is still striking, nevertheless, is the variety you find around you. In our row of six are archbishops from Ethiopia (Addis-Ababa), India, Canada, Argentina, France (Paris), and U.S. (Orleans). Immediately ahead I have the brother of President Diem of Viet-Nam, along with other archbishops from Brazil, Basutoland and Indonesia. I can only wave at my fellow bishops from Canada. As you move out of St Peter's at noontime, you can go "around the world in 80 seconds."[11]

In a more serious vein, Flahiff remarked on the improvement in the voting system, thanks to the installation of electronic machines, and on the greater serenity of the council proceedings. He commented on some of the spectacular reports in the press, which conveyed the erroneous idea of there being parties and factions within the council, although he admitted, there were "sharp differences of opinion." Even taking into account Flahiff's tendency to see things positively, one could probably get a true idea of the atmosphere prevailing at the second session of the council when he wrote:

Everyone is struck by the seriousness with which all speakers, without any least evidence of "party" spirit, exchange views and put forward arguments to clarify the truth about matters under discussion and to formulate it in language that is both precise and readily understandable. Again, the experience of last Fall has been valuable. Members of the Council did not know one another when they arrived in October, 1962. There was, as a result, a good deal of fencing. Now there is an atmosphere of great trust; differences of opinion seem less to conflict than to complement one another. One has the impression, too, that a good deal of studying was done during the 9-month recess; the general level of talks is definitely higher.[12]

This splendid letter ended with a kind of celebration of Rome, the city in which he found himself so much at home. He might become a bit weary of the work of the council, but he was never weary of the Eternal City: "Let me add simply that Rome is still charming. For the sake of exercise and also because I love it anyway, I go for a walk every afternoon (when we do not have committee meetings) in the older parts of Rome. The places, the people, indeed the whole atmosphere is interesting; I never tire of it. Maybe the weather helps. Outside of one rainy stretch of five days, it has been beautiful; sunny and warm."[13]

A number of the Canadian bishops were lodged at the Hotel de la Ville, beside the church of the Trinitá dei Monti, where they said mass each morning. As one would expect, there was much healthy interchange of ideas among them, and probably a good deal of discussion about the Church in Canada and how it related to the council. Several of the national groups of bishops, including the Canadians, organized conferences for themselves with noted theologians, with whom there could be dialogue and questions. They learned a great deal from the council and not all of it in the aula. They travelled to and from the basilica together in a bus which took twenty minutes in the morning but forty-five minutes to an hour to return at lunchtime during Rome's horrendous rush hour. Flahiff was usually the last one on the bus in the morning; when he arrived the driver knew there was no one else. No amount of jeers or wisecracks from his brother bishops disturbed his serenity, or made him change his habits.

During the second session Flahiff had been elected president of the Canadian Catholic Conference (of Bishops) at the Canadian bishops' plenary meeting in Rome. This meant added responsibilities, mostly of an organizational kind. He returned to Rome in March of 1964 for a meeting of the Conciliar Commission on Religious life. On his arrival back in Winnipeg he came down with an attack of shingles and was hospitalized for the first time in his life. As a consequence he missed all the ceremonies of Holy Week. He recovered quickly, however, and was able to meet his commitments during the late spring and summer: the confirmation tours; presiding at the May Day Marian Procession in Windsor, Ontario; receiving an honorary doctor of laws from St John Fisher College, Rochester, New York, in June; and giving a major address to the Canadian Religious Conference in Ottawa in July. He was buoyed up by what he felt was developing in the council for the life of the Church in Canada and the world. He was eager and ready to return to Rome in September of 1964 to continue the council's work.

A great event for Flahiff shortly after the beginning of the third session was the invitation he received from Pope Paul vi to a private audience. The invitation was unsolicited and unexpected. He attributed it to the fact that he was then the president of the Canadian Bishops' Conference. Paul vi was making an effort to meet bishops from all over the world. The audiences were held late in the day, for the mornings were taken up with council sessions. Flahiff took note of the beauty of the refurbished papal apartments, which reflected the tastes of the new pope. The heaviness of traditional appointments and hangings had given way to a lighter atmosphere created by fresh paint and modern furniture.

"The Holy Father was as fresh as the setting," he wrote. "I was surprised to find him looking so well and so bright. He follows the Council proceedings each morning on a closed circuit, even if he does not come into the Council Hall." He remarked how busy the pope had been that day and yet how "keen and alert in conversation." He found Paul less spontaneous and more intellectual that his predecessor, but engaging, simple, direct, and humble. "He puts you at your ease and, from the outset, you are made to feel that you are talking with a friend rather than with a Superior (not that the two are mutually exclusive). He creates a brotherly relationship without any effort ... I have the impression that Pope Paul is particularly conscious of the reality and the presence of Christ at all times."[14]

The conversation with the Holy Father seems to have been entirely enjoyable:

It turned out to be more of a chat than an audience or interview. He talked about things in Canada, sometimes questioning, sometimes making observations of his own. His intention of establishing direct contact of a personal sort rather than through reports and intermediaries was quite evident. Need I say that I enjoyed the experience thoroughly? Looking back, I am astonished at the ease with which it went off and at the freedom from constraint, even if I did find myself tongue-tied once or twice at the mere thought of what was happening. We have a different Pope from the last two but a great one and, to my mind, a Christ-like one.[15]

One can hardly fail to notice that the qualities he admires in Pope Paul are precisely the qualities many admired in Flahiff himself. They were kindred spirits and would develop a firm friendship over the years.

While the papal audience was a high point of the third session for Flahiff, it was but a momentary variation in the work of the council. Late in October 1964 the council undertook a discussion of family life which was the occasion of some interesting remarks by Flahiff on the thorny question of birth control. The commission to study this matter had already been set up by Paul vi, outside the framework of the council. Flahiff hoped for great things from the commission and from the discussion in the council. He was confident that the council's decision to face the issue squarely and openly would be a comfort and reassurance for faithful Catholics. He thought that even if there were no change, the fact that the matter was openly taken in hand would be a step forward. He also believed, probably until the day he died, that the whole matter of marriage and marital relations needed to be studied from a much broader viewpoint. "There is no question," he wrote, "of altering basic truths and principles; however, it is quite possible that we have been trying to apply these to situations about which insufficient knowledge existed, with the result that not the truths or principles but the applications of them were faulty. It is also possible that in putting the truths into human language, we have used expressions or placed emphases that involuntarily have been misleading. Certainly there is grave need of more information."[16] These are revealing remarks. They tell us a good deal about Flahiff's convictions and manner regarding a very delicate topic. We shall return to this topic in a later chapter.

Just a few days prior to writing the words quoted above in a letter to his family, Flahiff wrote to Father Laurence Shook at the Pontifical Institute in Toronto on the same subject:

To-day we reached the section on Marriage. Cardinals Léger and Suenens and Patriarch Maximos ix gave speeches that make Archbishop Pocock's letter of last June look relatively innocuous.[17] They sounded more like the new book *Contraception and Holiness*.[18] No one of the three was proposing a teaching on the subject but they went a long way to expose the problems and to sympathize with the anguish of many couples and to urge a thorough reinvestigation from every point of view. Cardinal Suenens used the expression: "one Galileo case is enough!" ... I am sure that the vast majority [of the council fathers] will seek a careful reassessment of the Church's teaching on the whole matter not only of family planning but of the ends of marriage, which may have been viewed too mechanically ... without sufficient consideration of the *total* view of its purpose.[19]

Three years later Flahiff would develop the same argumentation in a letter to the pope. His letter was acknowledged by the Vatican, assuring Flahiff that the pope had read it carefully.[20] What eventuated with regard to the question of birth control must have been a disappointment to him.

Flahiff found himself very busy during this third session. His main occupation, of course, was the daily assistance at the sessions in St Peter's, which involved study of the documents beforehand, concentration on the speeches, which were certainly not all electrifying, and the twice-daily bus trip across Rome. There was also his work on the Commission for Religious Life, with meetings, discussions, revisions, and some research. There were various social events, such as an invitation from the British or the Canadian ambassador to the Holy See, though in the light of Flahiff's penchant for socializing, these invitations can hardly be seen as chores. Liturgical events, special and routine, also took time. The colourful and boisterous ceremony for the canonization of the martyrs of Uganda, when St Peter's vibrated to tom-toms and African chants, was notably one of these.[21] Doubtless he found pleasure and satisfaction in the busy life he was leading. The thought that back home in Winnipeg he had excellent administrators in whom he had full confidence relieved him of a good deal of concern. It was a well-known fact that his favourite place was not behind a desk. He considered himself doubly blessed in being replaced there, and replaced by competent people.

But archdiocese out of sight was not archdiocese out of mind. He felt very close to his people, both in his consciousness of their prayers for him and the council, and in his conviction that what he was doing was going to affect their lives deeply. There is a fine example of his pastoral solicitude in a long letter "To the Members of the Religious Communities in the Archdiocese of Winnipeg" written on 11 November 1963. He had been asked by the Canadian Religious Conference in Ottawa to outline the work of his Commission on Religious Life, and to tell them where things stood with regard to possible changes in religious life. "When I finished," he wrote, "the thought struck me that of all the religious I know, those of my own archdiocese mean more to me than any others. Why, therefore, should I not share this same information with those who are dearest to me? I can only hope that it may prove to be of interest."[22] It probably did, perhaps more for the spirit in which it was sent than for the content itself.

Flahiff spoke only once to the assembled council fathers during the whole of Vatican II. It was on 2 October 1964, during the third session, when the council was discussing the schema on "Ecumenism." His speech was short and clear, obviously well thought out and well written. His point is unusual, and yet typical of the man. He began by stating his agreement with what had been said before him on the question of ecumenism. Then he suggested another approach to the whole question, an approach which lifted the discussion to a higher level: "Yet it seems to me that there should be more emphasis on the historical aspect of the unhappy division among Christians," he said. He backed up his historical approach with a theological justification, stating that schisms among Christians should be described dynamically, for they are allowed by the Spirit of God for learning, conversion, and purification of the people of God. Schisms can remind the Church that "she is not yet as holy as she should be and not yet perfectly obedient to her vocation to be catholic."

He saw a second dynamic in divisions among Christians: "Through the division of the Churches [God] wants to give many gifts of the Holy Spirit to his people in the contemporary situation." It is another statement of his much-loved dictum of Claudel, that "God writes straight with crooked lines." The positive approach of finding good coming out of evil was typical of Flahiff. He concluded: "This dynamic aspect, which highlights the work of the Holy Spirit, seems more important for an understanding of the ecumenical movement than a listing of the ecclesial values which have been preserved in other communities. Through ecumenical activities, the Spirit of God himself brings forth the varied fruit he wishes and leads all Christians to greater fidelity to the will of God." The point was well taken and was appreciated. Flahiff's was one of the speeches that Hans Küng, Yves Congar OP, and Daniel O'Hanlon SJ selected for their book *Council Speeches of Vatican II*.[23]

What progress had been made on the document concerning religious life with which he was more personally concerned and on which he and members of his commission had been working for well over two years? It seems to have met with some difficulties. In November of 1964 it was not near to being accepted, or even to being presented again to the general assembly of the council fathers. Flahiff wrote that it "has been sadly truncated as a result of successive reductions on orders from higher authorities and now lacks both organic unity and inspiration, dealing as it does with a limited number of more or less unconnected practical aspects of our life."[24] He was happy, however, that the topic of religious life had found an important place in the constitution on the Church, where it had been seen as an integral part of the life of the Church, and not as something extra. A full chapter in this, the most important document to come out of the council, *Lumen Gentium* ("The Dogmatic Constitution on the Church"), is devoted to presenting a summary of the theology of religious life. In later years, when Flahiff spoke on the subject, he frequently returned to the fact that the council situated religious life squarely and firmly at the heart of the Church itself. *Lumen Gentium* was promulgated on 21 November 1964. The document on religious life itself would have to wait for the final session of the council in the following year. Flahiff wrote that a good deal of work would have to be done on it in the meantime. The work must have been done, and well done, for *Perfectae Caritatis* ("The Up-to-Date Renewal of Religious Life"), was promulgated on 28 October 1965 and found wide acceptance and approval.

About the final session of the Vatican Council in the fall of 1965 there is very little in Flahiff's correspondence. Probably he was so busy, along with the rest of the council fathers, in bringing the remaining documents to completion, that he had little time for writing. No fewer than eleven of the sixteen documents emanating from the council were promulgated in the final session, four of them on the day before the closing on 8 December 1965. The final activity of the council fathers must have been feverish. It does appear, however, that all the documents were given the time they needed, in spite of the crush of approvals at the end. The Second Vatican Council was a tremendous achievement by anyone's calculations and, in the realm of religion, one of the great moments of the century and of the history of the Church.

Flahiff turned sixty as the council was ending. For him it had been the experience of a lifetime. Its most important effect was to instill in him a greater understanding of the Church and a keener sense of mission in his pastoral office. He used the documents of the council constantly in his preaching and his speeches. It is hard to find a talk or homily of his after 1962 that does not mention the council. Some speeches are devoted entirely to the event, presenting particularly its spirit and its meaning for our times. "Vatican II and Religious Life," given at the Basilian Pre-Chapter Convention in Rochester, New York, in 1966 is one example of this type. Others examine and explain one or other of the documents. Here his skill in manuscript study, his precision in the use of words, and his acquaintance with the genesis of the final texts, come into play. Not only did he witness the birth and the growth, the pruning and the flowering of the documents; he was an agent in the process. He knew the documents thoroughly. His scholarly instincts and skills found their full scope in his presentation of them.[25]

There was nothing pedantic in his manner of presentation. Flahiff had caught the spirit of John XXIII, a spirit of renewal and hope. He saw the council as a whole and insisted that each document be seen in the light of all the documents. They were all of a piece, with principles common to all, as he wrote to one person seeking his opinion on some matters of religious life.[26] He was absolutely thrilled, to use his own word, with the new point of view on the nature of the Church reflected in *Lumen Gentium*, where the older juridical perceptions, important enough in their time, had given way to more spiritual and inspiring ones. "The People of God" and "Mystical Body of Christ" were expressions which struck sympathetic chords and rang like messages of hope. True to his character, he was open to new ideas and to new points of view as the council progressed. We can catch some of his enthusiasm in his reaction to the document on revelation: "But what strikes me personally most forcefully in the new text is the emphasis on the *personal* element in Revelation. It may always have been obvious to others, but I had not adverted sufficiently to the fact that Christ Himself *is* God revealed and that this is the fundamental notion of Revelation, with the result that the latter is to be conceived of less as a book or as a series of clearly formulated truths than as a Person who still speaks and acts and with whom we have present contact through faith."[27]

Next to the document on the Church, what moved Flahiff most deeply was the document *Gaudium et Spes* ("The Constitution on the Church in the Modern World"), promulgated on the last day of the council, and last in order on that day, 7 December 1965. The Latin title, meaning "Joy and Hope," was like a clear hurrah at the end of the great event. What was especially gratifying to Flahiff was the call to the laity to realize their dignity as Christians, and their baptismal right to proclaim the gospel in their own walk of life, whatever that might be. The right does not come through clerical mediation but through the sacrament which initiates them into Christ. "The apostolate of the laity," he wrote, "grows out of the baptized condition of Christians and has a distinct finality of its own, especially in the sanctification or consecration of the temporal order."[28] Nothing could have been more consonant with his own thinking and the style of his ministry. Member of the hierarchy though he was, and the bearer of many dignities, there was no clericalism in George Flahiff. The dignity which marked his person did not come from external agents. It was interior, and he believed he shared it with his fellow human be-ings. He was united to other Christians not by his priesthood or his episcopal state but by the baptism they had in common. This docu-ment was for him an opening to his people, and an urgent invitation to move forward with them in the work of realizing the Kingdom of God on earth.

CHAPTER TEN

Born for Friendship

When the Second Vatican Council ended in December 1965, Flahiff had been a bishop for four and a half years. He had had the inestimable experience of an ecumenical council, of the universality of the Church, and of the hopefulness generated by Vatican II. His health was excellent, his outlook positive and optimistic. If the council had made the first years of his episcopacy abnormal, in that his attention had been divided between Rome and home, it had also inspired him with confidence and new vision. The lack of confidence he experienced in 1961 when he took on the pastoral charge had been dissipated by what he had learned, by the friends he had made, and by his active participation in an historic event.

Before recounting the events and manner of his pastoral ministry, it would be useful to look at an aspect of his life of which we have seen evidence in what has gone before, and which takes on particular importance for him after the council: the matter of friendship. Flahiff was a man who lived by friendship, who needed it in order to realize his potential. At every phase of his life and in all circumstances he went out to others, made friends, and valued their friendship. Numerous and easy friendships might imply superficiality in his relations, but Flahiff's friendship, broad as it was, never was anything less than genuine, serviceable, and enduring. As the close friendship which he enjoyed in the Basilian community was removed from him, he moved into other areas of friendship to find an outlet for his innate sociability and benevolence.

Flahiff naturally found friends and companions among the Canadian bishops. The close association with his episcopal colleagues during the council, his participation in the Canadian Conference of Catholic Bishops (CCCB), and the various problems and projects the bishops worked on as a group, fostered friendship among them. Archbishop Joseph MacNeil[1] relates how, as a newly ordained bishop, on his first entry into the large room in the Chateau Laurier in Ottawa where the bishops were socializing, he saw a tall figure coming towards him from the other side of the room. "I'm George Flahiff," said the figure as he held out his hand, "welcome to the club." He had sensed that possibly MacNeil, as the new boy on the block, might be feeling uneasy, and his gesture began an enduring friendship. Flahiff made himself aware of MacNeil's work on various financial commissions, some of these on the national level, and never failed to encourage his colleague in this activity, for he recognized its value in the whole picture of the Church in Canada. With all the bishops, English-speaking as well as French-speaking, Flahiff showed the same kind interest, concern, and unfailing support.

A special bond of friendship was formed with four bishops in particular: Philip Pocock, Coadjutor-Archbishop, and later Archbishop, of Toronto; Alexander Carter, Bishop of Sault Ste Marie; his brother, Emmett Carter, Bishop of London, and later Cardinal Archbishop of Toronto; and Aurèle Plourde, Archbishop of Ottawa. With Flahiff making the fifth member of what came to be called "The Gang of Five," these bishops fell into the custom of meeting annually over the Labour Day weekend at the cottage of one or the other (but not of Flahiff, for he had no cottage and lived too far from the others to provide a convenient venue for the group). The weekend was for relaxation and camaraderie. Part of it, however, was given to discussion of current matters regarding the Church. Flahiff commented on their friendly association in this way: "One of the outstanding features of our gatherings is the conversation anywhere and everywhere; at times, wildly humourous, not to say crazy, with abundant teasing and 'kidding,' but a lot of very serious conversation – about Church problems, for the most part. I always find the conversations stimulating and challenging, whether or not you agree with everything put forward ... There is always one 'business' meeting."[2]

These meetings benefited the whole conference of the bishops inasmuch as the five members of the "gang" came to the plenary meetings each fall prepared to speak to the various issues from a basis of reflection and even of consensus. Their association had a positive effect beyond their own sociability, in spite of some mild feeling on the part of others that the friendship smacked of clique. The Gang of Five continued to meet regularly until 1984, the year in which Archbishop

Pocock died, when they decided that if they were no longer five the gang would be dissolved as such.

Flahiff's scope of friendship was not confined to those of his own faith. With the leaders of the other Christian churches in Winnipeg and in Manitoba he was on terms of easy and unaffected friendship. He held a pre-eminence among them, not primarily by his ecclesiastical status, but rather by his scholarly reputation, his faith, and his simple humanity. With political leaders it was the same. They held him in high esteem, and also thought of him as a friend. Two ex-premiers of Manitoba, Duff Roblin and Sterling Lyon, cherish warm memories of Flahiff as gentleman and friend.[3] Flahiff was on terms of special friendship with the Jewish community of Winnipeg. Two days after his nomination as Archbishop of Winnipeg he received a congratulatory letter from Richard D. Jones, national executive director of the Canadian Council of Christians and Jews, recalling "the friendship and understanding [Flahiff] extended to the Council in its early history."[4] Twice Flahiff was honoured by the council, once in 1977 during a celebration in Kamloops, British Columbia, and again in 1981 at a ceremony at the King Edward Hotel in Toronto. On the occasion of his being named cardinal, a forest of two thousand five hundred trees was planted in Israel, named the Cardinal Flahiff Peace Forest, on the initiative of the Jewish community in Winnipeg.[5]

These various groups, and the political and religious leaders in Winnipeg, provided for Flahiff and received from him what might be called friendship on a professional level. What source of friendship was there on a personal level? There were, indeed, the members of his family with whom Flahiff kept in close touch, though they were distant from him and moved in other circles. For the first twelve years of his episcopacy there was his vice-chancellor, Charlie Halpin, who came as close as anyone to being a confidant. Flahiff missed him sorely when Halpin was named Archbishop of Regina in 1973. His chancellor, Norman Chartrand, Flahiff's closest associate during his entire twenty-one years in Winnipeg, provided friendship of a special kind by his fidelity, his admirable practicality, and, at times, by his firmness.

During the last two decades of his life Flahiff enjoyed an enriching friendship with Lenore Sullivan, a Loretto sister whom he came to know just before the last session of the Vatican Council, under rather interesting circumstances. In June of 1965 Flahiff began a retreat to a group of sisters at Loretto College in Toronto. Being between sessions of the council, and naturally preoccupied with and enthused by what was happening there, he thought that his retreatants would be inter-

ested in hearing some of the suggestions being put forward in the
council on the renewal of religious life. He himself saw a good deal of
hope and possibility of renewal, and he wished to share his optimism
with the sisters to whom he was speaking. His ideas, however, were
not so warmly received as he had anticipated. Accordingly he began
to tone down his presentation, lest he exacerbate the fears of some of
the older sisters who sensed that a cherished way of life was being
threatened. Flahiff was particularly sensitive to such a situation. He
was convinced himself of the necessity of change, but not at the price
of offending such persons of good will as the sisters. On this occasion
he retreated into the tried and the true, into the style of conference he
had been accustomed to give to sisters before his experience of the
council.

His change of manner, however, did not please some of the
younger sisters who were looking to the council for a new vision of
religious life. One person in particular, Mother Dorcas,[6] a religious
thirty-one years of age and ten years in vows, was deeply disappointed at the shift in manner of the retreat master. In her dismay she
went to her superior to inform her that she would not be attending
further conferences because they had ceased to be helpful to her in
her prayer. Her superior suggested that she go and see the archbishop
and speak to him frankly about her difficulty. This she did, which
resulted in a lenghty conversation.

For Flahiff, this meeting was one of the turning points in his life. It
convinced him of the urgency of implementing the principles of
renewal that were coming out of Vatican II. What the young nun said to
him, far from causing him resentment, worked a kind of liberation. He
was hearing a clear voice of criticism or dissent or appeal, and he was
relieved to hear such a voice. He was affirmed in his understanding of
the council and in his conviction of the necessity of coming to a new vision of the Church in general and of religious life in particular. At the
same time he discovered in this sister a person who was on the same
spiritual wave-length as himself. He was impressed by her intelligence,
her honesty, her courage, and her desire for renewed religious life. It
was not a spirit of rebellion that prompted her initiative, but rather a
firm desire, shared by several of her sisters, including the superior at the
time, for a new and better way to live their consecration to Christ and to
the Church. The conversation was a case of *cor ad cor loquitur*, of "heart
speaking to heart," and the beginning of a close and fruitful friendship
which continued until Flahiff's death. As it turned out, Mother Dorcas,
or Sister Lenore Sullivan as she was soon to be called, was one of the
three people who attended Cardinal Flahiff on his deathbed.

Out of this friendship grew an extensive correspondence. There survives a large collection of letters and cards written by Flahiff and preserved by Sullivan. These communications are an invaluable record of his activities during the last twenty-four years of his life, as well as an insight into his emotions, perceptions, and reactions to persons and events. The letters give credence to the opinion expressed by Cardinal Newman that a volume of letters is the only true biography.[7] Flahiff did not keep a journal, and only on a few occasions, such as the period of the conclaves in 1978, did he write any lengthy account of what was passing in his life. His letters, however, are a biographer's bonanza, especially those written to Sister Lenore Sullivan, who has kindly permitted their use in this book.

The Sullivan letters are all hand-written, Flahiff's preferred manner for personal letters. They are generally quite long, running sometimes to eight closely-written pages with little marginal space around the text. Grammar, syntax, and punctuation are all carefully correct. He wrote in an unhurried and orderly manner. He obviously enjoyed describing persons, weather, events, and scenery, and did so with an admirable choice of detail. Clearly the writing of these letters provided Flahiff with something he needed: the opportunity to express his thoughts, his activities, and his spiritual aspirations. There is rarely a sour note, even when he is recounting a bout with shingles or some broken ribs. On the contrary, the tone is generally cheerful and optimistic. When, for example, he has related an event, such as a confirmation tour, or a visit to the native peoples, or a gathering of his priests, he invariably comments, "I thoroughly enjoyed it." He delights in sharing his joy in a liturgical event or in some text from the mass or his breviary. In his remarks about people – and the number and range are extensive – he is unfailingly charitable, usually perceptive, and frequently amusing.

At once both a model and a seeker of friendship, Flahiff found a good friend, perhaps *the* friend of his life, in Lenore Sullivan. Circumstances and events had removed him from his community where friends abounded, and from the academic milieu where there was the meeting of minds which he so relished. The spiritual companionship in which he could express and deepen his experience of prayer and indulge his native enthusiasm was no longer so easily available. He found himself, as John xxiii is said to have remarked upon his election as pope, "at the end of the line and at the top of the heap." Though Flahiff was not exactly at the end of the line, he was in a certain sense at the top of the heap, where the rarefied atmosphere made friendship difficult and sometimes dangerous. Authority is lonely and the higher it is, the lonelier it is likely to be. It is not unreasonable to think that Flahiff found the episcopal heights lonely. Nor is it hard to understand why he would accept and enter into a friendship at some remove from his area of work, and with a spiritually like-minded person.

If this friendship was special, it was by no means exclusive. Flahiff felt that his friendship with Sullivan intensified rather than limited his friendship with others. He found that it gave "a hitherto unknown dimension" to his relations with others and his service of them. He hoped that this was particularly true of his "families," those of blood, of his religious community, and of the people to whom he ministered as bishop. He hoped that this one friendship, far from driving a wedge between him and others, would give "an altogether new quality" to the love he owed them, and would make them closer to him for the special friendship with and in Christ.[8]

This spiritually oriented friendship between a man and a woman, both of whom had consecrated their lives to God by vows, and both of whom had professed publicly their adherence to a life of celibacy, finds its analogue in the celebrated friendships between such persons as Francis and Clare of Assisi, John of the Cross and Teresa of Avila, and Francis de Sales and Jane Frances de Chantal,[9] all of whom are recognized as saints and all of whom, it would appear, grew in the love of God by means of their friendship. Without assuming a sanctity comparable to the historic persons mentioned, we can see the friendship between Flahiff and Sullivan as of an admirably spiritual quality. Far from involving any infidelity to their respective commitments, it was a boon for both in their quest for sanctity and in their service of the Church.

Hundreds of people called George Flahiff friend. Once having met him, one felt that he was a friend. This had a good deal to do with his manner of giving full attention to the person to whom he was speaking, no matter who they were. He was genuinely interested in what the person was saying. Conventional questions about health and family were not routine for him: he really wanted to know. He had a remarkable gift for remembering names, and he worked at it. He would also remember details of health, or occupation, or ambition, or success in a person's life, and had an astonishing ability to recall these when he met the person on another occasion. This manner of showing interest and remembering had no other motive than that of respectful interest in every person he met. His height, his manner of bending towards the person to whom he was speaking, and his way of looking one in the eye, made for easy rapport. He had what the

Mexicans call *"el don de gente,"* literally "the gift of people," or, in popular terms, he was "a people person." Erasmus referred to Thomas More as "a man born and made for friendship." Erasmus specified More's qualities as "open-heartedness, generosity, fidelity."[10] One could substitute the name of George Flahiff for that of Thomas More in Erasmus's encomium and not be wide of the mark.

CHAPTER ELEVEN

Pastoring on the Prairies

Some months into his new office as Archbishop of Winnipeg, Flahiff had occasion to visit Toronto briefly. A friend there asked him, "Will you be home for Christmas?" to which he replied without hesitation, "Why, yes," rather puzzled at the question. Then it dawned upon him that the friend was referring to Toronto as home while he himself meant Winnipeg. The spontaneity of his reply pleased him. Winnipeg was now home, and he knew that was how it should be. It was characteristic of him to adjust to a new situation and to enter fully into it. No doubt he had his nostalgic moments, but they were never allowed to cloud his loyalty to the persons, the place, or the work which he knew were now his.

Being a bishop gave great scope for his strong pastoral instincts. If the administrative demands of his office were a cross for him, occasions when he met his people, ministered to them, preached to them, and strove to help them were sheer delight. He liked being a bishop and later a cardinal because it opened such varied possibilities of contact and service. The regions, not to say the wilds, of Manitoba, he found novel and interesting. The various ethnic groups of his vast and scattered archdiocese, with their different attitudes and customs, delighted him. He was always eager to learn, to experience, to know better, and to reflect upon whatever came his way.

The journeys outside the city of Winnipeg for the administration of the sacrament of confirmation, which were a feature of every spring and early summer, involved long trips, of as much as two thousand miles and as many as thirteen days away from the city.[1] He would drive with Norman Chartrand or Charlie Halpin, and later Ward Jamieson[2] through great lonely stretches of farm or forest, to the north and west of Winnipeg, or to the southwest corner of the province, stopping in small towns or villages where there would be a number of children and some adults to be confirmed. The churches were often poor and tiny, tended by a priest who may have been in residence, and who provided the archbishop with very simple food and lodging. The welcome was invariably warm and Flahiff enjoyed it. Best of all he appreciated seeing and encouraging his priests in these remote and usually poor places, and meeting the people. He catered to the native people's love of colour by arriving in town dressed in his purple cassock, or later his red one, complete with gold pectoral cross. In one case he spoke of stopping a few miles out of town "to put on every stitch of red" he had, because the pastor there had warned him that his people were looking forward "to seeing a real cardinal."[3]

On another occasion he wrote: "Often these mixed-bloods are remarkably beautiful; the children are charming. Bright colours predominate; my red was a great success with them – even better than the purple used to be. So I have found *one* good use for the cardinalatial red." There were hazards and hardships, of course. An example of these was the attack of the mosquitoes at Langruth, a prosperous Hungarian community of good farmers. He wrote glowingly of the reception, the ceremony of confirmation, the good community spirit, then added: "I enjoyed the whole thing immensely, except for one thing: Langruth is near a swampy area on the [western] edge of [Lake Manitoba] and we suffered a mosquito barrage unlike anything I have experienced ... I was able to bat at the 'dive-bombers' above the table, but I had no protection against the attacks launched at my ankles. Remaining calm became quite a problem. I was in misery."[4]

The tall archbishop with his charming manner and easy friendliness won the hearts of his people by his very presence. Whether he won their minds or even made contact with them is another question. Because his academic habits never left him, he sometimes spoke over the heads of both children and adults, and occasionally he went overtime, which his flock would appreciate only at hockey games. Returning home from one confirmation, Ward Jamieson, made bold to say, perhaps a bit exasperated: "Your Eminence, I don't think those good people understood a word you said – and neither did I!" To which Flahiff laconically replied: "You know, Ward, that very thought occurred to me as I was speaking." Another of his close collaborators was wont to remark: "George is better *being* George than *speaking* George."

Flahiff liked liturgical functions not so much for the splendour and pomp which those events imply as for the teaching and spiritual uplift which they could provide. He officiated at liturgies solemnly and beautifully. He was obviously conscious of what was going forward on a higher level than merely that of formal movements and music. He was sensitive to the "communion" aspect of a liturgical gathering.

For this reason he loved especially what is called the Chrism Mass, which took place the week before Holy Week and during which the sacred oils were blessed. Originally the ceremony was intended to unite the priests in a celebration of their priesthood on Holy Thursday. Flahiff was one of the two bishops in the world who pioneered concelebration (that is, a number of priests celebrating together) at this mass, a custom which is now common throughout the Catholic Church.[5] But also important for him was the inclusion of the laity in this particular celebration. Since Vatican II, the notion of the priesthood of the laity, that is, of all the baptized, had received increasing attention. Flahiff invited everyone to this mass and stressed both the ministerial priesthood and the baptismal priesthood in his homilies.[6] The Chrism Mass became popular and was probably *the* unifying ceremony for the Archdiocese of Winnipeg. People would come great distances to assist at it. On one occasion Flahiff wrote: "The Chrism Mass last night was very touching again, with priests and lay representatives from literally the farthest parts of the diocese. The pastor and three parishioners from Swan River were there and they set out again around 11.00 to drive the 325 (+) miles back. The Cathedral was overcrowded ... I had the impression that there was a very real sense of sharing on the part of all, laity as well as priests, in being 'the anointed of the Lord,' truly Christed."[7]

Occasionally, if one of his priests, for sickness or whatever reason, could not assure the services in his parish, the archbishop would replace him and function as a simple parish priest. The opportunity to minister to his people and to be close to them, without the burden of pontifical pomp, pleased him. "I spent a large part of to-day at our Italian parish," he wrote. "They were short of help, so the Pastor turned to me. My Mass was an English-speaking one, of course, but there was mixing with mostly Italian people afterwards." He goes on to say how he heard the children's confessions and then assisted in distributing communion at another mass, adding, "I should get back more often into that type of pastoral work."[8] And of another such occasion he wrote: "Last Sunday offered an interesting experience. The pastor of a small and rather poor parish was away and I offered to look after the Sunday ministry for him. It was truly refreshing ... Usually, when I go to a parish, it is for some particular 'occasion' and

I always have the feeling of being 'received.' But, last Sunday, I experienced the feeling of being 'with my people' … it was the utter simplicity of it that made it so attractive. And it was so easy to greet them and then to talk to them about the Good Shepherd."[9]

Flahiff was extremely kind in dealing with his priests. With few exceptions, they loved and admired him. They found him open, understanding, and trusting. If one was in difficulty of any kind, he knew he would get a sympathetic hearing and wise counsel from his archbishop. Flahiff was not one to censure or scold, and only with the greatest difficulty could he steel himself to discipline anyone. His reaction to a raised voice in a meeting of his priests was to leave the meeting, but if someone was complaining to him personally and even rudely, he would listen patiently, always looking for an amicable solution. In general assemblies of priests he presented himself as "George," and wanted to be addressed so. Few complied, however, but more out of respect than fear. He was habitually very relaxed with his priests and they with him. He would invite to Christmas dinner at his home in Charleswood those of his priests who had no place to go on that day. He was especially kind to priests in difficulty and with those who wanted to leave the priesthood and came to him to discuss the matter. His watchword was compassion; his *bête noire*, compulsion.

Flahiff was one who empowered others in that he would welcome an idea and encourage the person who presented it. If he assigned a task to someone he then left that person free to do it without interference on his part. He encouraged people to experiment with projects and programs even before asking him, satisfied to receive a report afterwards. He also challenged his collaborators with such sayings as, "If you are smart enough to see a problem, you are smart enough to find a solution." Nor did his frequent absences from the archdiocese diminish their respect. Something of his relationship with his priests is touchingly revealed in his description of their retreat with him in May of 1970. He wrote: "The Liturgy was particularly well prepared … About 55 concelebrated each day … All the way through there was great warmth, and each celebration brought a greater ease, closeness and real community, – noticeable spontaneity as the days went on … I took the homily on the last day; then each priest came up to place his hands in mine and expressed in his own words his dedication, obedience or what have you. I felt tears welling up more than once at the obvious sincerity and, if I am not mistaken, the real joy at what they were doing."[10] One small shadow on this good relationship of Flahiff with his priests was his habit of using the expression "our priests," meaning the Basilian Fathers! While the priests of his archdiocese had reason to wince, they had no heart to correct their courteous – and oblivious – archbishop.

Administration, however, was another matter; it was not Flahiff's long suit. He knew he was not good at it and he had no taste for it, or vice versa. He had the same aversion to making appointments and changing his priests as he did when superior general of the Basilians. This resulted in delays and uncertainties which exasperated all parties concerned. His hesitation was above all from a fear of offending. He wanted no one to be assigned to a position against that person's will. One young priest found himself in an assignment which was quite uncongenial, even impossible. Flahiff heard him sympathetically, telling him that the days of absolute commands and blind obedience were over. He assigned him to another parish, and then typically forgot to inform the pastor of the parish that the young priest would be coming. When the latter arrived at his new parish two weeks later at noon, he got a very cool reception and was only reluctantly allowed to stay for lunch. The matter was soon cleared up, however, with apologies from the archbishop.

His desk was chaotic, though he did manage to find things on it. He would frequently fail to replace files after he had used them. His own manner of filing was to make piles of papers everywhere in his office, and then in the adjacent washroom, where he ultimately blocked the ventilation system with mountains of paper. He had an absolute aversion to dictating machines. Fortunately he had a capable, intelligent and gracious secretary, Viola Specht, whose devotion and efficiency assured a smooth-running office. He too readily gave over and left to others matters, particularly financial ones, which he himself should have monitored constantly and carefully. His indifference to these things was a frustration for those around him, who perceived clearly the dire consequences of his neglect.

Prominent laymen who formed the archdiocesan board of directors respected and admired Flahiff as a person and as a priest, but wrung their hands at his ineptness and hesitation in administrative matters. Flahiff, unlike his predecessor, Philip Pocock, would never use his position to push a cause. Laymen or priests who were working for various causes for the Church would expect him to play a part in meetings more than just by his presence. He frequently let them down by his refusal to weigh in or "to stick his neck out," as the saying goes. There was one case at least of a prominent lay member of the archdiocesan corporation who resigned in disgust at Flahiff's refusal to act. Like the Fabians in early twentieth-century Britain,[11] he believed in "the inevitability of gradualness," with the added component of friendship. While never compromising on truth or justice, he lacked the aggressiveness, sternness, and even political acuity that these important matters demanded.

The Manitoba School Question was a case in point. This issue of government support for private schools and particularly for Catholic schools had vexed Manitoba since the government of that province absorbed the Catholic school system into the public system in 1890. It had been a cause célèbre in Canadian politics and even today it remains without a fully satisfactory solution. No doubt Flahiff's appointment to Winnipeg had been motivated partly because of his experience as an educator with knowledge of schools and school systems, and therefore one who might well advance the cause of the Catholic schools in Manitoba. He arrived on the scene at a time when once again the matter of government support for Catholic schools was being hotly debated and Duff Roblin's survival as premier was threatened. Archbishop Pocock had worked steadily to create a favourable atmosphere among leaders and elements of the population at the grass-roots level, though the matter was still emotionally charged and a flash point for controversy.

An article in the 15 April 1961 Toronto *Globe and Mail Magazine* (when Flahiff had been already named archbishop but had not yet arrived in Winnipeg) presented a picture of the political turmoil around the question of aid to Catholic schools and of what might eventuate for Premier Roblin. When the article appeared there was a lull in the controversy and the writer explained: "The lull, however, may be due to the change in archbishops. Most Rev. Philip Pocock has been posted to Toronto, and Very Rev. George Bernard Flahiff of the Basilian Fathers is to become Archbishop of Winnipeg. Despite the controversy, the charm and wit of Archbishop Pocock gained the church many friends in Winnipeg and the day may come when those friendships will yield dividends. What happens next will no doubt depend on the policy of his scholarly successor."

That policy seems unfortunately to have been "wait and see." Flahiff did not actively take up the question or make it a priority in his pastorate. It was not through a lack of interest or conviction; it was more a habit of mind and manner, which valued amicable relations more than political aggressiveness. There was a slight advance in the situation in Flahiff's time when, in July 1978, a bill went through the Manitoba legislature strengthening the existing system of shared facilities between public and Catholic schools, but the credit for this was hardly due to Flahiff's efforts. Perhaps little could have been done during the years of his tenure in Winnipeg. It remains a disappointment to many, however, that Flahiff did not see fit to use his exceptional talents and his enormous prestige more readily in the cause of the Catholic schools.

While those close to Flahiff could observe his deficiencies as an administrator, none would deny his wisdom and his insight. His view of the Church as a whole was magnificent, though his understanding of the workings of an ordinary parish was quite limited. The historical perspective which he brought to every situation bred a serenity in him and in others who heard his opinions. "He could see around corners," one of his close collaborators said. The past was, as it were, present to him, and he could see the future, though he might not have been able to see over the clutter on his desk. He "thought in centuries," someone said to him one day and provoked the quip, "O come now, I'm not *that* old."[12] And where human relations were concerned, he was peerless.

Flahiff was a born ecumenist. While firm in his adherence to the doctrine and practice of his own Church, he had the greatest respect for the faith, sincerity, and good will of those of other beliefs. His ecumenical mentality flowed naturally from his optimistic and benevolent view of the world. He saw all persons as good and worthy of respect. In Winnipeg Flahiff was looked upon as a unifying figure respected by religious, political, and university leaders alike, no matter of what religious hue.

In Winnipeg he fostered a first-ever ecumenical project with the establishment of the Assiniboia Christian Centre, in which Catholics and Anglicans built a facility in common for worship and for parish activities. The centre was home to two parishes, John XXIII for the Catholics, and St Chad's for the Anglicans. The worship area was common to both groups, each accommodating itself to the other for times of services. The other features – classrooms, gymnasium, and meeting rooms – were shared as well. The centre was inaugurated in November of 1968, and it is still functioning today. The project came from lay initiative, which pleased Flahiff greatly. It remains a striking example of ecumenism in action, the kind Flahiff preached and promoted.

A project dear to Flahiff which was not so successful was the Pastoral Training Centre called Wolseley House, inaugurated in the early 1970s. It was to be a place of study and formation for parish administration. Unfortunately it developed in such a way that it was eating up close to 50 per cent of the diocesan revenue. Flahiff was slow or perhaps unwilling to recognize that the centre was not financially viable and was not fulfilling its original purpose. It was his brain-child, perhaps the only initiative that was really his own. He decided that a drive was necessary to save the centre, though his advisors, notably Norman Chartrand, Charlie Halpin, and Joseph (Jakey) Driscoll SJ, were against the idea. The last of these three was deputed to see Flahiff and to explain as best he could why a drive should not take place. In what has since been often recounted as a memorable moment in the annals of the Archdiocese of Winnipeg Chancery Office, the habitually calm and reasonable Flahiff could be heard through the closed doors shouting: "I *know* the Centre is losing money; that is why we need a drive!" Driscoll came out slightly shaken, to the nervous grins of his colleagues. Someone said teasingly: "Now what do you say of your unflappable archbishop?" All were secretly pleased to have a glimpse of clay feet. The drive took place and failed. The centre also failed and was closed in 1983 by Archbishop Exner, Flahiff's successor.

Flahiff was a busy man who gave himself wholeheartedly to his work. He readily accepted invitations to parish celebrations, which in his richly diverse diocese were many and various. He gave a good deal of time to the communities of sisters as he had done during his years in Toronto. He was generous with his time for community celebrations or anniversaries among the sisters, and would even give days at a time to help in major meetings such as chapters, and this both within his archdiocese and outside it. Some remarked – complained? – that he gave more attention to the nuns in his diocese than he did to his priests. Be that as it may, Flahiff went a long way to be of service to all, without discrimination, without stint. Such was his outreach that at Christmas time he sent between six and seven hundred cards. Most of these bore a short note in his own hand. All were personally signed.

He was in demand as a speaker both at home and abroad. His passion for preparedness made these requests more of a chore than one might think, for he was not content to mouth banalities. He took the trouble to suit his words to the occasion and to say something of substance. Because of his position he was often the main speaker at an event; when he was not, he was invariably called upon "to say a few words." His gentle sense of humour and his ready wit served him in good stead on these occasions. Unless the occasion were particularly solemn or sad, he seasoned his remarks with pleasantries, often self-deprecatory. Above all, he could adapt to the occasion, never uncomfortable or causing strain, whether he was addressing his priests, a hospital convention, a university convocation, or pronouncing the

Invocation before the Queen of England and the assembled dignitaries of the province of Manitoba.

Flahiff maintained a demanding pace in his various functions. "Last week was quite busy," he wrote. "The special items included a meeting of the Bishops with our Manitoba Catholic School Trustees Association, the ordination of a Permanent Deacon … the inauguration of eleven new candidates for the diaconate, a special session with the Diocesan Financial Committee and advisors, etc. On the more social side was a dinner to honour a good lady who, for 42 years, has served as a Chaplain's volunteer at our Penitentiary. Then on Friday evening, we had the annual barbecue at St. Benedict's Convent to which Priests and Religious are invited."[13] At the time of writing this Flahiff was seventy-four years of age. Doubtless others in comparable positions kept as busy a schedule or even a busier one. What marked his ministry in a special way were the generosity, good humour, and graciousness with which he served his people. A word of weariness might escape him, but never one of complaint.

Each New Year's Day Flahiff held a levée. He would first attend that of the Lieutenant-Governor of Manitoba and then return hastily to the Cathedral Parish Hall to receive his own people. He would stand for hours, greeting each one in a way that recognized the specialness of that person. This was true of him any time he found himself in a receiving line; he would meet everyone and he himself would be the last to leave. Oftentimes his ring finger was bleeding from the pressure of four hundred or more handshakes! Of one occasion he remarked with pleasure how some young people began a sing-song at one of these levees, an indication of the kind of atmosphere his presence created, even on formal occasions.[14]

He was appreciated by the university community in Winnipeg. St Paul's College, which was run by the Jesuits, gave him an entry to the campus and he was always responsive to an invitation from there for any academic, liturgical, or social event. The university itself was aware Winnipeg's Roman Catholic archbishop was a renowned scholar. He was regularly invited to academic events, and for two years he occupied the position of honorary member of the Department of History. He did read some theses and attend some academic meetings, though he gave no regular course or lectures. The whiff of academic atmosphere was pleasant to him, and nostalgic. He would have been happy to exchange his mitre for a mortar board, had he been able.

Flahiff kept up this pace as archbishop of an immense but sparsely populated archdiocese for twenty-one years. He enjoyed what he and his doctor, Jacob Hollenberg, jokingly referred to as "monotonously good health," in spite of a few exceptional moments, which we shall refer to later. As he moved towards his seventy-fifth birthday he slowed down considerably, both in his activity and in his habitual élan. He was also haunted at moments by the thought that he was too active, too much given to trivialities, and that his work was really vain, because he felt that it was not sufficiently directed by the Spirit of God.

In September of 1976, while relaxing with the Gang of Five at Emmett Carter's cottage over the Labour Day weekend, Flahiff read in his breviary a rather moving passage from Pope St Gregory the Great, who is lamenting his own deficiencies in the service of God's people, his distractions, his lack of time for prayer, his many and various obligations that keep him from the peace he knew as a monk before he was made pope. Gregory knows he is called to be a "watchman" over the people of God, but finds himself mired in distractions, some from his work and some from his weakness. He writes in part: "With my mind divided and torn to pieces by so many problems how can I meditate or preach wholeheartedly without neglecting the ministry of proclaiming the Gospel? ... I often listen patiently to chatter. And because I too am weak, I find myself drawn little by little into idle conversation ... What I once found tedious I now enjoy. So who am I to be a watchman, for I do not stand on the mountain of action but lie down in the valley of weakness."[15]

Flahiff perceived immediately the parallel with his own life. He, like Gregory, was taken from monastic life to be an administrator. He could empathize with the great pope: they were both prelates with heavy responsibilities who perceived their human weakness and seeming failure. Flahiff commented: "I read and meditated on [the passage] on Emmett's lawn at Grand Bend. Rarely have I identified more closely with such a passage; it expresses a lot for a bishop [even] 1400 years after it was written."[16]

Like any person in a comparable position of responsibility, Flahiff felt at times his inadequacy and the fruitlessness of his efforts. He was not immune to the weariness of life that at one time or another overtakes even the most dazzlingly successful people. His failure, as he saw it, to foster vocations to the priesthood and his consciousness of being unable to face conflict and make it fruitful, were two things which especially weighed on him. But he was essentially a man of faith and hope; despair was not in his vocabulary and discouragement was never given its head. He remained ever conscious of his role as one who must encourage others; nor was he found wanting in this.

In June of 1975 Flahiff was named a Companion of the Order of Canada, the highest rank of the order. The honour pleased him greatly and from the time he received it from the hands of the governor general, Jules Léger, at Rideau Hall on 6 December of that year, he wore the insignia of the order on his lapel. He wrote of the occasion: "[The ceremony] was truly delightful and very pleasant to recall ... The medal itself is simple but quite beautiful; the heart of it (flower-shaped) is all white, so that it shows up well against the black."[17] His abiding love of country was increased by the honour shown him, which typically he thought of as more than personal: it was also an honour for the Church and for Winnipeg.

We have noted that Flahiff was physically present in his diocese only about half the time. The other half was spent on a broader stage – other parts of Canada, Rome, various cities in the United States, Latin America – where he journeyed and was present in various capacities: counsellor, executive, diplomat, speaker, teacher, apostle of Vatican II, or simply friend. Before looking at this broader activity, it would be well to look at a particular event in his pastorate which very much increased his prestige in Canada and placed him on the world stage: the cardinalate.

CHAPTER TWELVE

Red Alert at Midnight

Archbishop Flahiff returned home late on the evening of 27 March 1969, after a meeting with a group of priests, to find a telephone message which read: "Please call the Apostolic Delegate in Ottawa this evening, no matter how late the hour." The archbishop dutifully put through the call, in spite of the fact that the hour was even later in Ottawa than it was in Winnipeg. The apostolic delegate, Archbishop Clarizio, answered the phone, thanked Flahiff for calling, and said: "The Holy Father has named thirty-five new cardinals; their names will be published tomorrow morning. The Archbishop of Winnipeg is one of them."

For a moment Flahiff did not catch the full import of what the delegate had said to him, thinking that it was a fine thing that new cardinals be named, but wondering why the news merited a late-night call to him. Then it dawned on him, "*I* am the Archbishop of Winnipeg." He was thunderstruck. The delegate, wondering about the long silence on the other end of the line asked, "Are you still there?" "Yes, Your Excellency," said Flahiff weakly. "Well, congratulations, Your Eminence," said the delegate. "It is a great honour for Canada and for Winnipeg. The consistory will be held in Rome early in May. You will receive the information and documents in good time. Good night, Your Eminence; sleep well!" The delegate's wish was as vain as it was polite. Stunned and troubled, Flahiff managed to drop off about 3:00 a.m., his life once more jolted into a new course.

The new cardinal's phone began to ring at 8:00 in the morning, just as he was finishing mass, and continued to ring relentlessly throughout the day: the press, his family, the lieutenant-governor, dignitaries, friends. Fortunately he had a dental appointment that morning, which gave him a short respite. He said to a reporter later in the day that he had indeed thought of postponing the appointment after hearing the news, but did not think that would be fair, for "dentists are busy people." Telegrams, which ultimately numbered well over three hundred, began to pour in: from Rome, Belgium (Cardinal Suenens), Brazil, Ireland, England, France, Monaco (Prince Ranier), and from all over Canada and the United States. Flahiff was characteristically sensitive to the humorous aspects of some of the messages, one saying, "We feel more *hinged* to the Church." (The word cardinal comes from the Latin word *cardo*, meaning hinge.). Another read, "You don't have to leave Winnipeg to be a success." He commented: "Some are funny through misspellings. Some are *mildly* pretentious, to say the least. Some assign me the most fantastic roles; I suppose they are in good faith which makes me feel very small and almost hopeless." There were extremes in the messages: "In two successive greetings I am hailed as the one to hold the line as subversive elements seek to destroy the Church from within and then as one to assure that, at last, the liberal voice will be heard in the Church!"[1]

The deluge of greetings and good wishes is a measure of the great esteem in which Flahiff was held in Winnipeg and far beyond the limits of his archdiocese or even of his country. The appointment was extremely popular. He himself was genuinely surprised and taken aback; his friends and acquaintances were overjoyed. They saw in the appointment the recognition of a churchman who was intelligent, forward-looking, and of unquestioned integrity. He inspired hope, and his being raised to a position of great influence in the Church raised the hopes of many both in Canada and abroad for reforms and for progress. He was a symbol of the *aggiornamento* which had been the clarion call of Pope John XXIII in summoning the Second Vatican Council.

Neither his personal surprise, however, nor the euphoria which surrounded him, unbalanced him when he met the press. He found the right words and, true to form, deflected the honour from his own person. He was deeply touched, he said, by the gesture of Pope Paul in naming him; it was a great honour for Canada and especially for western Canada. And, to the inevitable question as to why one should be a cardinal, he replied: to proclaim ever more clearly the message of Jesus Christ.

In the Legislative Assembly on the afternoon of 28 March 1969 *Hansard* reported a series of short speeches paying handsome tribute to the new cardinal and ending with a touch of humour. After the session had been duly opened with prayer, and guests acknowledged, the Progressive-Conservative premier, Walter Weir, rose to move that the House recognize the honour that had come to a distinguished Manitoban, namely, Archbishop George Bernard Flahiff, who had been named that day a cardinal of the Holy Roman Church. Weir went on to give some information about the cardinal, pay some compliments, and ask the speaker to convey, on behalf of the House, "congratulations and the expression of our satisfaction at the news." Then the leader of the opposition, Gildas Molgat, addressed the Speaker supporting the premier's motion, and in a slightly shorter speech, commented on Archbishop Flahiff's broad-mindedness and how he had brought understanding among the various religious groups in the province. The leader of the NDP, Ed Schreyer, rose in his turn to support the motion. This left only the Social Credit member, Jacob Froese, obviously only vaguely conversant with what was being talked about, who added the following: "Mr. Speaker, having been unaware of the situation, nevertheless, I would like to join with the First Minister and other members who have spoken on congratulating the – and also expressing my best wishes to the person involved." The cardinal pencilled beside this paragraph in his copy of *Hansard*: "An honest man at last! Eureka!"

Outwardly Flahiff met the appointment cheerfully and with grace. It came at a very busy time so that there was little opportunity to ruminate or brood over the implications of his new status. Holy Week was to begin in two days with Palm Sunday, followed by the numerous and lengthy ceremonies leading to Easter. The Plenary Assembly of the Canadian Conference of Catholic Bishops was scheduled for the second week after Easter, and this meant leaving for Ottawa soon after Easter, since Flahiff was a member of the Permanent Council of the conference, the body charged with the preparation of the meeting.

Far from being elated by this great honour which had come upon him so unexpectedly, privately Flahiff was deeply dismayed and fearful. "It is difficult," he wrote, soon after the announcement, "to analyze my feelings over these first three days ... There was a very real degree of interior numbness; there was preoccupation and concern that didn't fix on anything very precise; there was a very sensible depression ... The feeling had been akin to what I once described to you about previous moments in my life when, trying quietly to mind my own business, I found something of weight and consequence, far beyond what I felt capable of, thrust upon me. This time was perhaps the worst of all."[2]

Various aspects and ramifications of the nomination came to trouble him. He wondered, for example, why he, a bishop for only eight years, heading a relatively less important see, should receive the honour, while Archbishop Pocock in Toronto, a man who had served longer and with greater distinction as bishop in no less than three dioceses and in difficult circumstances, should be passed over. The fact that Pocock was a close friend added to his chagrin. This "pass-over," as some called it, was an embarrassment to Flahiff all his life. It made no difference, however, to the strong friendship between the two men, a fact which attests to the magnanimity of both.

And then there was the fear of being named to a position in the Roman Curia with the obligation of moving to Rome. Flahiff realized that he might well be considered for the position of prefect of the Sacred Congregation for Religious and Secular Institutes, and that he had probably been named a cardinal with a view to one day occupy-ing that position. Much as he loved Rome, he had no desire whatso-ever to live there, much less to be saddled with the direction of one of the curial congregations. Nor did he have any ambition to be pope, a position for which he was now eligible. Basically it was his imagined lack of suitability for these positions which haunted him. It was also the fear of losing more of his freedom, the company of his friends, and the contact with his people.

In the days following the announcement, Flahiff went about his duties, cancelling none of the appointments he had made. He went through the ceremonies of Holy Week perhaps with a keener sense of the passion of Christ and its meaning for him. As time passed he grew more accustomed to his lot and more interested in the coming events of going to Rome and participating in the consistory, which was scheduled for the first of May. He contacted Gammarelli, the Roman tailor who had made his episcopal robes, to order a red cas-sock, a black one with red piping, and the magnificent red cardinal's cape. The tailor had his measurements on file, and when Flahiff came to try on the new robes, there was very little adjusting to do, thanks to his rigid life-long fidelity to the 5BX exercise program of the Royal Canadian Air Force. Flahiff flew to Rome on 24 April 1969 with a reti-nue of some fifty persons: Archbishop (Baudoux of St Boniface), ten priests, ten nuns, twenty-seven laymen and laywomen, including his brother Terry and his wife Françoise. Not all the laity in the entourage were Catholics. Sterling Lyon, then attorney general of Manitoba, for example, went as representative of the Canadian government, appointed by Prime Minister Trudeau and given ambassadorial rank for the occasion.

The historic, happy, and rather hectic ceremonies took place over four days, from 28 April to 1 May 1969. The first of these was the Secret Consistory at 9:30 a.m. on 28 April, when the pope met with

Cardinal Flahiff receiving the red biretta from Pope Paul vi,
30 April 1969. (Photo: Felici, Rome)

the existing cardinals and announced the names of thirty-three new
ones. Two names were not revealed, but were kept *in petto* or "in the
heart" of the pope, probably for political reasons. The cardinals
present gave their consent and the pope forthwith created the new
cardinals. According to ancient custom, messengers were then
dispatched with a letter to each new cardinal at his place of residence
in Rome. For convenience, and perhaps because of the impossible
traffic in Rome, the new cardinals were grouped in three or four
readily accessible places near the Vatican. Those from North and
South America were gathered in the Cancelleria Apostolica, which is
a building not far from St Peter's Basilica. When Cardinal Masella,
the pope's messenger to this particular group, arrived there with the
individual letters of nomination, the hall was filled almost to overflowing with the families and friends of the new cardinals and the
media in force. It was hardly a ceremony; it was more like a party after a successful election. The new cardinals remained in that same
hall for several hours to receive ambassadors and other dignitaries in
what is called *di calore* ("heart-warming") visits. "It was a long day,"
as Flahiff commented in an account he wrote of the events.[3]

Two days later, Flahiff and the other cardinals received the red biretta, rather a come-down from the traditional red hat, now no longer
used. This took place in the Hall of Benedictions, the enormous space

over the vast entrance porch of St Peter's. Present with the new cardinals were the existing cardinals, other prelates, the diplomatic corps, and the families and friends of the new cardinals. The text chosen for the scripture reading was that from St Mark's gospel (10:35–45) in which the sons of Zebedee, James and John, ask for a special place in the kingdom, and Jesus takes the occasion to say gently to all his disciples that the greatest among them is the one who is the servant of all. Pope Paul vi took this theme to explain to the assembly the role of a cardinal as one of service to the people of God. A photograph on this occasion, published in the *Osservatore Romano* of 8 May 1969, shows a solemn-faced Flahiff not looking directly at the pope but rigidly attentive.

Certainly the most solemn and beautiful of all the ceremonies and gatherings was the Public Consistory on Thursday, 1 May 1969 in St Peter's Basilica. Surrounded by the new cardinals, Pope Paul concelebrated a Mass of Thanksgiving at the Altar of the Confession (the main altar) over the tomb of St Peter. It was the feast-day of St Joseph the Worker, and the pope gave his homily on the virtue of poverty, the dignity of labour, and the need for Christians to strive for social justice.[4] After the homily each new cardinal approached the pope to pledge his fidelity and to receive a ring.

In a letter written very late that same day, Flahiff briefly described his feelings and his fatigue: "The official part of it is over; a fair amount of the social part remains; but to-night I breathe a sigh of relief after three days that have, I believe, no counterpart in my whole life, long though it may be ... you would have to experience them to realize what they have been physically, emotionally and spiritually ... I can hardly keep my eyes open. I am not sure whether the feeling is that of being punch-drunk or just weary. I think I feel a bit bruised, but there is no hurt."[5]

The following day, once again in St Peter's, the pope received in audience the new cardinals and ten guests of each, together with any accompanying bishops. The pope greeted the whole group briefly in seven languages and then spoke a few words to each as that person was presented to him – some four hundred in all. Later in the week, Cardinal Flahiff had a personal audience with the Paul vi. There were, as well, invitations from the British and French ambassadors to the Holy See, as well as other gatherings and dinners with members of his party and with friends in Rome. Flahiff enjoyed it all but felt the fatigue of such intensive and stirring activity. Possibly the most emotional moment of all was a dinner with the Winnipeg delegation. The cardinal rose to speak but his voice betrayed him and possibly fatigue had weakened him. He tried valiantly but only managed a few words when he broke down and was unable to continue. It was certainly the most effective speech he gave during all the festivities.

On 9 May 1969 Flahiff left Rome for Annonay in France, the small town in the beautiful hills of the Ardèche, where the Basilians began. Annonay is off the beaten track, being some forty-five miles from the nearest large city, Lyons. This did not deter Flahiff. Annonay was a historic spot as the birthplace of the Basilians, and he decided his first visit after a historic moment in *his* life would be there. Thus he was in Annonay on the tenth, in Paris on the eleventh, and in London on the twelfth to see the Queen.

The invitation to Buckingham Palace had come through the Canadian ambassador to Italy during the festivities in Rome. About the invitation he wrote light-heartedly: "I do not know whether this is standard procedure, or whether someone asked for it. All I have is the message notifying me. I feel like Dick Whittington, but without the cat!"[6] Curiously he had not wished, at first, to accept the invitation. Nor did he, for all his courteous ways, see any problem in refusing. His reaction was one of those mysterious quirks of his character which no one, perhaps not even he himself, could penetrate. He was gently but firmly bullied by Norman Chartrand, who went about making the necessary travel and protocol arrangements for the visit.

Once in London, of course, Flahiff was pleased, positive, and even excited about the visit, which came off splendidly, and which began a friendship and mutual admiration between two exceptional persons. Arriving at the palace in a chauffeur-driven car (which Flahiff had suggested they use, to the amazement of his chancellor), the cardinal was duly instructed in the protocol of his presentation to the Queen. He was shown into a waiting room where, after a few minutes, the Queen entered, opening the door for herself. Her first words to her guest after the exchange of greetings were, "My Lord Cardinal, what on earth does your Church mean by demoting our St George?" (The "demotion" of the saint had actually occurred about this time: the reformed calendar no longer included St George among the saints to be venerated with a feast day throughout the Universal Church.) Flahiff may have been surprised at the Queen's question, but he was not lost for words: "Your Majesty," he replied, "I should like to know myself. You see, my name is George."

Another interesting conversation with the Queen took place a year later when the sovereign was in Winnipeg for the celebration of the centennial of the entrance of Manitoba into Confederation. Flahiff had been invited by the government to give the invocation, which he

did splendidly, partly in English and partly in French. But in one way
he disappointed the Queen. "My Lord Cardinal," she asked, "where
is your red?" "So please Your Majesty," replied the cardinal, "the
invitation specified 'business suit.'" "Oh," said the Queen, "but
surely not for a cardinal." Her Majesty seems to have had a truer
sense of what was fitting and a better instinct for the meaning of a
directive.

Cardinal Flahiff returned to Winnipeg by way of New York and
Toronto, arriving home on 15 May 1969 to a magnificent welcome. He
was met at the airport by a cross-section of the citizenry: school children, sisters, priests, civic dignitaries, and friends. He was dressed, as
directed by the reception committee, in black cassock with red piping
and the flowing cape of red watered silk with his red biretta.
Winnipeg airport features a spacious staircase from the arrivals level
to the main floor, open to the view of all. Down came the imposing
figure in red and black, smiling, obviously immensely pleased, coming home to his own. On the main floor the children awaited him and
accompanied him applauding during his slow progress to the motor-
cade. The procession of cars moved off towards the centre of the city,
with slowdowns at various spots to receive the cheers of massed
school children. At the City Hall, where another crowd of children
awaited him, he was met by the deputy mayor, Slaw Rebchuk, a
Catholic whom the cardinal knew well, and whom he greeted with,
"Well, how are you, Slaw?" He was then conducted to the reception
area where a speech of welcome was read and to which he replied
briefly, more or less impromptu, for the notes he had jotted down on
the plane he had promptly lost in the fuss of the arrival. He said he
was touched by the welcome and that he was glad to be back in
Winnipeg. They had brought out of storage for the occasion the 196-
year-old chair that had belonged to the first mayor of Winnipeg,
doubtless thinking it only suitable for a prince of the Church. The cardinal appreciated the gesture, though he stood to meet the members
of the city government and their wives, and to have a word with
each, as was his wont.

The next stop was the provincial legislature. Walter Weir met the
cardinal as he emerged from his car, and the two, escorted by red-
coated Mounted Police, proceeded into the legislature and up the
grand staircase to the large rotunda, where the lieutenant-governor,
Richard S. Bowles, received Manitoba's man of the hour. Both the lieutenant-governor and the premier spoke "touchingly," as the cardinal
put it, and he replied equally warmly in a slightly longer speech than
the one given at City Hall. A reception line was then formed consisting

Cardinal Flahiff being welcomed in Winnipeg, 16 May 1969, with Mayor Slaw Rebchuck
and Monsignor E.M. Hubicz on his right and Monsignor O.J. McInerney on his left.
(Photo: Frank Chalmers, *Winnipeg Tribune*, courtesy of the Department
or Archives and Special Collections, University of Manitoba)

of the premier, the lieutenant-governor, and the cardinal. He received
the MLAs and their spouses and friends, members of the judiciary, the
consular corps, many of the civil servants, representatives of the other
churches, along with the twenty-five visiting bishops, as well as other
clergy and people in the audience. Some refreshments were served to a
smaller group in the premier's office. The cars then moved off to
St Mary's Cathedral, where the cardinal had a much appreciated respite before the liturgical reception scheduled for 6:00 p.m.

The reception at his cathedral church was simple and dignified:
formal welcome by the rector, Monsignor Roy Larrabee, scripture
reading, and a homily by the cardinal on the same text Pope Paul had
used at the ceremony of the conferring of the red biretta in Rome two
weeks previously, the key phrase being: "But whosoever will be the
greatest among you will be your servant." At a banquet in the
evening for the visiting bishops and clergy at the Fort Garry Hotel,
the cardinal spoke about impressions of Rome, the events of the past
weeks, and about Pope Paul's vitality and optimism, his sense of historical reality, his trust in the Spirit of God, and his exhortation to the
cardinals to return to their missions with renewed zeal.[7]

The following morning, when the Basilians who had come from Edmonton and Saskatoon for the occasion were about to leave, the cardinal insisted that they stay for lunch. One would have thought the festivities had tired him and that he would have preferred to spend the day quietly. But his love for the Basilian community, and his gratitude for the presence of his confreres in Winnipeg, would not allow him to let pass an occasion for some hours of companionship and conversation … in a fine restaurant, of course.

There were other events in connection with the cardinalate – visits, receptions, and liturgical services – which stretched out into the early summer. The great moments were over, however, and Cardinal Flahiff returned to his routine of confirmations and ordinary administration. He had given his adopted city a moment of glory and a much longer-lasting pride and joy. He made his people feel that what he had received was not just for him, but was everyone's joy, everyone's honour. In a word, the cardinalate brought him closer to his people because he really believed and felt that it was for them. The fears and apprehensions of his early reactions to his elevation gradually gave way to peace and ease in his new status. This was a regular pattern with Flahiff: the thing which at first loomed overwhelming and dreadful was faced, submitted to, and then conquered by his humility, his intelligence, and his desire to serve others.

To complete the ceremonies and duties of his new honour, Flahiff took formal possession of his cardinalitial church in Rome on 12 October 1969. He had scheduled the event to coincide with meetings of the Sacred Congregation for Religious and Secular Institutes which called him to the Eternal City at that time. From ancient times each cardinal has been assigned a church in Rome for, according to some historical theories, the cardinals were originally the high clergy of Rome.[8] The tradition is maintained in order to underline the close connection of cardinals to the Bishop of Rome. The relationship of a cardinal to the church assigned to him in Rome is merely symbolic, though custom has it that the cardinal make a gesture of monetary assistance to his church to mark his taking possession.

Flahiff's church, Santa Maria della Salute (Saint Mary of [Good] Health), a large modern building, is situated in a working-class area on the west side of Rome called Primavalle. The ceremony took place on a bright Sunday morning, with the Canadian chargé d'affaires, Pierre Dumas, present as well as officials from the Canadian embassy, and a number of Canadian bishops and heads of religious orders in Rome. The procession and entry into the church were quite splendid. The cardinal was flanked by papal guards and accompanied by a cohort of small boys dressed as crusaders, who took up a position around the altar and stood at attention all through the ceremony.

As impressive as were the pomp, the reading of the papal bull, and the figure of the enthroned cardinal himself, was the short homily he gave. While he doubtless enjoyed the fanfare and the colourful Italian crowd, Flahiff used the occasion to make a strong point about authority: "All the while," he said, in Italian, "traditions of value are being kept, yet I have the good fortune to be in Rome when something new is developing in the life of the Church typical of the constant renewal in its history. What is new is this attempt in modern times to determine how authority now is to be exercised in the Church and to update the relationship between the centre of the church and its periphery."[9]

With the help of some of his close friends among the Canadian bishops, Flahiff donated five thousand dollars to his church for a new marble altar and work on the sanctuary, to mark his assignment to this church.[10] One may see today a red granite plaque on the wall at the left-hand side of the sanctuary which commemorates the event of his taking possession and of the renewal of the sanctuary.

Why was George Flahiff made a cardinal? We have already noted that Winnipeg was not one of the principal dioceses of the country. Nor was Flahiff outstanding for his administration, innovation, or leadership in the Canadian church. His being honoured with the red hat, though universally applauded, came as a surprise. The idea that his work with religious would make him useful in Rome at the head of the Congregation for Religious and Secular Institutes, and that the cardinalate was given with a view to a curial appointment, has some weight. Documentation to support the idea, however, would be hard to come by; it is probably non-existent. It would be equally difficult to document the suggestion that the pope wanted to recognize and honour the Church in western Canada. Nor was it that Canada lacked cardinals; there were actually three at the time Flahiff was named: Roy in Quebec, Léger in Montreal, and McGuigan in Toronto, although Cardinal McGuigan was in declining health and the archdiocese was being administered by Archbishop Pocock. In the world picture, Canada was rather generously represented in the Sacred College. And if a fourth cardinal were to be named, surely it should have been Pocock. Friends in high places might have had a hand in promoting Flahiff, particularly Sergio Pignedoli, former apostolic delegate to Canada, a good friend of Flahiff and close to Pope Paul VI. But who knows? The most satisfactory answer is that Archbishop Flahiff was made a cardinal because he was an exceptional person in whom

Pope Paul recognized qualities which he wanted present in the highest echelon in the Church.

With his new status, Flahiff stepped onto the world stage. While the office of cardinal adds nothing to the holy orders which one receives on being ordained a priest or a bishop, it does put one in a position of immense prestige and influence. He was widely known as archbishop, but he now became truly an international figure, belonging as he did to the highest council of the pope, the members of which were chosen from around the world. As cardinal he would be called more often to Rome. He would represent the Canadian bishops in various special missions, to Poland, to Mexico, and to Rio de Janeiro. He would be heeded with more deference when he wrote or spoke. He would add a special lustre to any event he attended. And, above all, he would have a voice in the choosing of the next pope. But these things, these effects of his office, meant very little to him. He truly believed with Pope Paul that the cardinalate was neither for personal honour nor for public prestige, but for more effective spread of the Kingdom of God on earth.

It would be hard to imagine anyone less affected by position or pomp than was Flahiff. Though he wore his title with dignity and he enjoyed being a cardinal, he maintained the human touch which endeared him to so many. No one was distanced from him because of his status. He never personally used the Vatican limousines which were at his disposition whenever he was in Rome. The bartender at the café opposite the Canadian College in Rome was struck speechless when he learned that the tall affable cleric chatting with the students as though he were one of them while he enjoyed an espresso was a cardinal who had just stepped off the bus, late for lunch at the college. The clerks in Eaton's in Winnipeg were used to seeing Flahiff dropping into the store, shopping, or just getting out of the cold.

A delightful episode is related by the cardinal's former secretary, Viola Specht: "His Eminence had been invited to celebrate his birthday at St. Joseph's Vocational School run by the Sisters of Providence. When he arrived he joined the intermediate group of boys (aged 6 to 12 years) where they were trying to get the Chaplain's myna bird, Chester, to say 'Happy Birthday.' Chester was loud and usually a great talker. His Eminence joined in on the fun but Chester was getting tired of it all and clammed up. Then suddenly in his loud voice said, 'Aw, shut up!' The Sisters were embarrassed, but His Eminence laughed and said something about being put in his place by another bird! Chester did eventually perform."[11]

CHAPTER THIRTEEN

On the World Stage

George Flahiff was destined to play a greater role than that of a bishop of one particular diocese in Canada. Both in his own country and abroad his position, his talents, and his personality would call him to exert a wide influence. His frequent travelling gave credibility to the quip, "If you want to find the cardinal, go to the airport." The circumstances that put him on the world stage were his being a cardinal, his membership in the Canadian Conference of Catholic Bishops (CCCB), his appointment to positions in the Roman Curia, his zeal for promoting the teaching of Vatican II, his generosity in responding to requests to speak, and his gracious manner. Lester Pearson was perceptive and prophetic in 1926 when he suggested to the young George Flahiff that he pursue a career in diplomacy. Others have said that as archbishop and cardinal his particular talents would have found their fullest scope in the diplomatic service of the Church.

Flahiff took his place among his fellow bishops in the CCCB as an exceptionally gifted member and one who could make a valuable contribution. There was no other bishop in the conference with equivalent academic standing, nor were there many endowed with the wisdom and the spirituality for which Flahiff was known. His position among the bishops of Canada came to be more that of sage and pacifier than that of leader. Or, to put it another way, he exercised a moral leadership rather than a political one. His manner was quite different from that of such strongly assertive persons as Cardinals James Charles McGuigan, Paul Emil Léger and Gerald Emmett Carter, whose influence in the conference was characteristically political. Flahiff did not speak frequently but when he did rise, his fellow bishops knew they would hear something wise and thoughtful, and seasoned with gentle humour.

Flahiff had been named secretary of the cccb in October 1961. A year later he was elected vice-chairman of the conference, and the year following that, when the conference met in Rome during the second session of the Vatican Council, he was elected chairman of the conference, a position he held for two years.[1] As chairman he was conscientious, deft at handling delicate situations, and possibly too indulgent with repetitious or long-winded speakers, which was quite in keeping with his deep respect for others and his inveterate hesitancy. He was elected to the permanent council of the cccb again in 1969 and continued in the position until 1980, an unusually long period of membership, and an indication of how much his counsel was valued by the bishops. The sixteen-member permanent council prepared the agenda for the general assemblies of the bishops and handled business in the interim between assemblies. Flahiff also functioned on several committees, one of which was the preparatory committee for the International Theological Congress held in Toronto in June 1967 as part of the Canadian centennial celebrations. This congress brought leading theologians to Canada from all parts of the world.

On two occasions the conference elected Flahiff to represent the Canadian bishops at the Synod of Bishops in Rome. The synod was established by Pope Paul vi in September of 1965, even before the Vatican Council had ended, as a means of providing a regular forum for the discussion of matters of importance for the whole Church. The synod was not intended to be a decision-making body, but only an advisory one. It was an attempt to give substance to the principle of collegiality, one of the foremost principles to come out of Vatican ii, and was considered to be a major development in the government of the Church.[2] The first synod was held in 1967. Flahiff was one of four Canadian bishops sent as delegates. He was elected as a Canadian delegate to the synod a second time in 1971, at which time he caused the sensation which has been described in the prologue to this book, with his plea for a study of the place of women in the ministries of the Church. It is important to remember that no Canadian bishop was speaking merely in his own name at the synod, but only in the name of his particular conference.[3] The speeches of the Canadian delegates at each synod were carefully prepared by the whole body of the bishops of Canada during the year before each synod opened, to make sure that what was said expressed the thinking of the conference as a whole. Flahiff's explosive intervention at the 1971 synod, however, redounded to him personally and willy-nilly marked him internationally as a champion of the recognition of women's place in the

Church, and even of the ordination of women. His second presentation at the same synod on the matter of social justice, also the fruit of long deliberation by the Canadian bishops, did not create the earlier sensation he had caused. Nevertheless, Flahiff was personally lauded for the intervention; and for this and other pronouncements on his part he acquired a reputation as a promoter of social justice in the world.

Twice the Canadian bishops elected Flahiff to be one of their representatives at the Inter-American Conference of Catholic Bishops, an organization whose membership includes the bishops of North and South America, and which calls general meetings every two or three years. Its purpose is not legislative but simply informative; nevertheless, it has proven useful for the contacts and the exchange of ideas it provides. Flahiff was one of four Canadian bishops elected to attend the meeting in Mexico City in May 1971. While the agenda was rather intense, treating chiefly of the topics of priesthood and social justice, Flahiff found time to do a good deal of visiting and dining, which he enjoyed to the full. In a long and interesting letter he describes the city, the people, the markets, the famous Shrine of Our Lady of Guadalupe, and the pleasantness of walking about. He says little of the actual discussions, but he does give some general impressions of the meeting: "What was of chief interest to me was the light that Latin Americans threw on [the two topics]. Their point of view and their preoccupations were always stimulating and challenging. Moreover, every one of the bishops was a strong person ... Many of the things they had to contribute opened our eyes ... you became aware of the problems that are peculiarly theirs."[4]

Two years later Flahiff was again elected as a delegate of the Canadian bishops to the Inter-American Conference, this time for the meeting to be held in Rio de Janeiro from 24 to 29 June 1973. Flahiff took advantage of the occasion to visit other cities in South America, including São Paulo and Santos (Brazil), Buenos Aires, Santiago, and Lima. He met a good number of South American bishops, and talked to missionaries in some of the poorest favelas of the huge cities. Fleeting and necessarily superficial as they were, these visits nevertheless deeply impressed the cardinal and were an education for him. Writing from Santiago, after his visit to Buenos Aires, he stated: "We spent a good part of our day in a 'favela' (slum) area where people who have wandered in from the 'interior' live in a tightly packed style that defies any description but that of a honeycomb. How so many (50,000 in this case) could live in so little square footage defies the imagination. Yet there it is! Obviously, it is poverty; yet it is not misery, in the strict sense. They all look human; they have interests; they *belong*. The whole thing is fascinating."[5] He was doubtless constantly contrasting what he saw with the spaciousness, the wealth, the political stability, and the sparse population of his own archdiocese, whose whole Catholic population could be less than that of one favelas of São Paulo or Buenos Aires.

Flahiff's work with the CCCB took him to Ottawa on an average of five times a year in the period from 1966 to 1982. He enjoyed CCCB work, largely for the association it provided with persons he found congenial and stimulating. After his retirement in 1982 he attended the annual meetings as "Bishop Emeritus," though his active participation was minimal during these declining years. A sad moment came in October of 1988 when he was about to be driven to the Toronto airport for a flight to Ottawa after Eucharist and lunch with some friends. It became increasingly evident that the cardinal was not well and was becoming increasingly disoriented. He himself recognized that he was in no condition to go to the meeting, and asked to be driven home. It was the end of twenty-seven years of valuable service to his fellow bishops and of his presence among them.

A second aspect of Flahiff's international position began with his nomination in January of 1968 to membership in two departments of the Roman Curia: the Sacred Congregation for Catholic Education (SCCE), and the Sacred Congregation for Religious and Secular Institutes (SCRSI). These nominations were a special recognition of Flahiff, since it was the first time that bishops from around the world – seven of them to be exact – were named to the Roman Curia. He was not yet a cardinal, though he would be named one the following year. His nomination to the SCRSI was noted with special satisfaction in various quarters, particularly among religious women in Canada and the United States, who felt that through Flahiff their aspirations and desires for renewal would be heard in Rome. Flahiff's wide experience in giving retreats and conferences to religious women had made him known as a man of rich spirituality and as one who was accessible, sympathetic, and disposed to help. The superior general of a religious order of women based in St Boniface, Manitoba, wrote to him at this time: "Be assured, Your Grace, that your presence in the Commission [of the Roman Curia] gives new hope to consecrated women and inspires in them a new courage in their constant quest for a more efficacious and authentic gift of self."[6]

Another word of congratulation, a rather touching one, came from an interesting source in the person of John Howard Griffin (1920–80), the black rights advocate, and a friend of Flahiff, who wrote on the occasion: "I have never for a moment loved the Church less than completely, but I do feel an even greater hope when I see men like you being advanced, especially in a world where the great and wise men too seldom get any kind of hearing."[7] Flahiff served on the scce for five years and on the scrsi for nineteen years.

Membership in the Roman Curia meant presence in Rome for meetings at least once a year and sometimes more often. Flahiff took his curial work very seriously and prepared for the meetings with his usual diligence. One of the few letters in which he allowed annoyance to show is addressed to Cardinal Garrone, prefect of the Sacred Congregation for Catholic Education, who was late in sending some promised documentation in preparation for an upcoming meeting. Flahiff wrote:

I must say in all frankness that I am disappointed at the lateness with which I received the documentation. I had been waiting for it ever since your letter of January 26 indicating that it would be sent *citius* [rather soon]. I am sure there are many and good reasons for the delay; but as it now is, there remain only two weeks before I must leave for Rome and these completely taken up with other meetings in Canada and in the United States. There will simply be no time to make the careful study of the documents that Your Eminence's letter of March 5 so strongly urges.

He went on to inform the cardinal prefect, rather petulantly, that his first inclination had been to cancel his trip but, considering the importance to persons in Canada of the matters to be treated, he would follow through with his plans to be in Rome for the meeting.[8]

Flahiff's influence in Rome with regard to questions on religious life extended through the whole period of his episcopate. Two weeks before his ordination as bishop in May 1961 he had been named to the Preparatory Committee on Religious Life for the Second Vatican Council. Then, when the council began, he was elected to the commission dealing with the same topic. As we have seen in a previous chapter, this meant he was one of the framers of *Perfectae Caritatis*, the decree on religious life promulgated on 28 October 1965. After the council he was named to the Post-Conciliar Commission on Religious Life (1966), the body responsible for the implementation of the council's decree throughout the world.[9] Two documents particularly worthy of note issued by the scrsi during his membership, and in the writing of which he had considerable influence were *Renovationis Causam: An Instruction on the Renewal of Religious Life*, issued on 6 January 1969, and *Evangelica Testificatio: An Apostolic Exhortation on the*

Renewal of Religious Life, issued on 29 June 1971. These documents
were intended to guide religious orders in the process of renewal
according to the spirit and the teaching of Vatican II. The second of
these went out over the signature of Pope Paul himself, but it was
largely the product of the SCRSI, and thus had input from Flahiff.
Work on these documents was for him a labour of love. Being a religious himself and an ardent promoter of the teaching of the Vatican
Council, he was more than pleased to be part of a process which
would help religious, especially women religious, meet the challenges of the post-conciliar period, those years of agony for religious
orders, marked by defections, rebellions, and questionable experi-
ments and teachings. Flahiff never lived to see the ship of religious
life on a completely even keel, but his steadfastness and optimism in
turbulent times provided a strong moral support for many religious
orders and many individuals.

Flahiff's words in Rome were monitored with interest and in some
quarters with suspicion, since he had a reputation for liberalism.
Indeed, the Canadian bishops as a group were considered liberals.
Such a reputation was established largely by what has come to be
called the Winnipeg Statement of September 1968, which was drawn
up by the Canadian bishops as a pastoral directive to their people
after the publication of Pope Paul VI's celebrated encyclical on birth
control, *Humanae Vitae,* in July of that year. The Canadian statement
came out of an intense plenary meeting of the bishops in Winnipeg.
They had gathered there to participate in the one hundred and fiftieth
anniversary of the founding of the Archdiocese of St Boniface, the
mother diocese of all of western Canada. That the bishops met in
Flahiff's episcopal city in no way meant that his influence on the
statement was stronger than that of any other bishop. No minutes of
the meeting were kept, in order that each bishop might have the
greatest possible freedom to express himself. The statement which
emerged from the meeting professed loyalty to the pope and obedience to his teaching. It explained carefully, however, the crucial role
of the individual conscience in the difficult moral questions that con-
fessors and sincere Catholics would face. As with other such documents, reception was mixed, though favourable reaction tipped the
balance, and even the pope himself was said to have received the
document with satisfaction.[10]

The Winnipeg Statement, more than anything else, tarred the
Canadian bishops with the liberal brush. Flahiff encountered an
indication of this in a conversation he had in Rome after a meeting of
the SCRSI in September of 1971, just prior to the opening of the

Second Synod of Bishops. He wrote: "This morning we continued our Congregation meeting and we finished up this afternoon. There were farewells to a fair number of the members; a few are staying, like myself, for the Synod. When [Cardinal] Danielou said goodbye, he added: 'Be careful; I am a bit afraid of the Canadian bishops.' And he was not smiling. Do we really create that impression?"[11] Danielou's ominous attitude is offset by an incident occurring a few weeks later during the synod, which Bishop Alex Carter relates: "I remember leaving the hall and chatting outside with Cardinal Flahiff. We met Barbara Ward, a leader in the struggle for Social Justice in the United States. She had given a magnificent talk on the subject at the beginning of the Synod ... When she saw us there she planted a big kiss on each of us and said, 'I love the Canadian Bishops!'"[12]

The third factor which extended Flahiff's range of influence and his reputation was his ability as a speaker and his willingness to accept speaking engagements outside his own archdiocese. We can appreciate the extent of his generosity when we recall how conscientious he was about adequate preparation. Each engagement meant hours of work and a good deal of worry. Many of his speaking engagements were connected with religious life: general chapters, congresses, retreats, and other community meetings. His position in the SCRSI in the Roman Curia, his being a religious himself, his experience as a former superior general and former president of the Canadian Religious Conference, made him much sought after as a speaker where religious life was concerned. He also delivered major addresses on occasions which rose naturally from his position as a Catholic archbishop, including the meetings of organizations such as the Serrans (an association of lay people devoted to the promotion of vocations to the priesthood and religious life), the Knights of Columbus, the Catholic Women's League, and other groups in which pastoral care was involved, such as hospitals and prisons.

To give an idea of Flahiff's speaking activity, we can look at the period from March 1970 to September 1971 and count twelve major papers in eleven different cities: Edmonton, Windsor, Dayton (Ohio), Sault Ste Marie, London, Albany, Winnipeg, Hamilton, Winooski (Vermont), Philadelphia, and Atlanta. It was not, one might say, an overwhelming schedule for a professional speaker, but for one whose duties included the administration of an archdiocese, frequent presence in Ottawa and Rome, participation in numerous civic events and liturgical functions of many kinds, as well as lengthy confirmation tours, it is an astonishing record. No talk was simply warmed over for a second use; each one was prepared for the time and place and crafted to the audience and the situation, though naturally his main ideas and themes recur. It must be said that while he agonized over the preparation of his talks, he thoroughly enjoyed giving them and enjoyed whatever events attended them. He was born to socialize and he loved to travel.

Flahiff's numerous talks still await collection, editing, and publication. Some have appeared as part of the proceedings of the event he was attending, but the majority have still to find their way into an accessible form for the benefit of posterity. There is much in them which transcends the time and place of their origin, for Flahiff's mind moved in universals even though his language and examples were quite suited to the persons and the period of the particular occasion. Almost invariably he took an historical run at his subject, a method which made for great interest and sometimes great length. But in history he was at home and he was masterful. He swept with ease through the centuries, the civilizations, the philosophies, the leaders, the heresies, the problems, the gains and the losses. He liked to begin with a microscopic analysis of the title of the talk, and seemed a bit put off when he was not given a specifically worded title, or if the title which he had been given had been changed when it appeared on the program. But he did the analysis well and often humorously. He was attentive to the precise meaning of words and delighted in referring to the etymology or the composition of a word in order to clarify and sharpen his own thought. His typescripts were sometimes marked with light pencil strokes to indicate the word he wanted to emphasize as he spoke. His academic habits of order, clarity, and thoroughness are ever present in his sculptured sentences and in his nuanced thought.

Flahiff was a sought-after speaker not because he was an orator – there was a certain monotony, even a deadness, to his delivery, and a kind of hesitancy – but because what he said was wise, cogent, and wonderfully heartfelt. There was no hokum, no padding. Perhaps his strongest appeal was his positive and encouraging presentation of whatever subject he treated. He took his cue from St Paul: "Say only the things people need to hear" (Ephesians 4:29). What they needed to hear became by his wisdom and his manner what they wanted to hear. What, then, did he say? A summary consideration of his perception and his presentation of life would be helpful at this point, where we find him at the zenith of his career.

CHAPTER FOURTEEN

The Eminent Vision

George Flahiff believed that the world was good. This conviction accounts for his unfailingly positive and optimistic attitude in whatever he wrote or said. He came by this attitude connaturally; it had been fostered by his family, by his faith, as well as by his particular gift of openness to the world, to people, and to things. As his life unfolded, his belief in the goodness of things constantly illumined his thinking and his manners, it flowered in his ecumenism, in his respect for everyone, in his courage in the face of change or novelty, and in his optimism with respect to the evolution of the world.

He was fully aware of the two senses in which "the world" was used by Jesus Christ and by St Paul. In conflict with the Pharisees, Jesus accused them of "being of this world." In saying this he was excoriating their pride and self-centredness which caused them to pursue values and ends contrary to those of his Father: "You are from below, I am from above; you are of this world, I am not of this world" (John 8:23).[1] St Paul regularly uses the term pejoratively.[2] Thus did Jesus and the apostle imply that in one sense the world is in opposition to God and tends to draw persons into attitudes and actions inimical to goodness and salvation.

Much more frequently, however, Christ uses the world to mean God's creation, both material and spiritual. Because it is the object of his love, God has sent his Son into the world to redeem it, as Jesus reminds Nicodemus in that marvellous nocturnal conversation recorded in John 3:16: "God so loved the world that he gave his only Son, that whoever believes in him should not perish but have eternal life."[3] It is the world in this positive and fostering sense that Flahiff saw as good, that he enjoyed and wondered at, that was for him a manifestation of God in persons and things, in nature and events, in history and in mystery.

With his Creator, who had looked upon his work and "saw that it
was good," George Flahiff looked on the world smilingly, without
fear, without disdain, without prejudice. His spontaneous reaction to
the world, to people, events, and things, was benevolent. He was not
oblivious to evil; he was simply much more attentive to the good and
the potentially good. It is told jokingly that when someone said to
him, "O Eminence, you would see good in Satan himself," he
quipped, "Well, you must admit he does his job!" Some of the most
beautiful lines Flahiff wrote are on his understanding of the world:
"Nor is this world to be thought of as an implacable enemy. Still less
is it, of course, to be thought of as the measuring rod of our endeavour. We must know it in itself (and in *our*selves, where it is always
present) for exactly what it is: a great freedom, a great power, a great
loneliness and a great seeking; often muddled, often comic, sometimes tragic, always transient, as the pilgrim People of God pass
onward and in their passing build the Kingdom of Christ."[4]

With the goodness of things taken as his basic conviction and in
effect the basic theme of his writing and speaking, we can better
appreciate the specific themes of Flahiff's teaching. Without prejudice
to the range and variety of Flahiff's thinking, we can single out four
of these master themes to illustrate his vision. These are: the meaning
of history, the Church as the "People of God," ecumenism, and
"wholeness."

History was more than his area of academic expertise; it was a
habit of mind. The facts of history, the sense of history, and the wisdom of history pervaded his thinking. History was for him at once
his master and his friend; it would accompany him throughout his
life. His education in Toronto and in Paris gave him an enviable formation in the subject and to this formation he responded fully. While
yet a student in Europe he was concerned about the manner of teaching history and about how best to prepare himself for meeting his future students at the Pontifical Institute in Toronto. In two essays early
in his teaching years, "The Catholic Historian and His Critics," and
"A Catholic Looks at History,"[5] we find him preoccupied with the
problem of whether a Catholic, supposedly restricted by rigid dog-
mas, who may be tempted to use history for polemical purposes, and
who may have trouble being objective, can be a good historian. He
concluded that far from being an inferior historian because of his
faith, a Catholic can be a better historian thanks to his faith. He wrote:
"Indeed, there is every reason why the Catholic can and should be
the most objective of all historians in his researches, for he knows in
advance that the truth of the doctrines, which he holds as the most

vital thing in his life, depends in no way on the results of his researches; their truth is of an entirely different order, guaranteed by faith, and neither acquired nor to be defended by purely rational processes, historical or otherwise." In the same article he went on to look at the services of history, distinguishing and explaining three: history gives a "spirit of healthy criticism," provides a "philosophy of man," and, most important of all, provides for "the acquisition of truth."[6]

"A Catholic Looks at History," published in 1941, is Flahiff's profession of what history meant to him. We see why and how he imbued his thinking with history, and how it gave him security and serenity, not only in what he wrote, but also in what he did. For him history was the providence of God working itself out in time. His habit of approaching almost every subject he undertook from a historical perspective – even at the risk of being too learned for the comprehension of his hearers and too lengthy for their comfort – gave him direction and assurance. He was never disoriented by events, nor was he afraid of new things, largely because he felt with Teilhard de Chardin,[7] whom he had read enthusiastically, that the world was evolving beneficently.

In a brilliant speech given in Saskatoon in 1952, entitled "The Meaning of the Past for the Present and the Future,"[8] Flahiff developed his understanding of history, rejecting out of hand the conclusions of "scientific" history, which dehumanizes the study by seeing it only as a collection of facts without design or purpose. He quotes from T. S. Eliot's *Murder in the Cathedral*:

> And later is worse, when men will not hate you
> Enough to defame or to execrate you,
> But pondering the qualities which you lacked
> Will only try to find the historical fact.
> When men shall declare that there was no mystery
> About this man who played a certain part in history.[9]

Flahiff justified the notion that there is something more than mechanics in history by looking at what we are as human beings who have a sublime destiny. In other words, he saw history in the light of the Incarnation and in the spiritual destiny of humankind. He sums up his fascinating exposé in these words:

To conclude, there *is* meaning in history. Its full meaning is known to God alone. Ours to seek to penetrate it with the aid of all the truths that we possess. How much of it shall we grasp? That will depend upon many things:

the degree of our knowledge and of our wisdom, but the degree, too, of our prayer and our union with God whereby we come to see things more and more as He Himself sees them. In this sublime light, past, present and future must appear as a greater or lesser degree of the Christing of all things through the human instruments to whom God commits it. "All history is a series of footnotes to Christ."[10]

Flahiff never compromised on thoroughness or honesty in his study of history, as attest the exhaustive notes which survive both from his student and from his teaching days.[11] Though some might consider his "providential" view a distorting prejudice, he was never selective or polemical in his historical method. He was a master of the facts and could muster them skilfully to provide background and understanding of the subject he was handling. Sometimes his appeal to history may seem excessive: when, for example, in speaking to a group concerned with hospital care, he reviewed the history of how the human person had been understood through the centuries; or, when speaking to prison chaplains he went into an extensive history of prisons. On the occasion of the installation of a bishop, he recalls the vicissitudes of a bishop's office down the ages.[12] But he invariably extended the understanding of his hearers and showed great respect for them by presenting a carefully studied and brilliantly expressed panorama of events. His incarnational view of the world did not distort his presentation, but rather suffused his theme with meaning. Some of his audience may have yawned, but no one could say that they were not well served.

A high point of his talent for history was reached in a talk he gave at Villanova University on 19 June 1971. The occasion was a theological workshop entitled "The Pilgrim People: a Vision with Hope." Flahiff gave the keynote address which he called "Eras of Openness in the Ecclesiastical History of the Pilgrim People of God."[13] The three eras are those of Constantine (after 313), the twelfth century, and our own day. Flahiff's sweeping and ordered overview of the centuries, and his confidence in his theme are admirably satisfying. Just to read the talk is to feel his enthusiasm and conviction. He was quite at home in his material; he communicated to his audience, and still communicates in the reading, the optimism of his world view and the integration of his faith with his knowledge.

The second master theme to be considered is that of Flahiff's notion of the Church as the people of God. The scriptural phrase, "the people of God," has entered into common usage in speaking of the Church nowadays thanks to the Vatican II document, *Lumen Gentium*.

The Church as the people of God, however, was very much a part of Flahiff's thinking before the Vatican Council. It grew naturally out of his study not only of Scripture, but of the two great encyclicals of Pius XII, *Mystici Corporis* (1943) and *Mediator Dei* (1947). The first of these documents, the one which Flahiff had often referred to and spoken about in his conferences, sermons, and other teaching, from the time when the encyclical on the Mystical Body of Christ first appeared, emphasizes the union of Christ with his members after the Pauline analogy (Eph. 1:22, 4:15; Col. 1:18, 2:19) of the head and body in a human being. The second of these, *Mediator Dei*, which concerns the liturgy, emphasizes the role of every Christian in the worship of the Church, since the liturgy is the whole Church, priest and people, the whole body of Christ, being offered to the Father. The second document was in logical sequence to the earlier one: *Mediator Dei* described the Mystical Body of Christ at worship.

These two documents, among the most important of the pontificate of Pius XII, deeply conditioned the thinking of George Flahiff. By the time of Vatican II his understanding of the Church was that of an assembly of God's people, baptized in Christ, united in love, and striving for the good of one another and of all. He thought much less frequently of hierarchy than he did of the common gifts of grace, truth, divine life, and communion among the members. He was ready for Vatican II, and even was one of those who anticipated the teaching on the Church which was formulated by the council.

In a speech delivered at the Twenty-third North American Liturgical Week, held in Seattle, Washington, from 20 to 23 August 1962 Flahiff outlined in the clearest terms the role of the layperson in the Church. The speech is entitled "Salvation of the Nations."[14] He began by calling his audience to heed the words of recent popes admonishing Christians to resist the temptation to withdraw from the world. He quoted, with his own emphasis, the 1957 Christmas message of Pius XII: "Intervention in the world to maintain divine order is a *right and duty* which belongs essentially to a *Christian's responsibility* and permits him lawfully to undertake all those actions, private, public and organized, which aim at, and are suited to, that end."[15] Flahiff warmed to his subject as he developed the role of the layperson in the world as the one who sanctifies and saves it because that person as a member of Christ, "incarnates" Christ wherever he or she acts. He noted that the spirituality of the laity had been neglected. He wanted to see the role of the layperson understood as integral to the life of the Church, and as someone whose work consists, not in pastoral activity as such, but rather in the sanctification of the world.

Flahiff is at pains to make clear that the Christian in the world cannot be satisfied simply to believe and be good. He or she must also be competent. "This simply means," he wrote, "that you cannot have a good Catholic nurse, religious or otherwise, or a good Catholic teacher, unless she is first a good nurse, a good teacher; you cannot have a good Catholic artist or musician, unless he is first a good artist or musician; you cannot have a good Catholic college unless it is first a good college ... There is no substitute for technical skill and professional proficiency." He went on to state even more strongly: "While the importance of spiritual and ethical training can scarcely be exaggerated, it may well be that our failure to christianize human activities in certain fields stems rather from the lack of expert competence in these fields – from the fact, in other words, that Christ, Salvation of the Nations, does not find instruments properly prepared in a purely natural way, through whom to achieve His purpose of redeeming the time, of saving 'the world,' that is to say, the temporal order of things and activities."

Respect for the dignity and role of the laity characterized Flahiff's pastorate. He was ahead of many a contemporary in giving voice to the importance of these concepts. His actions followed his convictions, as was seen in his desire to consult the laity and to work with them in their various activities in the Church and in society. In assemblies of laypersons he preferred to keep a low profile and to participate rather as a fellow worker than as one who presided or who gave the final answer. Where he was unknown to a group, he might appear in his lumberjack shirt and introduce himself as George. This was the case in a very large gathering of people from all over the province and from the United States, meeting at Gimli, Manitoba, to hear Jean Vanier on 5 August 1973. This was not an affectation of camaraderie; it was a desire to communicate on the basis of a common baptism and a common membership in the Body of Christ. To have participated in the making of the Vatican document on the Church in the world, *Gaudium et Spes*, approved on the very last day of the Council, was a deep satisfaction to him. This document gave expression to the whole world of ideas he had cherished and implemented for years. He often found inspiration in it when speaking of the laity's mission.

Flahiff's understanding of the Church as the people of God, and his consciousness of the union of all through baptism and the Eucharist, are the bases of his concern for the recognition of women and their equality with men. While he adhered firmly to the hierarchical structure of the Church, he regretted the feeling of inferiority among women and their exclusion from the Church's governance and ministries. As we have seen, he became a world champion of the cause for women's rights (and even, in the mind of some, of women's ordination), by the accident of his having been the one who spoke for the bishops of Canada at the synod of 1971. But long before that time he had been sympathetic to the aspirations of women, and especially those of women religious, for recognition in the life of the Church.

His intervention at the synod of 1971, and the recommendation to the pope by the bishops of Canada that a committee be formed to study women and ministries, while made in the name of the bishops of Canada, was nevertheless of particular interest to Flahiff. It was he who developed the final draft of the intervention and it was well known that his sympathies were very much with the cause being pleaded. Though somewhat reluctant to be cast in the role of women's champion, Flahiff made it clear where his sympathies lay. He lent an ear to those who were agitating for the promotion of women in ministries and even for the ordination of women. There was an interesting exchange of letters between Flahiff and one of his fellow bishops, Jean-Marie Fortier, Archbishop of Sherbrooke. The latter wrote in French, asking Flahiff for a list of reading materials for a group in his diocese charged with the studying of women's rights in the Church. Flahiff replied in English, with just a slight edge of weariness with the matter:

Frankly, Jean-Marie, I am not, and never have been, an expert on the question of the role of women in the Church. My name seems to be associated with the subject because of my intervention at the Bishop's Synod of 1971. But the purpose of my intervention was merely to present a motion adopted less than three weeks earlier by the c.c.c. [Canadian Catholic Conference, former designation of the cccb] requesting that a study be instituted regarding the role of women in the ministry or ministries of the Church. I was not the author of the resolution and spoke in Rome as the mouthpiece of the Canadian Bishops only. I had done no research on my own on the subject before that time and have done no real research since that time. Any reading I have done has been of a very general nature (almost all of it in English) and I doubt if it goes beyond what the average bishop anywhere has done.[16]

He then added an annotated list of fourteen references, which seems to indicate a fairly extensive knowlege of the matter and to reveal once more Flahiff's modest opinion of his own capacities, and perhaps even a certain naivety in his estimate of his own knowledge and interest in the question. He never stated publicly or, so far as is known, privately either, that he was in favour of the ordination of women. He believed in the evolution of ideas and movements. He kept an open mind, while at the same time adhering strictly to the official teaching of the Church, confident that the Spirit would ultimately guide her to the truth.

In the fall of 1976, the Sacred Congregation for the Doctrine of the Faith (formerly the Holy Office) prepared a declaration, with the approval of Pope Paul VI, entitled "Women in the Ministerial Priesthood."[17] The basic statement of the declaration was that the Church does not have the authority to change the tradition of an all-male priesthood. The document goes on to argue that, since Christ was male, a male priesthood provided a more suitable image of the spousal relation of Christ with the Church. The document stated further that it was quite obvious from the actions of the Lord in his ministry while on earth that he intended the priesthood to be exclusively male, sociological arguments notwithstanding. The declaration was published to the world on 27 January 1977. Shortly thereafter a group of sisters at Loretto College, Toronto, were discussing the document, which they had found not at all to their liking and to which they wished to draw up some objections. One of the group offered to go out and make a number of copies of the document in order to facilitate the discussion. The sister went out into a raging snowstorm, made the copies at the St Michael's College printing office, and was returning to the group when she met a tall man in black, also defending himself against the wind and the whirling snow. It was Cardinal Flahiff, who happened to be visiting St Michael's College at the time. The sister knew the cardinal well; in fact they had been good friends for some years. But she could not help, in spite of the weather conditions, expressing then and there and in no uncertain terms her strong objection to the document she was carrying. A member of the hierarchy was obviously the most suitable person on whom to vent her annoyance. Considerations of friendship seemed to be in abeyance as the cardinal just as vigorously defended the position of the Vatican and, as usual, pointed out the positive side of the document and the sound reasoning it contained. There they stood, raging with the weather, and perhaps abetted by it, one as determined as the other. In later years they talked about the humour of the situation, though neither claimed any kind of victory. What it proved once more was that when Rome spoke, Flahiff was ever respectful, and instinctively defended the official position of the Church.

A third master theme of Flahiff's writing is that of ecumenism. We have already referred to his ecumenical stance and activity in his pastorate in Winnipeg, and have seen how it was integral to his work during those twenty-one years and how effective it had been. In an address to the faculty and students of the Toronto School of Theology, given at Victoria College in the University of Toronto on 16 March 1972,[18] we have what might be considered his manifesto on ecumenism. For its clarity, its strength, and its challenge, this is one of the finest speeches he ever gave. "The Toronto School of Theology represents a signal advance in practical ecumenism," he began. He then stated clearly the centrality of the person of Christ in any ecumenical endeavour as that which will ultimately draw people of differing Christian persuasions together. "It is therefore," he said, "not a gradual unification of our theological stance and terminology that we are seeking: it is a total union of hearts and wills in the love of Christ which *compels* us."

Nor is the ecumenism about which he was writing merely "clubbiness" or fellowship, but rather a challenge and a striving: "A school of ministry will always seek the genuinely unifying elements but will reject instinctively that dismal and dishonest levelling process that seeks the lowest common denominator and sets aside the precious differences of inspiration in favour of bland conformism." The phrase, "the precious differences of inspiration" is worth our pausing over. Flahiff saw the differences in belief as positive: they can all contribute to a deeper understanding of the truth. It is an echo of his speech at the Vatican Council, in which he saw the various heresies in the history of the Church as so many calls by the Holy Spirit to deeper understanding and to purification. He went on in this remarkable address at Victoria College to warn of the dangers of indifferentism and of becoming stereotyped; he pointed out that no ecumenical effort is of value without prayer. He spoke forcefully. One could wish to have heard this speech, in which he uncharacteristically left aside history in favour of a clarion call to a cause about which he seems to have been passionately concerned.

For Flahiff, ecumenism clearly was not a case of watering down one's beliefs. It was rather a rejoicing over what was held in common and then a concerted turning towards something greater than any one particular group, something more vital, powerful, and efficacious, namely, the person of Christ. In speaking at the Baccalaureate Service of the University of Winnipeg, held in Knox United Church, on 28 May 1972 he stated these convictions strongly and beautifully: "It is a cause for joy and thanksgiving that all can now enjoy the insights of each, that the variety itself surrounds with a humanly illuminating halo the blazing central core of revelation, which is God's love for mankind ... I know of only one sure path to Christian unity,

that unity so necessary to repair the scandal of a divided Christen-
dom. That path is a mutual concerted looking toward Christ." He insisted on this latter point as he moved to the end of his talk,
contrasting two conditions to strengthen his point: "If our sins
against one another throughout the dark past of religious strife make
us only apologetic to our fellow human beings, the result will be at
best a slight sweetening of the atmosphere. If those sins convince us
all of our overriding need for Christ, of the fact that without Him we
can do nothing good, the result may well be revolutionary."[19]

The two speeches from which we have quoted were both given in
the spring of 1972. A more practical talk, and in some ways a more
vivid one, was given four years earlier at Westwood Collegiate in
Winnipeg at what was called the Inter-Faith Service of Intercession
and Thanksgiving, arranged by the Assiniboia Ministerial Association, on Sunday, 11 February 1968. While the two later speeches keep
to a more typical theoretical approach, the earlier one made clear suggestions on practical issues of cooperation and action. First, Flahiff
expressed regret for the historic reluctance of the Roman Catholic
Church to be involved in the ecumenical movement. He recalled the
example which Pope Paul vi had given to the Catholics of the world
at the beginning of the second session of the Vatican Council by asking pardon of other Christians for the faults of Catholics against
Christian unity, and added: "We must never yield to the temptation
to accept division as inevitable merely because it has existed for many
centuries. It is still a scandal."

He then listed political, social, cultural, and economic areas in
which Christians can cooperate "to bring a Christian touch and a
Christian influence to the ordinary life of every day": efforts for legis-
lation which respects the human person; efforts for peace in the
world; elimination of all discrimination based on race, colour, or
creed; helping the poor throughout the world; and efforts for aiding
the countries in the course of development. In the central part of his
text he stated forthrightly the themes which are constants of his
teaching on ecumenism: "Any union based on compromise would
not only be unworthy of Christians; it would lack all solid foundation. On the contrary, each Christian and each Christian group should
strive to know its own position better and should examine its roots
more seriously. I am convinced that, under the guidance of God's
Spirit, we would then become more clearly aware of what is truly essential and be able to distinguish it from the only accessory which all
too often has been the beginning of division." He suggested a return
to the scriptures held in common, to a study of the Church Fathers

and of the early councils, and a re-examination "calmly and dispassionately," of the historical situations and the controversial issues over which Christians became divided. "And all the while we could seek a centring and a concentration of our lives upon Christ, the living Christ, 'the same yesterday, to-day and forever,' as real and vital to-day as he was nearly two thousand years ago."[20]

At the service of his teaching on ecumenism was his gracious manner and his universal benevolence. The messenger and the message were so fully one that it would be hard to say which was the more effective. On the main point of his ecumenism, the centrality of Christ in our lives, he offered a clear example in his own life. A resolution of the General Synod of the Anglican Church of Canada in July of 1986 expressed the sentiments of some who knew and worked with Cardinal Flahiff in a common Christian endeavour: "That this General Synod of the Anglican Church of Canada now meeting in Winnipeg send Christian and thankful greetings to our beloved brother in Christ, George Cardinal Flahiff, retired Archbishop of the Roman Catholic Archdiocese of Winnipeg on this the 25th anniversary of his Consecration. We remember the great leadership to the whole of the Church in the ecumenical field given by this Christian leader, and send fraternal love." The letter conveying the resolution to the cardinal is signed by the Right Reverend Walter Heath Jones, Bishop of Rupert's Land.[21]

Running like a symphonic strain through Flahiff's thought is the notion of wholeness: the integrity of creation, the interrelatedness of things, the importance of considering always the total person, be it in education, morality, or health care. His habit of history, which, as we have seen, was his way to complete understanding, fostered his quest for wholeness. Sectarian stances had no part in him. While he held staunchly to his own principles and convictions, he believed that no human philosophy had a monopoly on truth: he was open to all opinions and ideas as possible advances to wholeness, which he was ever seeking. Even when he is not referring specifically to wholeness in his writings, one senses the operative presence of this notion in his thought. Where he found wholeness he delighted in it; where it was lacking, he pleaded for it.

In 1959, speaking at a convention of teachers in Rochester, New York, Flahiff, at that time superior general of the Basilian Fathers, expressed himself rather strongly on the shortcomings of the contemporary "isms," which would have been familiar to his hearers.

Communism is not wrong because it is materialist but because it is materialist only. Secularism is not wrong because it is devoted to secular things ... but because it is devoted to these only. Naturalism is not wrong because it stresses the natural, but because it stresses the natural only and leaves no room for grace and the supernatural destiny of man. Humanism is not wrong because it insists so strongly on man and on human values, but because it insists on these only, to the exclusion of God's rights. What is wrong in every case is taking a truth, and making it *the* truth, the whole truth, taking what is assuredly a part of reality but mistaking it for the whole of reality.[22]

In the same speech he introduced the theme of what it means to be both "Catholic" and "catholic," a theme to which he would return time and again with some rather unusual implications. Here he said, "Catholic schools, if they are to be worthy of the name with a small 'c' as well as a large 'C', can be content with nothing less than the *full* truth and the *whole* of reality, with all parts in proper order." Almost twenty years later, in his homily at the mass marking the one hundred and twenty-fifth anniversary of St Michael's College, he said: "The role of Catholic education is not merely to indoctrinate, but rather to integrate. Fundamentally, it aims at a synthesis of culture and faith and a synthesis of faith and life; the first is reached by integrating all the different aspects of human knowledge through the subjects taught, in the light of the Gospel; the second is achieved in the growth of values characteristic of the Christian."[23]

Wholeness, then, and integration were crucial elements in Flahiff's vision, but that vision takes in more than Catholics and their institutions. He believed that any Catholic education worthy of the name should contribute to the education of all, and this in two ways: first, by fidelity to its own principles and by internal excellence, thus being a valuable part of the whole and thus advancing the common goals; second, by interest and concern for the whole work of education in society. "We actually owe it to the pluralistic society of which we are a part," he stated on the same occasion we have just referred to, "and therefore to education in that society as a whole to make our characteristically Christian contribution, otherwise we are failing our society and depriving it, its culture and its education of a contribution that only we can make."[24] And more directly still, to the Federation of Parent-Teachers Associations of Ontario: "We are never more truly Catholic than, while insisting upon our just rights, we are at the same time deeply concerned about the education of all."[25]

The object of education is the whole person, he insisted: "[Christian education] is meant to form the *whole* man. It may therefore neglect no part of the truth contained in what we call the material, the natural, the temporal, the secular and the human orders; but all of these must be presented in well-ordered conjunction with the spiritual, the eternal and the sacred aspects of human life and existence, and in the still fuller context of the supernatural and even divine destiny which is ours, so that all can be directed ultimately to this end."[26] He pleads for a "wholeness of outlook which far from rejecting scientific and positivistic methods or accomplishments, seeks rather to elevate their unprecedented contributions. It is just that, great and welcome though these may be, there is a far greater depth in the person of man than these disciplines can ever reach."[27]

When Flahiff turns his attention to health care, as he did on various occasions, he is equally ardent for wholeness of approach. In 1969 he spoke to the Catholic Hospital Association of Manitoba on "Preserving the Catholic Spirit in the Hospital." He reflects once again on the implications of "Catholic" and finds in it the call to wholeness: "The word 'Catholic' means universal. We make a special application of this word when we say the Church is called Catholic because it is represented in all parts of the world and so is Catholic in a geographical sense. The original Greek word does not have this meaning in its group sense. It has more to do with wholeness and the 'Catholic' means 'toward wholeness.' I would, therefore, hope that when we speak of the 'Catholic Spirit,' this notion of wholeness be in some way present."[28]

In a talk given a year later to the Hospital Pastoral Care Association of Alberta he made an interesting and useful reference to the Bible to support his case for wholeness in our approach to the sick: "Obviously," he says, "none of the texts of the Old or New Testament represents a conscious effort to produce a systematic anthropology from either a philosophical or a scientific point of view. But they do reveal man to us as a living, personal *whole*. To be sure, he is considered under various of his principal aspects as flesh (*basar*) and as soul (*nephesh*) or spirit (*ruah*). He is never represented, however, as a composite, as though there were component parts; he appears rather as a single, psycho-physiological organism, even if he be made up of two elements. In the Bible, man does not *have* a soul and body, he *is* a soul and body."[29] The points he made a generation ago are even more compelling today when specialization and compartmentalization of health services cause such frustration among us. It seems that for our great advances we pay heavy costs in precious humanity. But Flahiff was never pessimistic. He recognized that doctors were becoming ever more "sensitive to this integral ministration of the whole person." He went on to say: "The Church, which is the Mystical Body of Christ and the integral communion of all believers, witnesses in its health care role both to the inalienable importance of each individual (in this context the sick and therefore temporarily indigent human individual) to the whole, and to the importance of that whole to each individual, however apparently alienated or temporarily suspended from full participation in that whole. That is the very essence of Catholicism."[30]

It is in speaking of education and health care that the theme of wholeness recurs most frequently, but Flahiff made many other references to what for him was primary, both in pastoral care and in human relations in general. He characterizes the prison chaplain's role as "based on the recognition that a human person is one and whole, even though we may distinguish between physical, psychic and spiritual needs. Indeed we must distinguish; but we must not divide, and we must not reduce to one dimension alone. Enlightened cooperation and team-work in health-care can best serve the total good of a patient, and I am convinced that the same is true of the healing process that rehabilitation in our penal system is meant to effect."[31] Many years before this, in an article entitled "Toward a Theology of Sports," he commented: "What is all too commonly lacking is an overall orientation, a properly integrated outlook on this specifically human activity in relation to other human activities."[32] And after the Vatican Council, he cautioned his hearers to consider the work of the council as a whole, and not as narrowed by taking one document in isolation: "No single document, no combination of two or three documents, offers a complete answer to any one question; 'cross references' are constant."[33]

A sin against wholeness which was particularly painful to George Flahiff was the failure of some to read a document, or pronouncement from Rome, from himself, or from any authority whatsoever, fully and as a whole. He himself was scrupulous in being fair to the writer of anything he came across by considering the text in its wholeness, without being emotionally sidetracked by one particular point, and thereby being unfair in estimating the document. He was particularly grieved when Pope Paul vi, who was the object of many a brickbat for his writings and pronouncements, was pilloried for one point in what he said, while a consideration of the wholeness of his pronouncement was lost. It is possible that Flahiff did not always agree fully with what the pope was saying, but he was unfailingly fair in his balanced and integral consideration of the pronouncement as a whole.

The four master themes we have presented here obviously overlap, or better, dovetail, in the person of George Flahiff, who was himself an integrated person. The completeness of the man was attractive, his integrity more so. Every aspect of his vision was integrated with his incarnational, Christocentric understanding of the world. It will be noticed that the references to Flahiff's writings and speeches come from the period between the late 1950s to the late 1970s – that is, from the years when he was at his best. They were extremely busy and admirably fruitful years. They reach a climax in 1978 when once again Flahiff participates in the making of history, fulfilling his primary function as a cardinal, that of electing the pope. The course of events was to be not only exciting but traumatic.

CHAPTER FIFTEEN

The Making of Popes

On the beautiful sunny afternoon of 6 August 1978, Cardinal Flahiff was showing the Cathedral of St Boniface to two visitors from Toronto.[1] Just after they had visited the church and the tomb of Louis Riel in the churchyard, a young priest approached the cardinal and asked him to come into the cathedral rectory. A few minutes later the cardinal returned to his guests with the news that Pope Paul VI had died. This news effectively put an end to the visit. It also put an end to the cardinal's plans for his own vacation in New York State to begin the following week. It began a period of eleven weeks in his life which were to be interesting, emotionally charged, and highly significant.

Flahiff kept a written record of these weeks.[2] Though it was not his practice to keep a diary, the fact that he was about to exercise his primary duty as a cardinal and participate in the making of history moved him to write a daily account of the events as the drama unfolded. He could not know just how extensive and how gripping that drama would be, nor that he would participate in the making of not one but two popes, in the space of a few weeks. This chapter is based almost exclusively on what the cardinal wrote. As usual he is observant and detailed in his reporting, and his comments to himself are revealing. There is an intriguing mixture of the sublime and the mundane as he lived through and recorded these historic days.

True to form, the cardinal was hesitant to act when the news of the pope's death arrived. He thought he should wait for an official summons to the conclave before taking steps to go to Rome. Once again his chancellor, Norman Chartrand, urged an immediate decision to leave for Rome, and went ahead with the arrangements. The cardinal left Winnipeg on the following Thursday, the day on which the official summons finally came, and arrived in Rome on the morning of Friday, 11 August 1978. He was met at the airport by representatives of the Vatican Secretariat of State and driven to the Oblate Generalate at 290 Via Aurelia, where he knew from past visits he would be well received and find warm hospitality. The Oblate house was within walking distance of St Peter's Basilica and the Vatican and commanded a magnificent view over Rome. It offered a terrace on the roof where Flahiff loved to walk, say his office, think, pray or just enjoy the city he loved. The house itself was a fascinating crossroads, being the headquarters of a world-wide congregation, where there were always interesting people from distant parts coming and going. At that time there were also special guests, among them Cardinal Léger, the former Archbishop of Montreal and later missionary in Cameroon, who were there for the important events. The Generalate was conveniently served by buses, and Flahiff used them regularly. He never on his own made use of the Vatican cars which were at the service of the cardinals.

Upon his arrival, the first thing he did after lunch and a rest was to walk down to St Peter's to pay his respects to the dead pope. He took his place in the line filing past the bier. He was saddened at the loss of a good friend and an admired servant of the Church. At the same time he was appalled at the gruesome aspect of the dead pope's countenance, "gray to green, and shiny," as he described it. There were police everywhere, as he had noticed on his arrival at the airport, a reminder of the political and social implications of the death of a pope.

The funeral of Pope Paul the following afternoon provided an opportunity for Flahiff to meet and renew acquaintance with a number of the cardinals. As they were vesting together in the sacristy before the ceremony he found to his pleasant surprise that he knew quite a few of them and reflected that they looked older, adding as he recorded the fact, "Me too?" Cardinal Marty, the Archbishop of Paris, remembering Flahiff's famous intervention at the synod of 1971 on the ministries of women, asked him jokingly if he were going to vote for a woman for pope, a jest Marty would repeat when the conclave began.

The funeral mass was beautifully celebrated on the broad esplanade in front of St Peter's Basilica. The cardinals were seated in a long row facing the piazza, which gave them a splendid view of the altar, the crowd, and the city beyond in the late afternoon sun. The pope's body in a simple cedar coffin lay before the altar, surmounted by the book of the gospels. At the end of mass the cardinals and the family

of the pope, along with a few officials, moved into the basilica and
formed a guard of honour as the body passed down the nave. It was
then taken below into the crypt, where it was buried in the ground as
Pope Paul had wished, and later covered with a slab of granite with
only the bare inscription "Paulus VI." Flahiff appreciated the simplicity of it all. Later in the week he returned to the tomb to pray and to
ask Pope Paul for guidance in the choice of his successor.

With the burial of the pope concluded, Flahiff had few obligations
during the time before the conclave which was set to begin almost
two weeks later. For some reason the cardinals had decided on the
longest interval allowed by canon law before the election of the new
pope. The papal funeral had occurred just before the *ferragosto*, the
midsummer Roman holiday around 15 August, the feast of the
Assumption. Everything was shut down for practically the whole
week after the funeral, many Romans stretching the three days of the
official holiday into five. The cardinals worked, however, at least for a
few hours each day in meetings called congregations. These were intended as substitute government of the Church in the period of *sede
vacante*, that is, "while the Chair of Peter is unoccupied." The congregation met every morning at 11: 00 o'clock in the Vatican. The matters
discussed were preparations for the approaching conclave, finances,
and the Church in the world. These were not caucuses in which candidates and strategies for the election of the new pope were discussed. Such discussions took place informally and unofficially.
Flahiff found the monetary discussions in the congregations tedious
and was more satisfied when they got to reports about the Church in
various parts of the world. At one point the cardinals were calling for
a greater consultation of theologians by the bishops. Flahiff adds a
note in his diary, "Why not the *sensus fidelium*[3] as well?" implying
that the faithful themselves are a font of wisdom in the Church and
should be consulted, a principle that John Henry Newman had
favoured in the previous century. The role of ordinary baptized men
and women in the Church was a preoccupation with Flahiff and a
recurring theme when he spoke publicly.

He spent many hours walking about the city of Rome. He never
seems to have tired of retracing his steps to places familiar and beloved. He would, for example, take a bus to a certain part of the city,
then walk around that area and most of the distance home. One walk
he took often was to the Spanish Steps, where he climbed to the
church of La Trinità del Monte, then strolled in the Pincio Gardens,
returning by way of the Via Sistina, just to pass the Hôtel de la Ville
where he had spent so much time during the Vatican Council some

fifteen years before. He would visit the churches, watch the people, delight again in the architecture and in the enchantment of the colour of Rome in the sunshine of August. The heat did not seem to deter him, although it was going to be a major problem during the conclave.

He also met many friends, both those visiting Rome and those he knew in the city. He would often dine out in a restaurant, both for lunch and for dinner, something he enjoyed immensely. His favourite restaurant, however, L'Eau Vive, was closed during this time. He also went swimming. Flahiff was a strong swimmer; water sports had been part of his life since his boyhood days. He noted that he had not been in the Mediterranean since 1969 (the year of the cardinalate) and before that, since 1932, when he was a student in Paris. The Oblates took him to the area of the beach reserved for clerics where changing facilities and towels were provided. One could get to the beach from Rome in less than an hour. These rather leisurely activities were punctuated with interviews with various newspapers. Flahiff was not particularly keen on giving interviews, for he thought the exercise superficial and largely sensation-seeking. When he found a reporter who was evidently interested in the meaning of things he was pleased and enjoyed the interview. He felt that generally he disappointed the interviewers as he was absolutely tight-lipped with regard to predictions about *papabili* (possible candidates for the papacy) and about tendencies or factions among the cardinals.

Flahiff records only two conversations which he had with other cardinals regarding the impending papal election. On 21 August he wrote: "Then Card. Roy kept Card. Cooray and myself (Léger having already retired) to discuss what we felt were most necessary in next Pope. It was very stimulating, less re persons than re qualities, background, etc. After discussion in 'Congregation' re theology to-day, we agreed that someone with a sound theological background or with a keen feeling for its importance would be particularly desirable, altho' there were 4 or 5 other qualities or backgrounds that we also discussed."

The second of these conversations took place at the Séminaire Français, supposedly at the invitation of the French cardinals. Flahiff writes, this time on 23 August, just two days prior to the opening of the conclave: "An exchange re 'papabili:' Marty, Gouyon, Guyot (Toulouse, just arrived), Renard, Thiandoum, Roy and myself. Roy read off a list of some 15 possibilities and we all commented. Gouyon had"fiches"[cards] with what he had heard or could gather from various sources, but everybody contributed something. Very helpful! ...

Feeling for doctrine, spirituality, experience, attitudes, languages, administrative ability all came in … The two for whom there seemed to be greatest *general* approval were Luciani & Benelli! – No caucusing, however, or agreements. Very friendly & open spirit! Marty joked again about my 'voting for a woman' and Gouyon about my being born *à Paris*!"

One does not get the impression in reading Flahiff's notes on these days before the conclave that he was at all concerned that he might be a likely candidate for the papacy, or that others were hinting that he might be such. The only reference to himself in the highest office in the Church comes in the form of a gentle compliment from one of the Gammarelli sons. The famous ecclesiastical tailoring house of Gammarelli had been commissioned in view of the conclave to prepare three white cassocks, small, medium, and large. The cardinal's entry for 18 August reads in part: "Took '46' to Piazza Torre Argentina, then walked to Gammarelli's for repair of cord and to buy another (simpler & more durable). Offered my sympathy to the 2 sons on father's death in past year. A photographer was taking careful, detailed pictures of 3 white cassocks in window. Younger Gammarelli said one was for me!"

While the impending election was not a matter of personal concern for him, there *was* something that was keeping him from having a good night's sleep. He consistently records trouble sleeping and resorting to pills. At first it was the dogs barking and the traffic which he thought were the cause of his insomnia. But when these were dealt with by his moving to a quieter side of the house, he still had fitful sleep and troubled dreams, difficulties which were to be more marked as he moved into old age. Curiously, however, they never seemed to slow him down in his program of long walks, visits, and hearty dining. He did manage rather lengthy siestas and in that way met his sleeping needs.

The conclave to elect a successor to Pope Paul VI began on 25 August 1978. There was a solemn mass in St Peter's Basilica in the morning at which all the cardinals concelebrated. They returned to the Vatican at 4:00 p.m. to be enclosed for the purpose of the election. Flahiff had accepted a room beside that of the aged and infirm Cardinal Cooray from Sri Lanka, in order to be of assistance in case the older man should be in difficulty, since no one except cardinals could be allowed into the conclave. There were few concessions to comfort. The rooms were makeshift, having been converted from offices for the occasion, and furnished with only a cot, a chair, a wash-stand, and nothing else: no soap, no towel, no hooks for hanging, not even sufficient air, for the windows were sealed. The heat made things very uncomfortable, and there was no bath. The toilet was down the hall. It has been said that such conditions were allowed in order to encourage the cardinals to get the business over with as quickly as possible. Perhaps so. The dining room, however, was pleasant and spacious, being the famous Borgia apartment, and the food, wrote Flahiff, was excellent. It was served by white-gloved waiters. The wine was fine and abundant. But he did not sleep well, from the lack of fresh air, the impossibility of taking a bath, and, no doubt, the pressure, conscious or unconscious, of the impending election.

Flahiff records the voting with little commentary. It does not seem that there was tension in the conclave; the voting went smoothly. It took only four ballots to settle on a new pope, and that with a clear majority: Albino Luciani, the Patriarch of Venice, who took the name of John Paul, in honour of his two predecessors, John xxiii and Paul vi. He was a man of extreme affability. He had a ready and engaging smile, and evidently accepted his new responsibility joyfully. There was great rejoicing, first among the cardinals and then in the waiting crowd outside, who gave the new pope a thunderous ovation as he appeared on the balcony of St Peter's. After some time, the pope left the balcony only to return almost immediately, bringing with him some of the cardinals, one of whom was Flahiff, whose presence beside the pope delighted the people in Winnipeg who were tuned in to the world-wide broadcast. Then the pope returned to dine with the cardinals. Flahiff's place in the dining room was near the door. John Paul entered smiling broadly, grasped Flahiff's hand, shook it warmly, and then took his habitual place at the table, putting everyone at ease by his utter simplicity. The joy and satisfaction among the cardinals was general and sincere. They did not know, nor could they know, that they had elected a dying man.

It had taken just one full day with only four ballots to elect a new pope. Flahiff did not mind one more night in the incommodious conditions of the conclave, knowing that soon there would be freedom. After mass with the new pope in the morning, the conclave ended and Flahiff returned to the Oblate residence on the Via Aurelia. The first thing he did was to take a bath; in the afternoon he went to the beach for the second time. It had all ended well; now his only major concern was to procure a flight home as soon as possible after the inauguration ceremony scheduled for 3 September.

Flahiff spent the intervening week between the election and the inauguration enjoying Rome, visiting with friends, giving interviews to the various media, buying photos of the major events, and coaxing a

Cardinal Flahiff meeting the newly elected Pope John Paul 1,
August 1978. (Photo: Felici, Rome)

reservation out of Alitalia. During the week there were two general audiences of the cardinals with the pope, in which the cardinals gained
some indication of the character and direction of the new pontificate.
The inauguration of John Paul on 3 September 1978 fittingly termi-
nated the week of rejoicing over his election. The new pope, whose
motto was *Humilitas* (humility), dispensed with the traditional coronation and the tiara and with being carried in the *sede gestatoria*, the por-
table throne in which the pope is carried in papal processions. John
Paul assumed the office of pope by the simple imposition of the pallium, the mark of office of the Bishop of Rome. His papacy was to be
brief but the memory of his simplicity and his affability would linger.

Cardinal Flahiff left Rome on 6 September, travelling in first class
by courtesy of Alitalia. He stopped in Toronto until 13 September,
then flew on to Winnipeg and picked up in his work where he had
left off a month previously. On the weekend of 16–17 September he
did a confirmation in Roblin, more than two hundred miles from
Winnipeg, and on the return journey attended a celebration in one of
the Polish parishes. During the following week he went to Vancouver
for the episcopal ordination of the new Bishop of Kamloops,
Lawrence Sabatini, and the following Sunday, 24 September, left for
Ottawa for the plenary assembly of the cccb. Wherever he went the
talk was all of the new pope and the bright prospects for the Church.
The assembled Canadian bishops felt the optimism of the whole

Catholic world as they began their meetings. They were hardly prepared for the startling news of John Paul's death which came during
the last night of their meeting, on 28 September 1978. Flahiff, awak-
ened by a phone call in the early hours, could hardly grasp what was
reported to him. He was devastated by the news. What had been
accomplished by the cardinals in Rome just a few weeks previously
and had given such promise and hope to the Church had been wiped
out in a moment.

Flahiff left for Rome once again on 3 October. On the plane the
stewardess, at the request of the woman who was sitting behind
Flahiff, showed him a picture in *Maclean's* magazine and asked him if
the person in the picture were he. The issue was dated 9 October and
the picture had been taken on 29 September at the installation of
Father Peter Swan as president of the University of St Michael's College, the last ceremony Flahiff had attended before leaving. He
owned up to the picture, and then read the article which described
him as "a skilled negotiator and an independent thinker ... the only
Canadian who has a slight chance of being elected." The author of the
article did not explain this opinion. It should be noted that the other
two Canadian cardinals, Roy of Quebec and Léger of Montreal, were
senior to Flahiff, better known internationally, and highly respected
for their achievements both in Canada and abroad.

Coming into a cloud-covered and rainy Rome the next morning,
Flahiff was met by one of the Oblates who took him immediately to
view the body of John Paul. The cardinal once more was shocked to
see the change from the man he knew, had talked with, had laughed
with so recently. He wrote: "You would hardly recognize the smiling
face we had last seen a month before. Not only was the smile missing,
but the face had a leaden grey hue to it, – not quite as bad as Paul vi's
had been, but painful to look at, just the same."4 The funeral that
same afternoon was a sad affair, again on the esplanade in front of
St Peter's, under intermittent rain. The ceremony followed the same
pattern as that of Pope Paul's funeral, with none of the beauty or
serenity of the former occasion.

There was more than a physical cloud over Rome: there was a pall
of sorrow and malaise that seemed to cover both place and people.
Among the cardinals, Flahiff was not the only one to have been trau-
matized by the pope's death. Many were left disturbed by the shock,
and the discussions in the meetings of the cardinals reflected this general dismay. Moreover, the sinister hints in the media about the death
of the pope, though not given credence by the cardinals, added to the
uncomfortable atmosphere which prevailed. Flahiff was even less

impressed than he had been in August by the cardinals' discussions in the congregations, finding them disorganized and a waste of time. On 9 October he recorded: "'General Congregation' was not very important, esp. when we *might* be discussing role of Cardinals *qua* Collegium in life of Church." His own problem of troubled sleep had returned. He wrote: "Slept very poorly. All kinds of things kept coming up to preoccupy me and keep me from sleeping: almost like a kaleidoscope of things here (e.g. government of the Church, with role of 'College' of Cardinals, choice of Pope, etc., – and things in Winnipeg, Basil Symposium, etc.) I guess I got some sleep, but there was a lot of turning over and being awake. How do I improve that?" (8 October).

The interval between the funeral of the pope and the beginning of the second conclave was shorter by five days than that in August. Flahiff put in the time in much the same way as he had in August: congregations with the cardinals, interviews with the media, and long walks in the city. After the initial rainy days at the beginning of October the weather cleared and was pleasant. He speaks of one unofficial meeting with a group of cardinals, mostly the same ones with whom he had met informally in August. He recorded: "I walked the rest of the way to French Seminary and gathering there: Marty, Gouyon, Thiandoum, Gantin, Roy, Hume [Archbishop of Westminster] and *Arns* (São Paolo). Very interesting exchange (7:00–8:00) with general view of Benelli as *perhaps* first & *certainly not* Siri! If opposition too strong, maybe Poletti! Other names were considered, even Woytila [*sic*] and Lorscheider (heart is against him). Poma was mentioned but, again, health! In general, an Italian seemed desirable" (9 October).

The General Congregation on the following day seemed awkward to Flahiff and not well conducted by Cardinal Villot, the former secretary of state and acting pope. After a review of the late pope's September activities, there was a long discussion on whether or not to issue a statement with regard to John Paul's death in order to staunch rumours of foul play. Some thought it would be good to explain why there had been no autopsy. A decision was put over until the next day. (Two days later the cardinals voted negatively to a statement of any kind.) Flahiff remarks also on the change in Cardinal Pignedoli, his good friend, who seemed to have lost his characteristic cheerfulness and to have fallen into despondency. He found the same condition in Baggio. It is quite evident that the atmosphere before the October conclave was far more tense and uncertain than that which prevailed in August.

Some of the media interviews seemed to Flahiff to be more like exercises in sensation-seeking than contributions to the spread of useful information. But he gave of his time generously to the reporters and acknowledged the merit of the serious ones. It was with considerable relief that he entered the conclave on the afternoon of 14 October, to find himself in the same room that he had occupied in August, and again beside Cardinal Cooray to be of assistance if needed. He recorded: "Room has a 'tree' for hanging things, which helps; otherwise, unchanged. For some reason, no soap and no towel. I had brought a towel, but no soap" (14 October). These latter actually appeared the next day. But there was one important addition to the conclave area, an addition which affected everyone and was very popular. A bar had been installed at the entrance to the dining room. Cardinal Flahiff does not mention the hours of opening, but it seems to have been in service around meal times and in the evening. Needless to say, it helped considerably in a situation which was unpleasant in several respects.

The voting during the next two days proved difficult. Three leaders emerged on the first ballot and stubbornly kept their solid positions, with slight variations, during the first day of voting in which four ballots were taken. Of that evening Flahiff recorded: "I am conscious of strain & tension. Nobody seems sure what to expect. Slept poorly again. – Need of pill around 2.00." And of the next morning at breakfast he wrote: "Everybody (in couples or small groups) trying to see trend. I talked with Pignedoli. He thinks the three will not make it and that some one from 3rd World or a small country will have to be chosen and pushed. He even mentioned *W*" (16 October). Cardinal Pignedoli was prophetic: the decline of the big three and the rise of "W" began with the first ballot of the day. By the fourth ballot late in the afternoon Cardinal Wojtyla was elected pope by a majority almost as high as that of John Paul in August, much to the relief of all concerned, with the possible exception of the early starters whose support had melted all through the day. There was general rejoicing. After the formalities of the name-taking and the appearance on the balcony of St Peter's for the applause of the crowd – with Flahiff again clearly visible beside the pope – the cardinals sat down to a most convivial dinner where the champagne corks popped and songs rang out in many languages, notably Polish. John Paul II rose and made the rounds, touching the glass of each cardinal with his own.

The conclave ended with a concelebrated mass the next morning in the Sistine Chapel at which John Paul II spoke for thirty-five minutes on collegiality and basic notions of the Church. Flahiff returned to the

Oblate house and spent the rest of the day meeting reporters. On Tuesday there was a formal audience with the pope for the purpose of receiving the obedience of the cardinals. John Paul II spoke briefly in answer to the speech of Cardinal Confalioneri, the dean of the Sacred College. Then, instead of having each cardinal kneel before him to make obeissance, the pope moved about the room to speak to each one individually, a gesture intended to illustrate his theme of collegiality of which he had spoken the previous day. That afternoon Flahiff heard the good news that five of the Winnipeg priests would be arriving the next day to be present at the inauguration ceremony of the new pope on the following Sunday, 22 October 1978.

Once more there was general satisfaction and much jubilation at the election, with the added surprise and novelty of having a non-Italian on the Throne of Peter for the first time in four hundred years. The feared stalemate had not occurred; the second day of voting had seen the cardinals come together in a gesture that broke the four-centuries-old monopoly which should not have been part of a Church calling herself universal. The Italian populace, after initially being stunned by the surprising turn of events, received the foreigner as enthusiastically as they would have received an Italian. And the man they received, former actor that he was, knew how to present himself and endear himself to them. His famous self-correction, when he referred to his inability in "your" language, and then said, "our" language, was greeted with tremendous applause. It was consciously or unconsciously a stroke of genius. One suspects that John Paul II knew exactly what he was doing. The inauguration on the esplanade in front of St Peter's was conducted beautifully under fine weather. After the imposition of the pallium, the obedience of the cardinals, and the mass, John Paul II went down to bless the sick in the front row and came close to being mobbed. His guards soon learned that they were going to be busy with this man, who was a crowd pleaser and a crowd teaser. He finally went into the basilica, only to appear a few minutes later at the window of his office, high above the piazza, to recite the angelus. Then he told the crowd to go home and have some lunch for the ceremony had been long and they were probably tired and hungry.

In what Cardinal Flahiff wrote in his diary of the second conclave there is no indication that he had been a contender for the papacy. He reports the whole thing with little emotion and probably hides the fact that he might have had a vote or two in the first few ballots. There is, however, a clear impression of his interest, of his desire to discern the will of God in the voting process, and of his satisfaction that things eventuated happily. He was also quite content to leave Rome and to get back to Winnipeg. The shocking death of John Paul I affected him probably more than he was aware. In two years' time he would be seventy-five and would submit his resignation. During those years he would be as diligent as usual in his duties, but he would be disinclined to undertake new things, and there would be some difficulties with his usually robust health.

CHAPTER SIXTEEN

Resignation at Length

Cardinal Flahiff had been looking forward to the moment when he could submit his resignation as Archbishop of Winnipeg. As the years of his service wore on, the prospect of being free of the responsibilities and of returning to things he had known and loved looked more and more inviting. He did not, however, slow down in his zeal, but maintained the same generosity and thoroughness in his duties: the confirmation tours, the careful and prompt correspondence, the attention to his staff and his priests, and the numerous public appearances and functions which formed so great a part of his life. Yet it was with some relief that he sat down on 20 October 1980, and wrote to Pope John Paul II as follows: "Most Holy Father, On October 26, 1980, I shall have completed the seventy-fifth year of my life. In conformity with the Decree *Christus Dominus* (#21) of the Second Vatican Council and with the more precise statement of the *motu proprio* of Pope Paul VI, *Ecclesiae Sanctae* (Pars 1a, #11), I do therefore offer to Your Holiness my resignation as Archbishop of Winnipeg. With loving loyalty and the assurance of my prayers, I remain, Most Holy Father, Yours respectfully in Christ ."[1] That was the easiest part; the cardinal did not suspect, nor could he know, that the resignation process was going to be long and would cost him dearly.

On 30 October, while in Ottawa for a CCCB committee meeting, the cardinal had lunch with the pro-nuncio, Archbishop Angelo Palmas, at his residence. As usual, he enjoyed the occasion. They chatted about the mechanics of resignation. The pro-nuncio gave the cardinal to understand that the process could take some months, given the usual inquiries and investigations to be undertaken, especially if the person resigning were in good health and urgency were not a consideration. Flahiff took this quite cheerfully, and expressed his willingness to stay in office as long as necessary, for the good of all concerned, and to assure a smooth transition process. He returned to Winnipeg to prepare for the archdiocesan celebration of his golden jubilee of priesthood. This took place on 12 November 1980, in the presence of some forty-two bishops from all over Canada. It was an extremely happy and successful event, in which the outpouring of congratulations and good wishes could not have been more sincere, nor indeed better merited

During the month of November Archbishop Palmas, in accordance with the usual procedures, did some consulting among the Canadian bishops on the advisability of accepting Flahiff's resignation, to ascertain whether, for the good of all – the cardinal himself, the Church in Winnipeg, and the Church in Canada – it might not be better to ask him to stay on for a time. The general opinion seemed to be that in view of the cardinal's age, his fatigue, which some had come to notice, and his desire to return to his community in Toronto, it would be better to accept the resignation and free him from all episcopal duties.

This was duly reported to Cardinal Baggio, the secretary of the Sacred Congregation for Bishops in Rome, and the man who had been apostolic delegate to Canada when Father Flahiff had been named bishop in 1961. In the meantime, Flahiff received a letter from the secretary of state, Cardinal Casaroli, gratefully acknowledging in the name of the Holy Father his letter of resignation, and telling him that the matter was being considered by the Congregation for Bishops. On 9 December, Cardinal Baggio wrote to the pro-nuncio in Canada, informing him that the pope had accepted the resignation of Cardinal Flahiff and had appointed him apostolic administrator of the Archdiocese of Winnipeg until such time as a successor be named. Cardinal Baggio instructed Palmas to inform Cardinal Flahiff of the pope's decision. This he did on 16 January 1981:

Your Eminence ... as directed by the Sacred Congregation for Bishops, I am to inform you that His Holiness Pope John Paul II has accepted your resignation from the pastoral government of the Archdiocese of Winnipeg. By accepting your resignation the Holy Father took satisfaction in noting that you are greatly esteemed by the clergy and laity of the Winnipeg Archdiocese which you have governed faithfully for the past 19 years. Yet, as a result of your age and tiredness, His Holiness has accepted your prudent offer to retire.

As far as the date of publication is concerned, this determination, as in other similar cases, may be made by you in co-operation with the Apostolic Nunciature, which then has to inform the Canadian Hierarchy and the Sacred Congregation responsible for arranging the publication in *L'Osservatore Romano.*

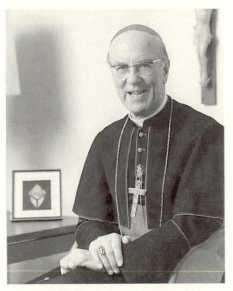

Cardinal Flahiff on the occasion of his golden jubilee
of priesthood, 1980. (Photo: Napoleon Studios, Winnipeg)

Hence, let me be permitted to ask you to please propose a date of publication and inform me at your convenience.[2]

It is curious that this letter says nothing about Flahiff's being appointed apostolic administrator, and nothing about waiting for a successor to be named. It seems to free the cardinal immediately from all responsibilities and allow him to leave Winnipeg. It asks him only to name the date. What went on in Flahiff's mind can be imagined if one considers his lifetime habit of agonizing over decisions and of exploring all the corners where a problem or a duty might lurk. It would probably have been much better for all concerned had the cardinal taken the letter at face value, set a date in the near future, and left Winnipeg. But this was not his way of doing things. Nor did he reveal this letter to anyone, or take advice on the matter so far as is known. What he did was mull over the matter for some two weeks and then telephone the pro-nuncio to acknowledge receipt of his letter and to arrange for a visit to Ottawa on 18 March.

In the course of the visit it transpired that Flahiff said he would like "a bit more time" to attend to many things which needed to be done. He seems also to have given some indication that he was not keen on being named apostolic administrator, and that he would like his resignation and the appointment of his successor to be simultaneous. On this point there seems to have been some misunderstanding. The cardinal was also concerned about where he should retire, mentioning what loomed for him as a problem, namely, that he saw reasons for remaining in Winnipeg and equally good reasons for returning to the Basilian community in Toronto.

Their conversation was reported to Rome, and on 23 April 1981, the pro-nuncio informed Cardinal Flahiff of the reactions of the Sacred Congregation, or, more precisely, of Cardinal Baggio: Cardinal Flahiff, so far as Rome was concerned, might freely choose his future place of residence; the announcement of his resignation would be published simultaneously with the appointment of the new archbishop, according to the "desire" of Cardinal Flahiff; and the whole matter would likely be concluded by the end of June. The use of the word "desire" in reference to himself touched a sore spot in Flahiff. In his reply to Palmas, after the usual courtesies, he wrote: "You refer in your letter to what was discussed in our last conversation at your residence on March 18, 1981. I do not recall having expressed any 'desire' that the announcement of my resignation take place at the same time as the announcement of the appointment of my eventual successor. Any 'desire' in this regard is similar to that of offering my resignation on my 75th birthday: I desire to do whatever the Holy Father himself or the Sacred Congregation for Bishops wishes of me." The hint of petulance in Flahiff's words might well be an indication of the tension his resignation was causing him.

He then went on to list the inconveniences of an announcement coming within the next two months, citing the confirmation schedule, which went on into July, the visit of Cardinal Ribeiro of Lisbon to the Portuguese community of the Archdiocese of Winnipeg, and his own expected presence at the General Chapter of the Basilian Fathers in July. "If I myself," he wrote, "and the priests and people of the Archdiocese of Winnipeg could be spared preoccupation with news of the appointment of a new Ordinary until the various events I have mentioned are over, it would mean a calmer time for us all."[3] He asked that nothing be done before the end of July.

Two weeks later, Palmas wrote to the cardinal, acceding to his request for time, and asking him for "information about the situation in the Archdiocese and its most important problems in relation to the appointment of a successor."[4] Flahiff replied presenting a picture of the Archdiocese of Winnipeg in terms both irenic and positive, without glossing over the problems: "I would say that the overall situation in the Archdiocese is satisfactory even if the situation may vary from place to place. The cooperation of priests, religious and laity is indeed impressive and that is all the more striking in view of the relatively large number of parishes of diverse ethnic origin (13 of 28 within the city of Winnipeg), even though the ethnic ones are not as large as the others in actual population."

He mentioned the decline in the number of priests and religious in the past twenty years as something which had affected all areas of the apostolate; for some time to come, he stated, relatively older priests would be in the majority. There were fewer religious involved in teaching and in the care of the sick, while on the other hand, the generosity of the laity in apostolic work was "impressive, encouraging and very helpful." The financial resources of the archdiocese, he said, were slim, and added that this was certainly one of the reasons why the number of Catholic institutions and services was relatively lower in Winnipeg than in many other dioceses. This was particularly so in the field of education, he said, Catholic schools having received no government help since 1890.

He commented on the vastness of the archdiocese. He was of the opinion, however, that since the great majority of Catholics lived in Winnipeg, any division of the archdiocese would be impractical from an administrative point of view. He went on to say that the number of French-speaking persons in the archdiocese, and the proximity to the Archdiocese of St Boniface, which is French-speaking, "would make the choice of a new Archbishop who speaks French not only desirable but even necessary." Furthermore, the new archbishop should also be prepared to be in close contact with the third archbishop in the Winnipeg area, the Archieparch of the Ukrainian Rite.[5]

This letter is vintage Flahiff in its tone and serenity, but hardly a guide to the choosing of a successor. He did not mention, for example, the very numerous demands on him from the academic and political communities. He was seemingly unconscious of how much his own success had depended on the friendly contacts and generous services by which he had carried on the humane and ecumenical traditions of his predecessor, Archbishop Pocock. He did not tell the pro-nuncio much that he did not already know. There is a certain detachment in the letter, and nothing of a spark. What comes through is not so much a lack of interest as a lack of urgency. Flahiff was obviously tired.

During this protracted correspondence with the pro-nuncio and the months of living in suspense with regard to his future and his authority, the cardinal did not reduce his normal activities, nor become less conscientious in his obligations. In fact, the intensity of his activity, for a man of seventy-five years on the brink of retirement, is surprising. In January 1981, with the other bishops of western Canada, he made a ten-day directed retreat at the Benedictine monastery at Mission, British Columbia. His commentary was enthusiastic: "The retreat was really superb. The setting is glorious and, for 6 of our 10 days, the weather was, too: sunshine from morning till evening, which enhanced the view, and temperatures (daytime) around +12 to 15 degrees ... Accomodations at the Abbey are very good; mine were among the best, thanks particularly to the view. Everyone was pleased with the spiritual part, too. It was, as it has been for 3 years, an S.J. 'Directed Retreat,' with one *Conference* only each day (evening) and one session with your Director, leaving plenty of time for prayer, reading and liturgy (with 'shared homily' that could last 3/4 hour and that was somewhat like an examination of conscience or an exchange on things important to each and every one.)"[6] The cardinal was pleased, too, that the two Jesuits directing the retreat were friends of his; one of them had actually worked in the Archdiocese of Winnipeg.

When Flahiff returned from this retreat, he learned of the death, at fifty-nine, of Father Elliott Allen, a Basilian professor of theology and dean of the Faculty of Theology at the University of St Michael's College in Toronto. Allen was a man of great ability and promise. The news, he said, left him "somewhat stunned, – 'depressed' would not be the word, – perhaps 'preoccupied' and 'sad.' " The cardinal appreciated Allen for his qualities of intelligence and spirituality and counted him as a good friend. His sadness, however, gave way to something more spiritual the next day, as, true to form, he saw the premature death of this capable and devoted priest in the light of providence:

As I reflected for a few moments before starting Mass, I suddenly realized that one of the chief sentiments should be that of thanksgiving to God for the person and the priest He had given us in Al and for all that Al had done for so many. I also accepted more sensibly the fact of God's love in sparing Al further suffering here and in welcoming him home. Unlike yesterday, I actually experienced a certain joy to-day, even if I was keenly aware of how much he will be missed. Altho' I have seen much less of him than formerly in the past 20 years, he has remained a very good friend and I always enjoyed my visits. Actually I was beginning to experience a definite anticipation of seeing more of Al once I get back. I guess I forgot to add: "Si Deus vult [If God wills]."[7]

"Once I get back" is one of the rare references we have during this time of the cardinal's anticipation of returning to Toronto. It implies a decision and plans. When the moment came to decide his future, however, he was far from decisive and at a loss for any kind of plan.

February took him to Houston, Texas, for a ceremonial visit to the University of St Thomas. As was his custom when the occasion offered, he called at all three Basilian houses in the city. In the same month, he attended the Scriptural Study days for the Western Bishops in Edmonton, Alberta. Early in April he went to Weyburn, Saskatchewan, by way of Regina, where he visited his good friend Charlie Halpin. The occasion in Weyburn was the silver jubilee cele-bration of a long-time friend, Father Len Sullivan, who "wanted his rural parish to *see a Cardinal!*"[8] Flahiff went along with the fun, taking with him all the paraphernalia he could that goes with the office. But by the end of the month he was suffering from fatigue and, on his doctor's advice, he cancelled meetings in Quebec City and Moncton, and took a few days' rest. But he was not kept down for long, for in May he went to Montreal for the fortieth wedding anniversary of his brother Terry, returned west to Regina for the silver jubilee of priest-hood of Charlie Halpin, only to go east once more in June for the one hundred and twenty-fifth anniversary of St Basil's parish in Toronto.

The cardinal's pace and activities during the autumn months were astonishing. On October 12 he wrote:

The Ukrainian celebrations are always long and heavy; the three days to mark the Silver Jubilee of their Archeparchy in Winnipeg outdid anything before it. Hardly was it over than St. Paul's College arranged meetings in connection with a special Memorial Lecture series, famous both for the speaker and for the social aspects. I enjoyed it and was delighted to meet the speaker, a Ger-man theologian whose name you have doubtless heard: Johannes B. Metz ... He is excellent, even tho' some authorities in Germany are not too happy. He certainly is not Hans Küng, but they are good friends, and the German bish-ops may not like that. We had a couple of very pleasant visits.

After a break of one full day, trips to the country became necessary for the 3 penultimate Confirmation dates ... The three earlier ones involved nearly 600 miles of travel, but the countryside was beautiful, as I mentioned, and there was a warm, friendly feeling in all the places I visited. Diminished sleep-hours were the only trying aspect to the trip. The first half was in the S.W. cor-ner of the province, – closer actually to Regina than to Winnipeg! After 2 full days there, we returned to Winnipeg for a few hours and then headed north along Lake Winnipeg. – Next weekend (blessing of church and Confirmation) will be a trip of no more than 200 or 250 miles. Everything has been, and will be next weekend, in thoroughly rural settings, – not at all unpleasant.[9]

These events are merely the highlights in Flahiff's busy life during this year when his resignation was pending. He followed his heavy confirmation schedules in both the spring and the fall, and attended the General Chapters of the Basilians and of the Loretto Sisters during the summer.[10] In spite of the usual positive tone of his letters, he was living and acting in an atmosphere of uncertainty. Knowing his departure was imminent, though as yet not precise, his characteristic hesitancy regarding decisions was accentuated. Nor was he the only one suffering from the situation and from the silence of the Holy See. In November 1981 the Senate of Priests of the Archdiocese of Winnipeg sent a letter to the pro-nuncio, urging action in the appointment of a new archbishop. The priests pointed out to Palmas that, on the one hand, the cardinal was suffering from the suspense, and on the other, the archdiocese was stagnating, appointments were not being made, and general administration was in crisis. To the credit of the Winnipeg priests, they added that if the delay was due to extra time needed to find the right man, they were quite reconciled to waiting.

This letter may have been precipitated by the cardinal's sickness. At the middle of November 1981 he came down with an infection of the inner ear, painful and even dangerous, given the cardinal's tendency to lose his balance. This obliged him to cancel his projected trip to Rome at this time and to take to his bed. Nor did he recover completely, for at the end of the month he suffered a second bout of the same problem and had to cancel a trip to Toronto and, what disappointed him even more, he was unable to go to San Antonio, Texas, for the episcopal ordination on 6 December of a fellow Basilian, Ricardo Ramírez, who had been named Auxiliary Bishop of San Antonio.[11] Palmas responded to the Winnipeg Senate of Priests' letter with regrets for the delay in the appointing of a new archbishop and an assurance that the matter was going forward.

At the beginning of the new year, however, a further delay set in. On 20 January 1982 the pro-nuncio wrote to the cardinal, with appropriate apologies, announcing that the Holy Father wished to explore the possibility of finding a suitable Polish candidate for the See of Winnipeg. Probably further inquiries were made, but this matter seems to have had no sequel.

Obviously the uncertainty of his position was an obstacle to any pastoral planning. "The question about how long I shall be scheduling things for the Archdiocese of Winnipeg remains open," he wrote early in February,[12] noting in the same letter that he has heard from the pro-nuncio but only that there will be no announcement for some weeks yet. Monsignor Ward Jamieson, his vice-chancellor and secretary, advised him that a tentative schedule should be prepared, at least for the important annual duties, such as confirmation, whether he were still in office or not. The cardinal did not reduce his pastoral activities nor his travels during this time. He seems to have been as busy as ever and he also seems to have been as wholehearted and as enthusiastic about all the things he was doing. He made one trip to Toronto in the course of January. At the beginning of February he attended an ecumenical service, his comments on which display his characteristic *largesse d'esprit*:

And now I have just returned from an ecumenical service at our St Mary's Cathedral to mark the 30th anniversary of Queen Elizabeth's accession to the throne. It had been planned by a group called the Monarchist League, two leaders of which are priests of our diocese who are converts and still have many friends (clerical and otherwise) in other Churches, especially the Anglican. They, too, had planned things well. I was asked to preside, since this year's ceremony was in our cathedral. Frankly, I was impressed with the strong ecumenical spirit, not only in the ceremony but also in the conversations afterwards at the very pleasant reception. Views expressed seemed very sincere and very desirous of a better understanding and a trend towards reunion. An Anglican preached the homily and it was excellent.[13]

In mid-February he went to Toronto for the ordination of a young Basilian, Mitchell Dowalgo, and was hardly back in Winnipeg when he was off to Edmonton for the meeting of the Western Canadian Bishops. He had intended to go to Vancouver early in March, at the invitation of Archbishop Carney, for the celebration of the founding of a Polish parish in that city by a priest who had served successfully in Winnipeg. The death of Archbishop Jordan of Edmonton intervened, however, and he found himself back in that city for the funeral, rather worried about whether he was doing the right thing by going to Edmonton, when the commitment to Vancouver had been of long standing. Flahiff, as we have seen on other occasions, was scrupulous about keeping his word. A striking proof of this came a few weeks later when he regretfully declined the privilege of saying grace at a banquet for the Queen during her visit to Ottawa. It is possible that the request for his presence came from the Queen herself, but he had promised to ordain Norbert Maduzia, a young Basilian from Houston, on that day, and he did not wish to go back on his commitment. Grace was actually said for the Queen by Cardinal Carter, though Cardinal Flahiff's name appeared on the program.

One catches a glimpse of the cardinal's preoccupation in a somewhat impatient note of 12 March: "Baggio continues to make visits to the Holy Father." Three weeks later came the abrupt announcement of the appointment of Adam Exner, OMI, Bishop of Kamloops, as the new Archbishop of Winnipeg and Flahiff as the apostolic administrator in the interim until the new archbishop would take over. Flahiff was absolutely devastated. Although one might have expected him to be relieved and even pleased, perhaps he was expecting more ceremony in the notice, or perhaps he was offended at being so abruptly demoted to the rank of caretaker. It is impossible to know exactly what takes place at such a moment in someone who has occupied a high position for almost thirty years, especially a person so emotionally controlled as was George Flahiff. In any case, it was the beginning of a very difficult period in his life and an indication of declining mental health. On receiving the news the cardinal was so emotionally jolted that he had to be hospitalized for several days.

April was taken up with Holy Week and Easter, and all that those days demand of presence and pastorate. Just after Easter he went to Houston for the ordination of the young Basilian, Norbert Maduzia. Then there was the preliminary visit of Archbishop Exner, whom the cardinal invited to come to Winnipeg for four days in the third week of the month, and for whom he spared no courtesy. Flahiff was pleased with the appointment of Exner, and naturally he wanted to make the transition as smooth and as gracious as possible. He wrote: "Adam seemed very pleased with everything and I have the impression that our priests, religious and people will be more than satisfied with him. Most conversations were group ones, but he and I spent a fair amount of time together and I think it was helpful to both of us. I have the impression that he will like Winnipeg and also that he will be liked here. He is well experienced and is a man of good judgment. The future looks bright."[14]

On 28 April Flahiff went to Chicago for the funeral of Cardinal Cody, for whom he seems to have had a genuine affection and whom he considered a good friend. "We sat side by side during the whole first session of Vatican II," he wrote, "and have known each other well. When he was moved from New Orleans to Chicago ... I was invited to Chicago for his installation and I was invited on other occasions too. Just last week, I had a letter from him, – probably one of his last. He didn't anticipate his death at that time; he talked more of my retirement and went on to say that, now that I would be having more free time, he looked forward to my use of it in a visit to him!"[15]

He was not back from Chicago twenty-four hours when he left for Sudbury, Ontario, for the celebration of Alex Carter's silver jubilee as bishop. Since Alex was a close friend, and had been so for many years, Flahiff did not wish to miss this event, and he went with great pleasure and anticipation. He loved the company of his fellow bishops. He might not have realized what a strain he was putting on his health, but found out very soon. When he returned to Winnipeg, he was suddenly stricken with intense headaches and disturbed sleep, to such an extent that he was hospitalized, and remained so for ten days.

Exhaustive testing revealed nothing serious. It was obvious that the collapse was the result of tension and fatigue. He was at this time preoccupied with two problems which would seem to anyone else to be of minor consequence, but which were to him extremely oppressive. One was the decision as to where he should live after leaving the office of Archbishop of Winnipeg. The other was, incredibly, the decisions to be made with regard to packing.

As to the first, it should be noted that almost two years previously, the then superior general of the Basilian Fathers, James Hanrahan, aware of the fact that the cardinal was approaching his seventy-fifth birthday, and consequently his time for retiring, mentioned to him that he would be welcome to come back to St Michael's in Toronto to live out his remaining years. At the time Flahiff was grateful and happy at the suggestion, but gave no firm commitment on the matter. Both men knew that normally a bishop who was a member of a religious order would return to his congregation upon retiring. When, however, the time actually drew near for leaving his position as ordinary, that is to say, after the announcement at the end of March 1982 that a successor had been named, a dilemma presented itself. Flahiff was invited and urged by his associates in Winnipeg to think of remaining there where he had lived for such a long time, and where he had so many friends. This was not merely conventional courtesy; it was a very sincere suggestion and a real desire on the part of the clergy and people of Winnipeg that the cardinal, much beloved as he was, should stay with the people to whom he had been ministering for twenty-one years. His many friends were quite prepared to provide him with comfortable retirement, and would have been delighted to have him in their midst.

This was the kind of problem with which Flahiff could not easily cope. His characteristic hesitation with decisions was now aggravated by age and ill-health. Nor was he good at externalizing the issue. He was torn between friendship and duty, there being a strong element of friendship in the duty, for the Basilians were his friends as were the people of Winnipeg. He was deeply afraid of offending, and this fear paralysed him.

At the direction of the new superior general of the Basilians, Father Ulysse Paré, Father James Daley, his assistant, wrote to the cardinal

Cardinal Flahiff, with Archbishop Hacault of St Boniface,
welcoming Mother Teresa of Calcutta, 26 June 1982, the last of
the cardinal's functions in Winnipeg. (Basilian Archives)

on 5 May 1982.[16] The letter of three full single-spaced pages began
with congratulations to the cardinal on his resignation, and on his
great record of service as ordinary in the Archdiocese of Winnipeg.
Daley then expressed the ardent wish of the Basilian Fathers that
Flahiff return to Toronto. In sensitive and courteous terms Daley
treated the "problem" facing the cardinal of choosing between
Winnipeg and Toronto. He acknowledged the kindness of the Archdiocese of Winnipeg, and the attractiveness of staying with friends. He
then assured the cardinal that he would have the advantages of both
places, enjoying the freedom and possibility of visiting his former
archdiocese whenever he wished, as well as living among his Basilian
brothers in surroundings familiar and dear.

This letter must surely have had some effect, but the final decision
was really occasioned by the visit to the cardinal of the Basilian superior general himself, accompanied by Father George Freemesser, who
was, as has been noted, a medical doctor and psychiatrist. They simply
said to him in substance, "Your Eminence, we are expecting you home
next month. Your rooms are ready and waiting for you." This took the
burden of decision off his shoulders. From that time on the question of
residence was no longer a problem. Doubtless he was sensitive to the
grace of religious obedience, and was happy to find a refuge therein.

The other problem of packing remained a bugbear. Flahiff has been described, not disrespectfully, as a pack-rat, and indeed he saved almost everything. By way of material possessions, such as furniture and objets d'art, he had practically nothing. But he did have books, papers, letters, notes, speeches, reviews, and reports. His problem was what to take and what to leave, what belonged to Winnipeg and what could be considered personal, what would be useful and what would be superfluous. "My great preoccupation," he wrote, "is still the packing and especially decisions about the packing. A couple of seminarians are doing most of the real work part of it, but I find myself very preoccupied and often afflicted with grave doubts, – especially *after* certain things have been packed."[17] These are not the words of a well man.

At this distressing time Cardinal Flahiff was shown much friendship and kindness by Debbie Kohen, a young woman in her twenties who had come to know the cardinal through Norman Chartrand, who was a close friend of her parents. This young woman had not only a supremely kind manner, but also tact and sensitivity. She loved to converse with the cardinal, whom she admired for the scope of his mind, the range of his interests, and the simplicity of his person, but she perceived that he was then going through a very difficult time. She was constantly attentive. She considered herself the granddaughter he never had, and he thought of her in the same way. From the end of March, when the announcement of his resignation was made public, until he left for Toronto, Debbie Kohen was called on frequently, and made visits at other times on her own, well aware of how helpful she was in the situation. She alone could calm him in the tantrums which beset him. She saw him through the trauma of packing; she was able to anticipate difficulties and meet them when they came. In a word, she was exactly the person needed for the great man in a difficult moment of his life. When, during the ceremony of installation of Archbishop Exner, the cardinal stopped dead in the procession, Kohen, close by and alert, slipped to his side to reassure him. Few noticed. The ceremony continued and concluded smoothly.

May and June were indeed difficult months. To relieve the cardinal of some of his work, five monsignori were appointed to do the confirmations. This must have both relieved him and saddened him, for this was his favourite pastoral duty. Twenty-four hours after his release from the hospital on 19 May, he went to join his priests on retreat under the direction of Adam Exner, to share with them at least the closing hours of this annual event which had been a joy to him. The priests were touched by his efforts to be with them, but they would not have been surprised. Then later in the month he wrote: "Preparations for Adam Exner's installation make the present schedule a bit heavy. I have got caught for several receptions, – more personal than public, and really very touching, even if they do take up a good deal of time, lessening somewhat the time I should be reserving for packing, – or, at least, for making selections. The headaches are not as bad as they were when I went to the hospital two weeks ago, but I am still quite conscious of them, and there is a repeated weariness that is not natural to me at all. Maybe it is chiefly a psychological effect of the many preoccupations, – yes, and occupations, too."[18]

One notices a slackening of firmness in the cardinal's handwriting at this time, and there were lapses of memory and failures in recognizing people. On one occasion, when Archbishop Exner had come for a short visit preparatory to his installation, the cardinal asked his chancellor after Exner had left, "Who was that priest, and what did he want?" His gentle nature and external serenity sometimes gave way to expressions of resentment at being "rejected" and "put on the shelf." Those were feelings that would plague him later in his retirement in Toronto. He was experiencing the trauma so common to those in positions of authority who must let go of command and even of independence.

He was also pressed with invitations, which, had he been better physically, he would have relished. He tried to fulfil them as best he could, but it was a great strain, and more duty than delight. To compound the difficulties Archbishop Exner decided to come a few days earlier than originally agreed, which was probably not a big problem, but which loomed so for the cardinal, given his psychological and physical condition. He was worried at the prospect of three persons living in the house, two of whom would be in the process of packing or unpacking. And he was concerned about the various functions coming up, his own farewell ceremony, and the installation of the new archbishop on the following day. However, these events all went well, and were organized and carried out with little onus on Flahiff himself.

Archbishop Exner was installed on 23 June 1982. The cardinal had planned to leave on that day or the following one. He consented, however, to remain in Winnipeg for the visit of Mother Teresa of Calcutta who was expected on 26 June. He left for Toronto on 28 June, accompanied by Monsignor Norman Chartrand, arriving that evening at St Michael's College where a gathering of his Basilian confreres and some friends awaited him. The cardinal came in leaning on Chartrand's arm. He still commanded attention as he always did when he entered a room, but he was not the man who had left St Michael's twenty-one years before.

CHAPTER SEVENTEEN

The Sunset and the Sorrow

The cardinal was warmly welcomed into the community at the University of St Michael's College. He was home in a very real sense, and he was among brothers and friends. His accommodation at the college was the best the Basilians had, though it was far from palatial. He was given a suite in the Charbonnel wing of Elmsley Hall, which consisted of a sitting-room with bedroom and bath. He was also provided with an office on the first floor of the same wing. The landing on the staircase between the two floors opened onto a small chapel which proved convenient for him, particularly when he had visitors with whom he wished to celebrate mass. He was obliged to walk outside, a distance of some seventy to eighty yards to Brennan Hall to join the brethren for prayers and meals. Though going from building to building was something he had been accustomed to during the years in which he lived at the college, it was to prove inconvenient in his retirement years, especially in winter, now that he was older and less steady on his feet. His living arrangements, on the whole, pleased him, however, and with easy access to a car which was put at his disposal, and parked conveniently close to his residence, Flahiff settled into a new phase of his life.

It was not one of inactivity. He soon recovered from the trauma of leaving Winnipeg, and while having nothing of the burdens of episcopal office, he found a good deal of activity both social and ceremonial. He continued to attend the annual meetings of the bishops in Ottawa up until October of 1988, though his participation was mostly that of simple presence. He was invited by the bishops of Ontario to attend their meetings as well, a gesture of recognition which touched him. He also continued to participate in the deliberations of the Congregation for Religious and Secular Institutes[1] in Rome, making in all five visits to Rome in the first four years of his retirement. He was officially a member of the congregation until his eightieth birthday on 26 October 1985, and was asked to come to one more meeting after that in January 1986. It proved to be his last visit to Rome.

His taste for travel did not diminish even though he was not disposed to travel for speaking engagements. Visits and ceremonies were fine; obligations of any kind became increasingly burdensome, and the cause of much anxiety in anticipation. In August of 1982 he visited Peterborough, Ontario, for the centenary of the cathedral there; in September he attended the CCCB meeting in Ottawa; in November he was in Rome for a special synod on finances; and in December he went to Winnipeg to receive the Caritas Medal from the Catholic Foundation of Manitoba. The latter part of the following year shows a similar pattern of travel activity: to Ottawa in September for the CCCB meeting; to Hamilton in November for the fiftieth anniversary of the cathedral, and to Gary, Indiana, for the golden jubilee of priesthood of Bishop Grutka, the man who had received the Basilians in Gary when Flahiff was superior general; and again to Rome at the end of the month and into December.

The year 1984 reveals a slowing down in ready and extensive travel: the cardinal went twice to Ottawa, once in January and once in October. In March he went to Boston for the installation of Archbishop Bernard Law, and in May to Hamilton for the installation of Bishop Tonnos. In September Pope John Paul visited Canada. "Much preoccupation here has to do with the Holy Father's visit," he wrote on 2 September, "I am grateful to be on no committee having to do with plans or with their implementation, but the preoccupation is a reality even for me."[2] The cardinal participated in the events in and around Toronto though he had no official functions. At the time of the visit of the pope, someone had asked Flahiff to procure a papal blessing for a couple about to be married. Such blessings were usually done through correspondence with Rome. Flahiff, however, took advantage of his position beside the pope as they were dining in Cardinal Carter's house. He leaned towards the Holy Father and asked him personally for the blessing, explaining that there was no time to go through Rome. The pope, of course, was pleased to grant it, charmed, no doubt, with Flahiff's simple humanity.

There were many happy moments in Flahiff's years of retirement. First of all and most enjoyable was community life with the Basilians. Flahiff was regular at morning and evening prayers and meals with the community. He frequently concelebrated with the confreres at mass, but he rarely gave a homily. He would attend community meetings, but would speak only when asked. He listened, however, very attentively, for everything about the community and religious life interested him. His manners and affability were appreciated by all. He would never leave the breakfast table without a courteous word, such as, "Well, let's see what the Globe and Mail is offering us this morning." (Flahiff was a newspaper reader all his life; the sports section was particularly important for him. When in Rome, he would buy two or three newspapers, French, Italian, or English.) It was a great suffering to him when his remarkable memory for names began to fail him. In the dining room he would sit at a place which commanded a view of the door. As people came in he would ask Father Joseph Wey or another of his usual table companions the name of the person entering, who very often would come over to speak to him. Thus he could continue to do what he had done all his life: greet everyone by name. He loved the community, and the confreres were pleased and honoured to have him in their midst. But there were shadows, as we shall see presently.

Another source of joy to the cardinal during this time was the proximity and attention of his family. His sister Catherine lived in Toronto, sharing a beautiful apartment on Jackes Avenue with Mary Murray, her life-long friend. From time to time the cardinal would go there for Sunday mass, celebrating on the coffee table in the living room which looked over the city and beyond to Lake Ontario. He loved this kind of mass, without pomp and without strain. Catherine and Mary had often received him when they lived in New York; he was entirely at home and comfortable with them. His brother Terry Flahiff carried on his custom of organizing family parties, usually at the Park Plaza Hotel in Toronto. Terry had done this with great success on the occasion of George's seventy-fifth birthday in October 1980; he did the same in 1983, 1984, and 1985. These were gala events which brought three generations of the family together and which gave Flahiff a good deal of enjoyment.

There were also frequent invitations to dinner from friends: various groups of sisters, the Jesuits, visitors from Winnipeg, old and new acquaintances in the Toronto area. He was a sought-after guest and a willing one. On the occasion of his silver jubilee as a bishop in May of 1986 a number of Winnipeg priests came to Toronto and arranged a dinner with the cardinal. Though it was intended to be informal, the priests thought clerical dress would be proper. They were somewhat surprised when Flahiff appeared in a sports shirt.

For the convenience of the cardinal, who did not relish driving at night, various seminarians volunteered to drive him when necessary

Cardinal Flahiff with Pope John Paul II meeting native peoples at Midland, Ontario, September 1984. (Photo: Osservatore Romano)

on these social occasions. Flahiff was not a good driver at the best of times. In his retirement he became increasingly inept and even dangerous to himself and to others. Efforts to get his licence cancelled were unsuccessful. His bad driving was a cause for concern among his confreres, his family, and his friends, but the streak of stubborness in Flahiff seemed to defy the aging process. He refused to give up his car until physical incapacity forced him to do so, just eight months before his death.

Though Flahiff gave few public speeches and wrote little during his retirement years, he did accept the invitation to give the opening address at a symposium organized by the Jesuits in Toronto to mark the twenty-fifth anniversary of the convoking of the Second Vatican Council by Pope John XXIII. His talk was entitled "Recollections of a Council Father," and was later published along with the other talks given at the symposium on ten of the council documents.[3] Faithful to its title, "Recollections" is personal and interesting without pretending to be scholarly. What Flahiff remembers particularly is the growth of the ecumenical spirit during the council, the increase in the number of non-Catholic observers, and their contact with the council fathers. He also remembers the increase over the sessions of the number of religious women included as observers. He recalls vividly the interventions and the influence of Archbishop Lefebvre[4] in the council and indicates that the council itself was the cause of the schism into which Lefebvre's followers fell. What one notices in Flahiff's speech is the lacklustre treatment of his theme. The spark and vim of his post-conciliar talks is gone. He is questioning the impact of the council and presenting, in his careful manner, the two sides of the problem of its effectiveness. There is no impression that he thinks the council has been a resounding success. He refrains from enthusiastic comments or predictions. Perhaps more interesting than his comments made in the talk is one he made afterwards about the symposium as a whole and the people there who gave the papers: "I think they improved my understanding of Vatican II."[5]

The years in retirement were not the happiest years of Flahiff's life, mainly because of his failing health. During his active years he had enjoyed remarkably good health; he could work or travel for hours, and then sit up talking into the wee small hours of the morning. His record for avoiding hospitals was broken only in April of 1964 at the age of fifty-eight when he came down with shingles and was hospitalized for the first time in his life. From the hospital in Winnipeg on that occasion he wrote to Father Robert Scollard, secretary general of the Basilians, with whom he was in competition for avoiding hospitals: "We battled for a long time as to who would have the longest unbroken record. I guess you win. I had never before been a patient in a hospital. Moreover, I had not missed a day through illness in more than 29 years, but I am now out of competition. And so inglorious a thing as 'shingles' was the cause."[6]

In December 1972 Flahiff fell in the bathroom at his home in Charleswood and broke two ribs, something which caused him a great deal of pain and inconvenience during the Christmas season that year. This, too, was but a passing incident from which he recovered with no ill effects. It was six years after this that decline in general health seems to have become evident. In July 1978 he uncharacteristically speaks of a "lessening of energy."[7] That was the year of the conclaves: they took their toll of his energy and of his spirit, as we have already noticed. In September 1980 he suffered a serious fall during the bishops' meeting at the Chateau Laurier in Ottawa. A nightwatchman found him unconscious and bleeding in the staircase between the assembly floor and the floor on which his room was located. Evidently he had decided to use the stairs instead of the elevator and somehow missed his step because of insufficient lighting.

Athletic though he was, and agile in his movements, Flahiff was prone to lose his balance. As a result of the fall in Ottawa his head and hand had to be stitched. From this time on, the pressure he had been feeling at the back of his head was accompanied by a persistent buzzing or ringing, which became accentuated with fatigue and stress.

What he went through during the resignation process was certainly painful in many ways. The mental anguish of those days, occasional forgetfulness, and moments of disorientation, were symptoms of a gradual breakdown of brain cells which would ultimately prove fatal. It is not surprising that in his retirement he had no inclination to write and very little desire to read. Many of the books he brought from Winnipeg to Toronto remained in their shipping boxes. Nor is it surprising that his participation in the bishops' meetings was nothing more than simple presence All activity in his retirement years must be seen against this background of deteriorating health. Most of the time he would appear well, very much himself, gracious and in command. His health was degenerating, however, and gravely affecting his moods, his memory, and his peace of mind.

Thomas Wolfe's theme of "you can't go home again" was borne out in the case of Cardinal Flahiff. The community to which he returned in 1982 was not the community he had left twenty-one years ago, nor could it have been. Not only were many of those whom he had known closely no longer there for reasons of death or departure to another house, but religious life itself had changed. Vatican II had intervened, and no religious community in the world was unaffected. In Flahiff's case there was a further component: he had left his religious community as a confrere, but had returned as a cardinal. The Basilians with whom he lived loved and respected him, but their respect caused some distance. He longed to be called George but few addressed him so, for those who might have addressed him familiarly were gone. In a letter he wrote to his sister Margaret ten months after his arrival at St Michael's, we can read between the lines some of the loneliness or strangeness he was experiencing in spite of the sincere kindness being shown him, and which he acknowledged and appreciated:

You were very sensitive to my "living situation" back here with my "Basilian family." It certainly is completely different from what things were in Winnipeg for 21 years, but it is far more than just tolerable. So much of the situation is very much different, even physically, from what I had known and experienced in that "same family" nearly a quarter of a century ago. But that is normal, I suppose, and I don't really suffer from it, Margaret. There are awkwardnesses of various sorts but they are certainly not painful. You speak of my being cut off from "community life"; even for the others, "community life" is not what it was long ago. If I am separated physically to some extent, many of the others are, too, with all the changes that have taken place. Yes, there are things that I miss, but I am certainly not excluded by my confreres. But thanks for your concern.[8]

Apart from his correspondence to which he was faithful, and the one talk mentioned above, Flahiff did no writing. Any hopes of doing memoirs or reflections on various aspects of his episcopacy or on the Church in general and the great moments when he was witness or participant were confounded by his mental state, which was not exactly one of depression as much as melancholy. He was at sixes and sevens, as are many who go into retirement psychologically unprepared. He had dreamed of some kind of intellectual or academic activity, but when the time came he had no heart for it and no incentive, nor the mental capacity. Apart from the newspapers, he read little. He was troubled by his inability to pray and spoke of this to George Freemesser, looking to the priest-doctor-psychiatrist friend for some guidance. Once a spiritual director for so many, Flahiff was now a troubled seeker of direction himself. He would often take a walk in the afternoon, usually following the same route, up Avenue Road to Bloor, west on Bloor to St George Street, south on St George to the Newman Centre. He would go into Newman to talk to Father Dave Katulski, the director of the centre, and reminisce about old times when his brother, Ed Flahiff, lived on the fourth floor of that building while doing medicine at the University of Toronto, and where George would visit him. He would repeat himself, telling the same stories over and over. He would take a cup of tea or coffee and then return to St Michael's College. A friend was greatly saddened to see the cardinal striding along Bloor Street one day as though beside himself, a man whose gait and mien had once been so dignified. This is not to say that Flahiff was not most of the time much his usual self. But it is to say that there was a good deal of interior suffering, both physical and psychological.

A great sorrow for Flahiff at this time was the sickness of his brother Norman who was admitted to Sunnybrook Hospital in January of 1984 with Alzheimer's disease. George and Norman had always kept in touch over the years and there was respect, admiration, and much affection one for the other. The progress of Norman's illness was a great trial for his wife Simone, their son Terrence, and for all the family. Flahiff faithfully visited his brother, but the experience was excruciating. As he watched his brother grow steadily less able to move, and then to speak, Flahiff would leave the hospital and return to his car in tears and had to spend some time composing himself before he could start out for home. Norman died in November of 1985 just after George had left for Rome. It was a further sorrow for him that he was unable to attend his brother's funeral. He deeply appreciated the qualities of this fine man to whom some referred as "the saint of the Flahiff family."

On 28 July 1985 Flahiff suffered what was described by his doctor as a "minimal stroke." The attack left no permanent damage but was an indication to him of the frailty of his own health. He was told that he would feel the effects of the stroke for some time."That, I suppose, is why," he wrote, "I am still conscious of the pressure at the back of the head and occasionally of the lack of balance, but the overall condition is very good and I can be quite active. I have called off a number of commitments I had had in the future, – chiefly for comfort in anticipation."[9] He recovered satisfactorily, however, and was in fine fettle for his eightieth birthday party in October, which was reported in the social column of The *Globe and Mail*. He left for Rome on 17 November for a plenary session of the College of Cardinals to discuss the finances of the Church. It was his second-last visit to Rome. He would return just once more, in January 1986, for a meeting of the Congregation for Religious and Secular Institutes, invited out of courtesy, since his official membership had ended the previous October when he reached his eightieth birthday.

The cardinal had done some service for the bishops of the Archdiocese of Toronto in the way of confirmations or filling in at ceremonial occasions during his retirement. This did not amount to a great deal, but it made him feel useful and still in the swim of things. In this connection there arose a misunderstanding in his relationship with Cardinal Carter, whom Flahiff considered a good friend. It seems that Carter spoke to Flahiff shortly after the latter's arrival in Toronto to the effect that the practice among the bishops in Toronto, that is, Carter and his four auxiliaries, was that ordinarily only one of them would attend a public ceremony, funeral, anniversary, or other. The purpose for such an agreement was to avoid competition among the laity in collecting bishops to grace an occasion. Flahiff somehow construed this as a restriction on his activities in the Archdiocese of Toronto, a kind of restraining order which he did not expect from his good friend. Though not given to complaints, Flahiff spoke to several people about this situation and about the fact that Carter, who used to be in frequent contact with him, now seldom called or wrote him. Carter on his part always considered Flahiff a close friend and never had the slightest intention of excluding him from the life of the archdiocese. In one case, for example, Cardinal Carter replied to an invitation from a prominent lawyer in Toronto explaining his policy and stepping aside to let Cardinal Flahiff be the guest of honour at a certain event. The letter is worth quoting for the light it casts on the "problem" from which Flahiff was suffering:

There is only one difficulty in the requests which you have made from me. When Cardinal Flahiff decided to come to live in Toronto for the period of his retirement, he and I, old friends of long-standing, sat down and discussed the practical problems attendant upon his residence in a city already well endowed with Prelates. We agreed that it would be unwise for us to allow ourselves to be paired in public events and in fund raising endeavours. You know, as well as I do, the tendency of people to play the game of one-up-manship. For that matter, the you-had-one Cardinal – but we-had-two Cardinals syndrome has already appeared in the land.

As you mention, Cardinal Flahiff has been most correct and fastidious in his reactions to invitations to duplicate our presences or our participation. I feel that to make an exception in your case would be unwise. Hence, I am only too happy to authorize you to invite him to act as Patron of whatever he chooses to accept and to be present at your dinner ... I gladly withdraw in his favour.[10]

In an interview with Cardinal Carter in November 1995 I raised the question of Carter's relationship to Flahiff during the latter's retirement. It became abundantly clear that Carter's friendship with Flahiff was solid and faithful and that there was never on his part the least intended offence. Cardinal Carter's manner can sometimes be misinterpreted. On the other hand, Flahiff's deteriorating health and his feeling of having been put on the shelf would account for the expressions of discontent which uncharacteristically escaped him.

A few months after the above letter was written, Carter and Flahiff took a decision which caused a good deal of sadness to the members of the famous "Gang of Five." They put an end to their annual Labour Day rendezvous, the source of so much enjoyment and mutual benefit to all the members: Emmett Carter of Toronto, Alex Carter of Sault Ste Marie, Plourde of Ottawa, Flahiff in retirement, and Pocock, also retired. Archbishop Pocock was terminally ill and it did not seem likely that he would be present at the gathering scheduled to take place at Plourde's cottage that year. It was decided, on a motion from Emmett Carter, "that the Gang of Five be considered as dissolved if it cannot meet as Five." Flahiff, responding to the motion in a letter to Plourde, recognized the wisdom of the proposal but wrote: "At the same time, the purely emotional effect on me is such that I find it hard to volunteer to *second* the motion."[11] Archbishop Pocock died in September of that year and with his death the Gang was dissolved. They had been meeting annually for some twenty years; it was a sad moment for the survivors.

Flahiff carried on valiantly. Not many knew of the things he was suffering, though a number were aware of his failing powers. In July of 1986 he was hospitalized for a week for observation, the discomfort of dizziness and pressure in his head being persistent. Twice more that year he complained in his letters of the pressure: "The last few days have not been so good for me. The pressure on the back of the head seemed to increase and has produced a general discomfort ... Not that my overall physical life or activity is greatly affected, but it is truly bothersome."[13] He wrote few letters through 1987 and 1988; those he did write show a noticeable degeneration in his fine handwriting. He attended what turned out to be his last meeting of the CCCB in Ottawa in September of 1987 and found it a wearying experience.[13] In April 1988 he had the great joy of attending the ceremony in Halifax in which his sister Margaret received an honorary degree. But by October his faculties had diminished noticeably and was unable, in spite of his efforts, to attend the CCCB meeting in Ottawa because of serious disorientation.

On 18 December 1988 Father Francis Sheahan celebrated his golden jubilee of priesthood at the University of St Michael's College in Toronto. A banquet was held in his honour in Brennan Hall which the cardinal attended and enjoyed. As the evening wore on, however, it became evident to those sitting near him that Flahiff was not well. He was accompanied to his room. The next morning, alarmed by his serious disorientation, the superior of the college had him taken to the hospital. He was kept in St Michael's Hospital for a few days and then returned home, but not to his rooms at the college. He was admitted to St Basil's Residence, the Basilian infirmary on the fourth floor of the building at 95 St Joseph Street. He needed surveillance and special care. What had been observed was a failure in his mobility and periodic disorientation, simply another and critical stage in the breakdown of brain cells which had been increasing for some years. He never returned to his rooms at St Michael's.

During the next eight months deterioration was steady. He soon needed a wheelchair. He fell into a lethargic state and a querulous one, very untypical of him, with constant anxiety, the cause of which neither he nor others could identify. It was heart-rending to watch the relentless ravages of his illness, no respecter of dignity or titles, reduce this once noble figure of a man to that of an invalid both in body and mind. At this time the director of the infirmary was Sister Irene McDonald of the Sisters of St Joseph. McDonald saw personally to the needs of the sick man and he became very dependent on her. She has recorded how in these last months, when she would take him to Queen's Park in the wheelchair, Flahiff would have some bright moments, commenting on the university buildings, harking back to his interest in architecture and his extensive knowledge in that domain. She also noted how sad it was to see the cardinal attempting to answer the doctor's questions smartly, but not well, in a vain effort to cover up his failing powers. He received excellent care from all, notably from the young doctor who attended him, Greg De Marchi, who was particularly respectful and sensitive, not suggesting – as he might have done, given the patient's condition – that the cardinal be moved to another facility where unfamiliar surroundings might have been a further suffering. Nor had such a move ever been considered by the residence staff.

Flahiff was taken to St Michael's Hospital Emergency on the afternoon of 17 August 1989, the fifty-fourth anniversary of his ordination as a priest. An infection in the urinary tract had been diagnosed. He no longer recognized acquaintances and did not respond to his environment. He was admitted to the hospital and started on intravenous antibiotics. On 21 August he had an acute episode of respiratory distress but responded well to drugs and oxygen. At that point, in a discussion with family members concerning his rapidly deteriorating condition which did not appear to be reversible, he was declared DNR ("Do Not Resuscitate"). Early next morning, 22 August, the cardinal had chest pains but stabilized through the day. At about 4:00 p.m. his sister Catherine, Mary Murray, and Lenore Sullivan were gathered at his bedside, but there was no communication with the cardinal. They began reciting the rosary, meditating on the glorious mysteries. Just as they were completing the fourth mystery, the Assumption of Mary into Heaven, a lab technician came into the room seeking a blood sample, but with no success. The cardinal's breathing pattern suddenly changed, and then his breathing stopped altogether. It was 4:15 p.m. Catherine went to the nursing station to inform the persons there that the cardinal had died. The three women then resumed their prayer, meditating on the fifth mystery, the Coronation of the Blessed Virgin Mary. Coincidently, it was the feast day of Our Lady, Queen of the World, the feast on which Flahiff had been ordained bishop; with the revision of the liturgical calendar after Vatican II the feast had been transferred from 31 May to 22 August.

Cardinal Flahiff was laid out in the chapel at St Basil's College, the building later to be renamed in his honour. The dignity and nobility of which sickness had robbed him were restored. He was, so to speak, too big for his casket, his mitre extending some distance beyond the limits, as though death were unable to contain him. During the vigil service held on Sunday evening, 27 August, Father John Gallagher, superior general of the Basilian Fathers, developed the theme of Flahiff as shepherd, recalling the cardinal's talents and achievements in the context of the shepherd image which so aptly typified the faith, the life, and the achievement of the man who lay before him. It was also a farewell from the Basilians who were about to surrender their confrere to Winnipeg for a second time.

Cardinal Flahiff on the occasion of his silver jubilee as bishop, May 1986.
(Photo: Couvac, Toronto)

EPILOGUE

His life was gentle, and the elements
So mixed in him that Nature might stand up
And say to all the world, "This was a man!"

Julius Caesar v, 5:73–5

Cardinal Flahiff's funeral mass took place in a packed St Michael's Cathedral, Toronto, on Monday, 28 August 1989. There were twenty bishops present, with the apostolic pro-nuncio representing Pope John Paul II. Notable among the civic dignitaries was the former lieutenant-governor of Ontario, Pauline McGibbon, who had been a personal friend of Flahiff. Cardinal Carter presided; his brother, Bishop Alexander Carter, gave the homily. The Gospel was read from Matthew 5:1–12, the proclamation of the beatitudes. Bishop Carter pointed out how this charter of the Christian life was realized in Flahiff: poverty of spirit, meekness, mercy, purity of heart, peacemaking, and the pursuit of justice.

A second funeral was held in Winnipeg later in the week. The cardinal lay in state in St Mary's Cathedral all day on Thursday, 30 August. That evening Monsignor Roy Larrabee, rector of the cathedral and Flahiff's close collaborator during the whole time of his episcopacy, presided at the wake service. In his homily Larrabee, commenting on Romans 8:28–39, where Paul asks what could ever truly separate the Christian from Christ, specifying the various human potencies and pitfalls, emphasized the constancy of the cardinal: "As I read that passage," he said, "I am reminded of how much the Cardinal trusted in God implicitly. Trials and difficulties didn't unduly depress or discourage him. Christ was truly his strength." Then moving to the Gospel reading from Matthew 11:25–30, where Jesus counsels learning from him because he is meek and humble of heart, the speaker aptly stated: "Certainly gentleness and humility were two outstanding characteristics of our late Cardinal, who despite his great learning and the many degrees he had acquired, always remained very humble and retained a great simplicity."

Flahiff had come back to Winnipeg, the scene of his great pastoral years, to the people he had served so fully and so faithfully, the people who cherished his memory and who claimed him as their own. That he belonged to Winnipeg was the thinking of Archbishop Exner, Flahiff's successor, who insisted that the cardinal be buried among the people for whom he had been pastor for so many years. Both the Flahiff family and the Basilian Fathers deferred to the archbishop. Exner spoke of Flahiff at the funeral mass on 31 August as "a distinguished churchman, a distinguished Canadian, a special human being … a man called by God, led by God, gifted and empowered by God."

In the course of his homily he read the telegram of condolence from Pope John Paul II who referred to the late cardinal as "a caring and untiring pastor." Though Flahiff had been gone from Winnipeg for some seven years, such words from the pope resonated in the hearts of the people as true and apt: that is precisely how they remembered their much-loved cardinal. After the funeral mass the body was taken to St Mary's Cemetery where burial took place in the priests' plot. All that distinguishes the cardinal's grave among the priests is a slightly larger bronze plaque in the line of graves: a modest marker for a modest man.

Flahiff's passing did not receive much attention from the media. The seven years of his retirement had taken him out of the public eye. Since he rarely spoke in public and did not write at all, he attracted little attention. An editorial in the *Prairie Messenger* of 11 September 1989 under the title "Cloak of Silence," took exception to the media's indifference to the cardinal's death, funeral, and contribution to the nation, characterizing it as "indefensible and an insult to Catholic viewers, listeners and subscribers." It is possible, however, that Catholics found the humbleness of his passing quite in keeping with the example he gave of humility during his life.

A beautiful and moving memorial mass was held in Rome in the Capella Santa Maria of the Governor's Palace in the Vatican gardens, on 28 October 1989, presided over by Archbishop Marchinkus, a long-time friend of Cardinal Flahiff, and attended by Cardinal Gagnon, by the Canadian ambassador to the Holy See, and by other friends of the late cardinal residing or visiting in Rome. Father Tom Rosica CSB, organizer of the mass, said in his word of welcome: "The Canadian

Church mourns Cardinal Flahiff's passing and the world Church has lost a credible and powerful voice for the poor and the marginated."

The tributes to Cardinal Flahiff at the time of his death focused on his kindness, his gentle manner, his devotion to the causes of the laity, the recognition of women, ecumenism, and social justice. One commentator, a person who knew the cardinal quite well, referred to him as a radical, because he was a promoter of causes for the deepest root-reasons of things – justice and humanity – and did so before some aspects of these ideals became popular.[1] The article referred particularly to Flahiff's speaking out on the ministries of women and on the necessity of solidarity with the poor by direct experience. The writer's point is well taken: Flahiff was ever one to go to the root of things, and one to speak out courageously, if always courteously.

He did much more by his being and his presence, however, than he did by his notable actions or even by his words. In the last analysis he was more influential simply by his person. The late Cardinal Bernadin, reflecting on his long friendship with Flahiff, wrote: "I remember Cardinal Flahiff as a very gentle, humble (in the best sense of the word) person ... The Cardinal gave me the impression that he was at peace with himself. No matter how volatile the issues or circumstances might have been, he always approached them calmly and rationally. He was convinced that in the end, good would win out over evil. This calm, insightful approach to things was what I needed at the time; often – even today – when I am confronted with serious problems I think of Cardinal Flahiff."[2]

A similar reflection came from a sister working in the Archdiocese of Winnipeg who remembered that one felt assurance and drew strength merely from the thought that Flahiff was their archbishop, and that he was approachable and understanding.[3] A lecturer on lay spirituality who had the cardinal in his audience – this was after the cardinal's retirement to Toronto – wrote: "His presence alone was a kind of leadership ... for it was the manner of this man, an eminent, able and quiet man."[4]

David Hockman, a Jewish friend and ardent admirer of the cardinal, recounted to the author in November of 1994 how he would go to the cardinal's grave of an afternoon, taking a folding chair. There he would sit and "communicate" with the man who had meant so much to him during his years in Winnipeg, thinking over the memorable moments of their acquaintance. Hockman had written about Flahiff in an article published just a year after Flahiff became cardinal: "My cardinal believes in the One and Only God. This Jew has riveted the spirit of Cardinal George Bernard Flahiff to his heart with straps of steel. My cardinal loves all mankind – regardless of race, colour or creed."[5]

Flahiff was a witness on an even deeper level than that of friendship, or ecumenism, or stability in a stormy world. Faithful all his life to his incarnational spirituality, he witnessed to the person and mission of Christ to an extraordinary degree. One bishop said of him, "You always knew he was a religious," meaning that his way of life, even as a bishop, reflected his commitment to Christ, made at his first religious profession of poverty, chastity, and obedience in September 1927. It could be said with equal truth, "You always knew he was a Christian," so clearly and consistently did he seem to be conformed to the person and teaching of Christ.

His Christ-like manner was not only evident in his obedience to what he saw as God's will at every turn in his life, or in his docility in accepting the difficult calls on his freedom. There was also a clear configuration to Christ in his person. As a director of souls he counselled the importance of putting on Christ, of the Christian being conformed to Christ, of his or her being completely "Christ-ed," as he was wont to say. He deeply realized this process in himself, or rather, this process was deeply realized, even bitterly realized, in him. Like many holy and generous persons before him, whose lives he admired, he got more than he bargained for when he entered so willingly into the "Christing" process. Much more would be asked of him and taken from him than he imagined.

The chronology of Flahiff's life has shown that he entered into a time of uncertainty, of physical deterioration, and of moral darkness about the time of the shocking death of Pope John Paul I. After that event, Flahiff was never quite so buoyant and self-assured as he had been in the years before. Circumstances played a part in his dark night, as did age and failing health. Along with these there began a stripping away of the things that had supported him. His friends, indeed, remained loyal, but friendship itself, in which he had put so much store, became less a support than it had been. Interest in things of the mind, in reading, in new ideas, faded away. Any intention of writing memoirs or of lecturing, things mentioned before as possibilities, had no sequel. His marvellous talent for remembering persons and names failed him, leaving him insecure. Perhaps heaviest of all was the distress which came over him at the loss of comfort in prayer.

In a certain sense, all this was his glory, for it completed and fulfilled the putting on of Jesus Christ. The doctrine he preached had its fullest realization in his own person, both in the power and serenity of what he said and did through his life, and in the suffering and humiliation of his last years. The witness he gave was perhaps most powerful at the end when no title, or position, or pomp – things on which, in any case, he never counted – evaporated to leave only the man, weak and dependent, but very much a reflection of the Saviour. George Flahiff gave himself entirely, and it was all accepted. This is his glory, his success, and his heritage.

On the fourth floor of the building which now bears his name, the Cardinal Flahiff Basilian Centre, and where he spent the last eight months of his life, there hangs a painting, the first thing one sees as one steps off the elevator at the west entrance. This painting, which belonged to Flahiff, is all that remains to mark his passage in that place. The scene is western Canadian: mountains, snow, trees, cerulean sky, with just a touch of pink, a sapphire lake, all creating an impression of peace, freedom, and joy. The painting was the gift of the Western Region of the Canadian Religious Conference, on the occasion of the Cardinal's golden jubilee of priesthood in 1980. The inscription on that painting must have pleased him greatly:

"To Cardinal George B. Flahiff:
Authentic Witness to the Humanness of Christ."

NOTES

PROLOGUE

1 See "New Ministries Limited to Men?" *Origins* 1, no. 17 (1971): 295–6.
Pope Paul VI did, in fact, establish such a commission in 1973 which functioned until 1976. Flahiff was not a member. Rome issued "A Declaration
on the Question of the Admission of Women to the Ministerial Priesthood," *Origins* 6, no.33 (1977): 94–7, which reaffirmed the exclusivity of
male candidates for the major ministries in the Church.

2 Cardinal Flahiff Loretto Collection to Sister Lenore Sullivan IBVM, 17 October 1971; Flahiff's letters to Lenore Sullivan are referred to in the notes
as CFLcol-(date). The letters remain for the present in the possession of the
recipient. They will ultimately be entrusted to the Archives of the Institute
of the Blessed Virgin Mary (Loretto Sisters) in Toronto. See chapter 10,
p. 109, for a commentary on these letters.

3 The international edition of the New York *Herald Tribune* of 12 October
1971 published an article on the front page entitled "Cardinal Considering Women in Priesthood."

4 CFLcol-17 October 1971. Flahiff was not the only one to flutter the dove-
cotes at the synod. Bishop Alexander Carter gives a fascinating account in
his *A Canadian Bishop's Memoirs* (North Bay, Ontario: Tomiko Publications,
c. 1994), 210–28, of the various interventions concerning the priesthood
and social justice, with a description of the role played by the Canadian
bishops and others and the reactions in Rome and beyond which followed.

5 It is not known to what these telegrams refer. Among the notices, more or
less sensational in the Canadian press at the time, was an article in the
Montreal Gazette (14 October 1971) entitled "Canadian asks for women
priests," and which contained the statement: "[Flahiff] suggested it was

time to consider ordaining women into the priesthood." An editorial applauding the intervention of Flahiff appeared in the same issue. On the same day a much more balanced editorial was carried in the Toronto *Globe and Mail* under the heading "Canada's bishops lead," in which the ordination of women was not mentioned. The writer focused on the initiative of the Canadian bishops in raising the question of women's equality.

6 CFLcol-17 October 1971. Flahiff occasionally underlined passages in his letters or text of his talks for emphasis. Such underlinings are printed here in italics and in every case the emphasis is in the original passage.

7 The letters Flahiff received following his intervention were almost exclusively from women. The two men who wrote, one Italian, the other Spanish, but both living in the United States, denounced him roundly for teaching heresy and misleading God's people. See CFLcol-23 October 1971.

8 Some of the departments of the Roman Curia were called Sacred Congregations and the head of such a department, Prefect. See Terminology on page 227.

CHAPTER ONE

1 One of the group of "receivers" of the first call is said to have been Terrence Flahiff, the grandfather of the future cardinal, whose signature can supposedly be seen on the document testifying to the historic event in the Brant County Museum in Brantford, Ontario. This information was communicated to the author by the cardinal's brother, Terrence Flahiff. Unfortunately, verification of the facts, both at the museum in Brandford and with the Historical Services of Bell Telephone in Montreal, has proved unsuccessful. It is quite probable, however, that Terrence Flahiff was indeed present at the event.

2 Syl Apps was born 18 April 1915, ten years after George Flahiff. Apps was famous early in life for being a gold medalist for pole-vaulting in the 1936 Olympics in Berlin. He is best known as a hockey star, having been captain of the Toronto Maple Leafs in three Memorial Cup wins. After his athletic days, Apps went into politics.

3 This brief geneology of the Flahiff family is based on research done principally by Norman, Terrence, and Catherine Flahiff, the brothers and sister of George, during the 1960s and 1970s. They sought to find the roots of the family in Ireland and to trace the various branches of the family in Ireland and in the new world. Their work, which involved considerable correspondence and visits to the Genealogical Office in Dublin Castle and visits to the various places in Ireland where Flahiffs might have been found, was complicated by the various forms of the name (Flahiff, Flahiffe, Flahiv, Flahive, etc.). The condition of genealogical records in Ireland is in

general unsatisfactory, largely due to the political unrest and catastrophic social conditions in Ireland in the nineteenth century. Their work produced reliable results only from the period after the mid-nineteenth century. The interesting, if limited, results of their research can be found in the Cardinal Flahiff Collection (CFcol) in the General Archives of the Basilian Fathers (CFcol-4/1, 4/2).

4 See the unpublished memoir of Terrence Flahiff entitled "Our Father" (CFcol-31/3) on which the details of the family here related are based.

5 The top floor of the hotel no longer exists as the result of a fire sometime in the 1930s.

6 Verbal communication from Terrence Flahiff to the author. Efforts to verify the story have not been successful. Edward's daughter, Mrs Mary Smith, has consulted military sources in both Canada and the United Kingdom without results. Her father was not inclined to speak of his military experiences. Mary heard the story from her uncle, Terrence Flahiff.

7 CFcol-4/2, Terrence Flahiff to Margaret Flahiff, 21 July 1990.

8 CFcol-2/6.

9 CFcol-4/2, letter to Terry and Françoise, 25 November 1983.

10 Peter Gzowski, "This Country in the Morning," CBC, 28 January 1974.

11 See D.A. Smith, *At the Forks of the Grand*, Vol. II (Paris: Advance Printing, 1982), 288.

12 Flahiff would relate jokingly that the first words he learned to read were those of the caption to an old boot on display over the bar in his father's hotel: "If water does this to a boot, what must it do to your stomach?"

CHAPTER TWO

1 Academic Records, University of Toronto Archives, A89–0011.

2 See Robert J. Scollard, *Dictionary of Basilian Biography* (Toronto: The Basilian Press, 1969), 20–3.

3 See *Basilian Annals* 5, no. 8 (1981): 603–5 for a brief account of McCorkell's life.

4 CFLcol-5 January 1973.

5 Born at Pembroke, Ontario, in 1906, Trottier was a brilliant left wing for the Montreal Maroons from 1928 to 1938.

6 See *Basilian Annals* 4, no. 5 (1971): 209–10, for a brief account of McLaughlin's life.

7 At St Michael's the term president only came into use some years later when the offices of superior of the religious house and academic head of the institution were distinguished, with a different person in each office.

8 CFcol-4/1, letter to Father Tom Rosica, 28 September 1986.

9 See *Basilian Annals* 5, no. 3 (1976): 190–2, for a brief account of Sharpe's life.

10 See ibid. 4, no. 5 (1971): 482–3, for a brief account of Bondy's life.
11 The others were Alexander Denomy (1904–57), Thomas Vernon Kennedy
    (1907–49), Vincent Lorne Kennedy (1899–74), and Terence Patrick
    McLaughlin (1903–70).

CHAPTER THREE

1 Etienne Gilson (1884–1978), possibly the most renowned mediaevalist of
   his time and a member of the Académie Française, was co-founder and
   director of studies of the Institute of Mediaeval Studies in Toronto, where
   he lectured almost annually from 1929 to 1972. For a concise account of
   the founding of the Institute of Mediaeval Studies see Laurence K. Shook,
   Etienne Gilson (Toronto: PIMS, 1984), 192–5. The prestige and wise guidance which Gilson lent to the Institute of Mediaeval Studies, later the Pontifical Institute of Mediaeval Studies (PIMS), did much to establish its
   international reputation as a centre of teaching and research.
2 While the Institute of Mediaeval Studies had been formally begun in 1929
   at St Michael's College in the University of Toronto, a full program of
   courses would not be offered until 1935, when the young Basilians sent on
   graduate studies returned to teach there.
3 CFcol-2/1, to Maurice Lavanoux, 29 March 1948.
4 Some of these books were: F.J. Tout, *The Study of Ecclesiastical History*
   (Manchester: Manchester University Press, 1905); Maitland, Guatkim,
   Poole, et al., *Essays on the Teaching of History* (Cambridge: Cambridge University Press, 1901); F.M. Powicke, *Historical Study at Oxford* (Oxford: Clar-
   endon Press, 1929).
5 E.T. Williams and C.S. Nicholls, eds., *Dictionary of National Biography,
   1961–1980* (Oxford: Oxford University Press, 1981), 857.
6 CFcol-28.

CHAPTER FOUR

1 Information communicated from the Department of Statistics of the University of Toronto, October 1997. The figure for the student body is based
   on the total for 1996.
2 The two young men were Paul Glynn and William Lewis. Both subsequently withdrew from the Basilians. They related the incident to the author in 1996 and 1997.
3 See, for example, the correspondence between Flahiff and Victor Brezik
   regarding the situation at the University of St Thomas in Houston in 1957
   (GABF-sup.gen.-Flahiff C.3134, 1947–1951). See also pages 43-4 where
   scholarly expectations are discussed.

4 Oral communication from Father Walter Principe to the author.

5 CFcol-28, letter from Father Victor Brezik to the author, 24 September 1996.

6 Oral communication from Msgr. E.A. Synan to the author, October 1994.

7 Oral communication from Sister Caroline Dawson IBVM to the author, November 1994.

8 *Mediaeval Studies (MS)* 2 (1940): 104–26; *MS* 9 (1947): 162–88.

9 *MS* 6 (1944): 261–313; 7 (1945): 229–90.

10 *MS* 9 (1947): 162–88.

11 *Proceedings of the Canadian Historical Association,* Report 19 (Winnipeg, 1954–5): 65.

12 "The Art of Saint Sulpice" refers to a kind of religious art which developed in Paris around the church of Saint Sulpice in the nineteenth and twentieth centuries. It is characterized by saccharine representation of Christ and the saints, more inspired by sentimentalism than by authentic religious feeling.

13 "Can Art Be Christian?" 10.

14 This statement is based on an oral communication from McCorkell to the author sometime in the late 1940s or early 1950s, as well as on a conversation in the early 1950s (reported to the author) between McCorkell and Father Ambrose Raftis when discussing the course of studies of the latter at Laval and Cambridge, with a view to Raftis's possibly succeeding Flahiff as professor of history at the Pontifical Institute.

15 James McConica, the noted historian and today Praeses of the Pontifical Institute of Mediaeval Studies, while recognizing that Flahiff's scholarly career was cut short, sees him nevertheless in the line of the Christian humanists such as Juan Luis Vives (1492–1540), Erasmus (1466–1536), and Thomas More (1477–1535), for the manner in which Flahiff harmonized learning, scholarship, art, and spirituality, in his appreciation of all things human (conversation with the author, November 1997).

CHAPTER FIVE

1 CFcol-2A, letter to Helene Darte, 6 January 1944.

2 Ibid., 24 April 1946.

3 CFcol-32/5:8 "Instaurare Omnia in Christo" ("To Restore All Things in Christ"), *Resumé of Seminarians Study Week,* 27–31 August 1950, St Michael's College, Toronto; CFcol-25/2.

4 Probably his chief reference was Joseph Anger's, *La doctrine du Corps Mystique de Jesus Christ d'après les principes de la théologie de Saint Thomas* ("The Doctrine of the Mystical Body of Jesus Christ according to the Theology of Saint Thomas") (Paris: Beauchesne, 1929).

5 The doctrine has its roots in St Paul (1 Cor. 6: 15; 12: 12–13, 27; Rom. 12: 5; Col. 1: 18) though he does not use the term mystical.

6 Gibson was ordained to the priesthood by Flahiff at the Shrine of the Immaculate Conception, Washington, DC, on 24 August 1963, for the Archdiocese of Winnipeg. Flahiff, however, did not give him an appointment in Winnipeg, but allowed him to teach at St Michael's College in Toronto. Gibson died in Toronto on 17 January 1980. Flahiff presided at the funeral and burial.

7 Born 1912 in Welland, Ontario; BA and MA in Modern Languages from the University of Toronto; professed in the Sisters of Charity of Halifax in 1941; teaching and administration in Halifax and Bathurst, NB; presently (1997) living in Halifax.

8 Sister Helene Darte has confided this valuable collection of letters and cards which she received from Flahiff to the General Archives of the Basilian Fathers (CFcol-2A). Quotations and references to the letters throughout this chapter appear with her kind permission.

9 For many years this work circulated among the nuns for whom it was written before it was recognized as a work of value for the general believing public. Henri Ramière SJ edited and published the work at Le Puy, France, in 1861. Flahiff used an English translation by Algar Thorold (London: Burns Oates and Washbourne, 1935). His copy shows the discreet pencil markings in the margin. He also came by Father Henry Carr's copy of the same work which is heavily and copiously underlined. The two copies are at present in circulation at the John Kelly Library, University of St Michael's College, Toronto.

CHAPTER SIX

1 This seems to have been the opinion of Father McCorkell, one of those who was disappointed in Flahiff's scholarly performance.

2 Kevin J. Kirley, *1922, Before and After* (Toronto: Basilian Press, 1992), 38.

3 Some years later, as Archbishop of Winnipeg, he wrote to Father Laurence Shook: "While I accept without question His providential disposition of all things, I cannot but experience considerable regret at the prospect of definitive separation from the Institute" (10 November 1961, University of St Michael's College Archives).

4 CFL-15 August 1970, "[Changing appointments] is something for which I have no taste whatsoever. I did not like it as a Basilian and it is the thing I find hardest now. I don't mind talking with the priests, no matter what is at issue; but I find it very difficult to move a man, – at least, when it is tantamount to criticism of what he is doing now."

5 CFcol-2/2, 20 July 1954, 31 August 1954.

6 *Basilian Annals* 2, no. 4 (1954): 156–8.
7 The Congregation of Priests of St Basil was founded at Annonay, France, in 1822, by ten priest-professors at the Collège d'Annonay. The congregation made its first foundation in Canada, St Michael's College in Toronto, in 1852.
8 Charles Léon Luc Roume (1901–66), professed in the Congregation of St Basil in 1927, and ordained to the priesthood in 1929, was elected superior general of the French Basilians in 1950. He wrote a history of the early years of the congregation, *Origines et Formation de la Communauté des Prêtres de Saint-Basile* (Privas, 1965). Father Roume died as the result of an automobile accident in 1966. He is considered the refounder of the Basilian community in France. See Robert Scollard, *Dictionary of Basilian Biography* (Toronto: Basilian Press, 1968), 139–40.
9 See Scollard, *Dictionary*, 102–3, 148–50.
10 *Basilian Annals* 2, no. 5 (1955): 208–9. For an eye-witness account of the reunion, see pages 205–7.
11 GABF, C.3114, 10 October 1955.
12 His letters to the congregation in the *Basilian Annals* 2, no. 7 (1957): 308–9 and 2, no. 8 (1958): 337–8, provide good examples of this.
13 Verbal communication from Father David Belyea, October 1994.
14 CFcol-31/1, written communication from Father Victor Brezik, March 1996.
15 GABF, C.3134, 11 November 1955.
16 GABF, C.3114, McGuigan to Flahiff, 7 January 1955; Flahiff to McGuigan, 10 January 1955; Flahiff to McGuigan, 5 May 1955.
17 CFcol-31/1, written communication from Father Terence Forestell, February 1996.
18 GABF, c2.3134), Flahiff to Father Matthew Sheedy, 2 April 1960. The Junior A team was suspended the following year and remained so for thirty years. It was revived at St Michael's in the fall of 1997. For a view of the principles and issues in the matter, see John Wallner, "Athletics and Academics: St. Michael's College Withdrawal from Ontario Hockey Association Junior A Competition" (MA thesis, Carleton University, Institute of Canadian Studies, 1990).
19 GABF, C.3114, Flahiff to Bishop McCarthy, December 1955.
20 Ibid., Flahiff to Bishop Leo Pursley, 25 November 1956.
21 Ibid., Flahiff to Bishop Andrés García, 6 September 1956.
22 This talk was published later as *The Pursuit of Christian Perfection* (Ottawa: CRC Publications, 1956).
23 GABF, C.3114, Flahiff to Scollard, 12 April 1959.
24 Verbal communication from Father George Freemesser, October 1994.

25 Migne, *Patrologia Latina*, vol. 182, letter 237, 425–7. Albino Luciani, Pope John Paul I, used the same quotation when he was elected pope in 1978; he apologized to the cardinals afterwards for its use.

26 *Basilian Annals* 3, no. 2 (1961): 58.

CHAPTER SEVEN

1 In 1961 the papal representation in Canada was called the Apostolic Delegation, and the representative of the pope, the apostolic delegate. The office was raised to a Pro-Nunciature in 1969 by Pope Paul VI, and the pope's representative then became the apostolic pro-nuncio. In 1985 full diplomatic status was awarded; the office is now the Apostolic Nunciature, and the pope's representative is called nuncio.

2 This account is based on an interview with Cardinal Flahiff published in the Franciscan review, *Companion of St. Francis and St. Anthony* (Toronto), XLVIII 8 (September 1985): 5–7.

3 CFcol-1/2.

4 When a religious is named a bishop, he does not lose his membership in the religious congregation or order to which he belongs, though his vows of obedience and poverty are suspended.

5 The names of these two great scholars were often linked in conversations about the Pontifical Institute of Mediaeval Studies. Gilson we have already identified in chapter 3, note 1. Jacques Maritain (1882–1973) was a French neo-thomist whose works, such as *The Degrees of Knowledge* (1937), *True Humanism* (1938) and *Art and Scholasticism* (1939), had a great influence among thomists of the time and were much in vogue at the Pontifical Institute. Maritain was an occasional lecturer there (1933, 1944, 1946, 1950, 1955), and published articles in *Mediaeval Studies* (1941, 1942, 1943). His presence, his lecturing, and his writing gave the institute prestige and fame. He was a friend of Flahiff, who considered himself a disciple of Maritain in his teaching of art.

6 Kennedy has left a short memoir in which, among other things, he recounts his reaction to the nomination of Flahiff (GABF-Kennedy, V.L.).

7 CFcol-2/3, Gilson to Flahiff, 16 March 1961.

8 Ibid., Bickersteth to Flahiff, 11 May 1961.

9 In 1961 the word used for the making of a bishop was consecration. After Vatican II it was changed to ordination, to be more in line with the teaching that the perfection of the priesthood is in the episcopacy. Priests are ordained.

10 CFcol-13/4.

11 L.S. Suenens, *Memories and Hopes* (Dublin: Veritas, 1992), 237.

12 John Joseph Wright (1909–79), an urbane and witty man, had become known to Flahiff through Alex and Emmett Carter. He was noted as a

theologian and orator, and later as an ardent promoter of the teachings of Vatican II. He was ultimately called to Rome to head the Congregation for the Clergy, receiving the cardinalate with Flahiff in 1969. The two became close friends.

13 The phrase is part of the doxology which ends the canon of the mass and is based on several texts in St Paul (Rom. 11: 36; 1 Cor. 8: 6; Col. 1: 16–17).

CHAPTER EIGHT

1 Archives, Archdiocese of Winnipeg.

2 See Raymond Huel, "The Irish-French Conflict in Catholic Episcopal Nominations: The Western Sees and the Struggle for Domination Within the Church," Canadian Catholic Historical Association, *Study Sessions* (1975): 50–70.

3 At one time the Archdiocese of Saint Boniface stretched westward to the Pacific and northward to the North Pole. It is thus the mother archdiocese of the whole of western Canada.

4 In the late 1940s there were two archbishops in Winnipeg, Sinnott and Murray; two in Saint Boniface, Belliveau and Cabana; and the Ukrainian Eparchy had an archeparch, Ladyka, and an auxiliary bishop, Hermaniuk. The Anglican Archbishop at the time was the Most Reverend Louis Ralph Sherman.

5 Today there are seventy-eight parishes, with twenty-three missions; seventy-two diocesan priests and thirty-seven regular priests; five religious orders of men and twenty of women, according to the *Archdiocese of Winnipeg Directory* (1996).

6 These statistics are taken from the *New Catholic Encyclopedia*, over the signature of C.A. Halpin. They reflect the situation as it was in 1965, that is, four years after the coming of Flahiff.

7 CFLcol-10 June 1975. After meeting Halpin at an event in Vancouver in January 1974 Flahiff remarked on how well he looked after less than a month as Archbishop of Regina, and added "I do not recall that that was the way with me when I began here in Winnipeg and I surmise that the reason is that, for years, he has already known more about running a diocese than I ever will" (CFLcol-4 January 1974).

8 CFLcol-26 September 1972.

9 CFLcol-16 October 1976.

10 CFLcol-9 December 1977. This particular occasion was not in Winnipeg but in Regina, a place of comparable temperatures.

11 CFLcol-4 January 1974.

12 CFLcol-2 February 1974.

13 CFLcol-17 September 1979.

CHAPTER NINE

1 *Basilian Annals* 2, no. 9 (1959), 397.
2 *Basilian Newsletter,* 1 November 1962, 1–2.
3 CFcol-1/2, to the author, 25 October 1962.
4 *Basilian Newsletter,* 1 November 1962, 6.
5 Ibid., 5.
6 Ibid., 12.
7 CFcol-4/1, "Dear Family," 17 October 1963, 2.
8 *Basilian Newsletter,* 1 November 1962, 7.
9 CFcol-4/1, "Dear Family," 17 October 1963, 1.
10 Ibid.
11 Ibid., 2, 3.
12 Ibid., 3.
13 Ibid., 4.
14 CFcol-4/1, "Dear Family," 1 November 1964, 4.
15 Ibid., 1–2.
16 Ibid., 2.
17 In July 1963 Archbishop Pocock addressed a confidential letter to his priests in the Archdiocese of Toronto regarding the manner of counselling penitents in the confessional on the matter of birth control. The gist of Pocock's letter was that leniency should be the rule where people were obviously acting in good faith. It is said that his letter was not well received in Rome.
18 *Contraception and Holiness: the Catholic Predicament* (New York: Herder and Herder, 1964) is a book of essays by moral theologians, introduced by Archbishop Thomas D. Roberts, SJ, arguing for a reconsideration of the teaching on the morality of artificial birth control. The book caused considerable stir at the time of publication.
19 Archives, Pontifical Institute of Mediaeval Studies, "Flahiff, Cardinal," Flahff to Laurence Shook, 24 October 1964.
20 CFcol-14/5, "To His Holiness, Pope Paul VI," 29 October 1967; to Cardinal Flahiff, 4 December 1967.
21 CFcol-4/1, "Dear Family," 1 November 1964.
22 CFcol-5/4.
23 Hans Küng et al., eds. *Council Speeches of Vatican II* (Glen Rock, NJ.: Paulist Press, 1964), *185–7.*
24 *Basilian Newsletter,* 3 November 1964.
25 Two speeches by Flahiff in which he analysed and explained the council document on Christian Education (*Gravissimum Educationis*), one given at the Catholic Information Centre in Toronto on 2 March 1969 (CFcol-32/4), and the other to the Parent-Teacher Association of Ontario at their Annual

Convention in Hamilton, Ontario, 1 May 1971 (CFcol-32/2), provide excellent examples of Flahiff's mastery and method.

26 CFcol-5/3 copy, letter to Sister Irene Farmer, 31 July 1965, 3.

27 *Basilian Newsletter*, 3 November 1964, 5.

28 Ibid., 6.

CHAPTER TEN

1 Native of Sydney, NS, Bishop of St John, NB, 1969, Archbishop of Edmonton, 1973.

2 CFLcol-6 August 1980.

3 Interviews with the author, October 1996.

4 CFcol-3/2.

5 According to information received from the Israeli Consulate in Toronto in November 1997, the Cardinal Flahiff Peace Forest has been relocated to what is called the Canada Park in the area of Latrun, just outside Jerusalem.

6 The title Mother was used for sisters in perpetual vows. This usage was dropped in the 1960s when many of the sisters reverted to their baptismal names. Mother Dorcas was soon to be known as Sister Lenore Sullivan: born 1934, Albion Township, Ontario, the sixth of nine children; professed in the Institute of the Blessed Virgin Mary (Loretto Sisters), 1953; doctoral studies in classical philology at Harvard, assistant professor of classic humanities, York University, 1965–78; dean of Loretto College, 1982–3; teacher at Indian Reserves in Northwestern Ontario, 1983–8; general councillor IBVM, 1987–91. Sullivan had met Flahiff some years before the particular interview in June of 1965, but only in the context of a conference or visit to the whole community of sisters.

7 C.S. Dessain et al., eds., *Letters and Diaries of John Henry Newman*, vol. XXVI, (London and Oxford: Oxford University Press, 1961–84), 375.

8 CFLcol-16 November 1967.

9 Francis of Assisi (1182–1226) founded his brotherhood in 1206; Clare of Assisi (1194–1253), with the encouragement of Francis, founded the female counterpart of the Franciscans, the Poor Clares, in 1212. John of the Cross (1542–91) with great difficulty undertook the reform of the Carmelites in Spain; Teresa of Avila (1515–82) sought out John for the spiritual direction of her nuns in her work of reform. Francis de Sales (1567–1622), bishop and spiritual guide, founded the Order of the Visitation in cooperation with Jane Frances de Chantal (1572–1641) and provided spiritual direction for the religious for many years.

10 Gerard B. Wegner, *Thomas More: A Portrait of Courage* (Princeton: Scepter Publishers, 1995), 61.

CHAPTER ELEVEN

1 To Bernard M. Daly, 30 July 1963 (Archives, University of St. Michael's College Alumni, 1926: F55).

2 Ordained 1968, in St Boniface for Winnipeg; parish work from 1970–3, then called to the Chancery Office when Halpin went to Regina as archbishop; accompanied Flahiff to Rome for the first conclave, 1978; named chancellor in spiritual matters, December 1978.

3 CFLcol-24 November 1970.

4 Ibid. July 1969.

5 Flahiff asked Pope Paul VI in a private conversation during the second session of the Vatican Council if such concelebration would be possible on a trial basis. The pope replied that it would indeed be a good idea for someone to experiment. Thus Archbishop Flahiff and Archbishop Baudoux of St Boniface introduced concelebration at the Chrism Mass one year before it became common practice for the Universal Church.

6 CFLcol-18 April 1973.

7 CFLcol-8 April 1977.

8 CFLcol-13 February 1977.

9 CFLcol-26 April 1970.

10 CFLcol-17 May 1970.

11 A socialist society founded in London by Sydney and Beatrice Webb in 1884 named for Quintus Fabius Maximus (275–203 BC), called Cunctator, "the Delayer."

12 Verbal communication from Sister Sheila Madden, a sister working in the Archdiocese of Winnipeg, October 1994.

13 CFLcol-17 September 1979.

14 CFLcol-8 January 1972.

15 Homily on Ezekiel, *Roman Breviary III*, Second Reading for 3 September.

16 CFLcol-13 September 1976.

17 CFLcol-17 December 1975.

CHAPTER TWELVE

1 CFLcol-31 March 1969.

2 Ibid.

3 CFcol-1/2, letter to the author, 8 December 1969.

4 *Osservatore Romano*, 9 May 1969.

5 CFLcol-1May 1969.

6 CFLcol-8 May 1969.

7 The foregoing account of the cardinal's return to Winnipeg is based on one of his letters (CFLcol-6 May 1969) and on contemporary local newspaper reports.

8 This is to state the matter very simply; the history of the cardinalate is complicated and uncertain in many respects; what is certain, however, is the long-standing tradition of each cardinal "possessing" one of the churches in Rome. See K.F. Morrison's article on the history of the cardinalate in the *New Catholic Encyclopedia* 3 (New York, 1967), 104–5.

9 The text of the cardinal's homily as well as the events recorded in the ceremony are taken from an article by Mollie McGee in the *Winnipeg Free Press*, 13 October 1969, pp. 1, 4.

10 CFcol-2/5, Flahiff to Most Rev. Louis Joseph Secondo, TOR, 5 March 1971. The participating bishops were Alex Carter, Emmett Carter, Philip Pocock, and Francis Marrocco.

11 CFcol-31/1, letters to the author, 7 November 1994 and 22 September 1997.

CHAPTER THIRTEEN

1 During the second, third, and fourth council sessions the Canadian bishops met in Rome instead of Ottawa where they usually met.

2 See "Lumen Gentium: The Dogmatic Constitution of the Church," 22, 23, in Austen Flannery OP, ed., *Vatican Council II, The Conciliar and Post-Conciliar Documents* (NY: Costellor Publishing Co., 1992), 374–5.

3 It was following an appeal to the pope on the part of the Canadian bishops, with Alexander Carter, Bishop of Sault Ste Marie, as their spokesman, that the interventions made at the synod could represent the voice of the whole conference of bishops of a particular nation and not merely the opinion of an individual bishop. See Bernard Daly, *Remembering for Tomorrow* (Ottawa: CCCB Publications, 1996), 163–4.

4 CFLcol-23 May 1971.

5 CFLcol-4 July 1973.

6 CFcol-13/2, trans., Soeur Lorraine Préjet, Superior General of Les Chanoisses Regulières des Cinq-Plaies du Sauveur to Archbishop Flahiff, 25 January 1968.

7 CFcol-13/2, Howard Griffin to Archbishop Flahiff, 16 January 1968.

8 CFcol-1/1, Flahiff to Cardinal Garrone, 16 March 1973, copy.

9 In February of 1966, after a meeting of the Post-Conciliar Commission on Religious Life, Flahiff submitted a six-page typewritten commentary on *Perfectae Caritatis* (CFcol-14/3) which for its clarity and perceptiveness was of considerable value to Pope Paul in his instruction *Ecclesiae Sanctae* on the implementation of the council documents issued to the whole Church in August 1966.

10 A good account of the drama in the genesis of the Winnipeg Statement is found in Bernard Daly's *Remembering for Tomorrow*, 126–32.

11 CFLcol-28 September 1971. An editorial in the Toronto *Globe and Mail*, "Canada's reforming bishops" (9 November 1971), which reviewed the work of the 1971 synod, commented favourably on the reputation of the Canadian bishops as progressives and referred once more to Flahiff's contribution to the question of the equality of women.

12 Alexander Carter, *A Canadian Bishop's Memoirs* (North Bay, Ontario: Tomiko Publications, *c.* 1994), 221.

CHAPTER FOURTEEN

1 See also John 15: 19, 16: 33, and 18: 36.

2 For example, in 1 Cor. 3: 19, 6: 2, Gal. 6: 14.

3 See also John 3: 17 and 8: 12.

4 CFcol.32/3, Address at the Closing Exercises of the Toronto School of Theology (third anniversary), Victoria College Chapel, University of Toronto, 16 March 1972.

5 *The Basilian* 4, no. 2 (1938): 27–8; *Catholic Historical Review* XXVIII, no.1 (1941): 1–15.

6 "A Catholic Looks at History," 9, 12, 13, 14.

7 Pierre Teilhard de Chardin (1881–1955), French Jesuit, anthropologist, and palaeontologist who presented a global vision of the universe wherein matter and spirit, body and soul, nature and supernature, science and faith, find their unity in Christ. See *New Catholic Encyclopedia* 13 (New York: McGraw Hill, 1967), 977–8.

8 CFcol-32/5, address to the Newman Association of the St Thomas More College Guild, Bessborough Hotel, Saskatoon, 12 October 1952.

9 T.S. Eliot, *Murder in the Cathedral* (New York: Harcourt Brace, 1935), speech of the Second Tempter, 39.

10 "The Meaning of the Past for the Present and the Future," 19.

11 The General Archives of the Basilian Fathers hold Flahiff's notes from courses taken during his studies in Paris, as well as his lecture notes from his teaching years in Toronto at the Pontifical Institute. There is also a copy of the notes taken by one of his obviously very diligent students, Andrew McLean, which gives a good idea of Flahiff's thoroughness and order. See CFcol-20, 21.

12 CFcol-32/3, "The Person to Whom We Minister," address to the Hospital Care Association of Alberta, Edmonton, 11 March 1970; "Closing Address to the Manitoba Prison Chaplains' Conference," Winnipeg, 29 February 1972; CFcol-32/4, "Sermon preached at the Installation of Archbishop Joseph N. MacNeil," St Joseph's Cathedral, Edmonton, 5 September 1973.

13 CFcol-32/4.

14 CFcol-32/3.

15 V.A. Yzermans, ed., *The Major Addresses of Pope Pius XII*, vol. II: *The Christmas Addresses* (St Paul: North Central Publishing Co., 1961), 243.

16 CFcol-1/1, Flahiff to Fortier, 6 January 1977.

17 See *Origins* 6, no. 33 (3 February 1977): 46–52.

18 CFcol-32/3, "Third Anniversary Closing Exercises."

19 CFcol-32/2.

20 CFcol-32/3.

21 CFcol-3/3.

22 CFcol-32/3, "Shooting for More than the Moon," 55th Annual Teachers' Conference, Rochester, N.Y., 28 September 1959, 6–7.

23 CFcol-32/2.

24 Ibid., 4. This same sentence occurs in his speech at St John's College in the University of Manitoba, 1 November 1977.

25 Ibid., Hamilton, 1 May 1971, 4.

26 "Shooting for More than the Moon," 8.

27 Ibid., "Address to the Graduates, St. Thomas College, University of New Brunswick," 10 May 1976, 4.

28 CFcol-32/3, 17 November 1969, 5–6.

29 "The Person to Whom We Minister," 9.

30 CFcol-32/3, "Role of the Church in Health Care," Winnipeg, 31 May 1976, 11–13.

31 "Closing Address to the Manitoba Prison Chaplains' Conference," 5.

32 *Basilian Teacher* 2, no. 5 (1958): 22.

33 CFcol-32/1, "Vatican II and the Religious Life," Rochester, 1966, 5.

CHAPTER FIFTEEN

1 The visitors were myself and my brother, Reverend Edwin J. Platt, a priest of the Archdiocese of Toronto. The Cathedral of St Boniface, a once magnificent building, now but a shell since the fire of 1960, is a monument to the faith of the French-speaking population of the area; it now encloses a smaller church but remains by far the most impressive building in St Boniface.

2 CFcol-14/7; no further references to the archives will be given since the various quotations can be easily found by following the chronological order.

3 Literally, "the understanding of believers." Such general understanding possessed by the faithful throughout the world is considered to be one of the guarantees of truth in the Church. John Henry Newman's famous essay, "On Consulting the Laity in Matters of Doctrine," is considered the classic text for the explanation of this theological notion.

4 CFLcol-5 October 1978.

CHAPTER SIXTEEN

1 cFcol-14/5, copy.
2 Archives, Archdiocese of Winnipeg.
3 cFcol-14/5, 4 May 1981.
4 Ibid.
5 Ibid., 8 June 1981.
6 cFLcol-24 January 1981.
7 cFLcol-28 January 1981.
8 cFLcol-8 April 1981.
9 cFLcol-12 October 1981.
10 General Chapters of religious communities are usually rather lengthy, extending from two to four weeks, or longer. The Basilian Chapter of 1981
   went on for three weeks.
11 In the history of the Basilians only two other members besides Flahiff
   have been named bishop: Denis O'Connor, Bishop of London, Ontario
   (1889–99), Archbishop of Toronto (1899–1908); and Ricardo Ramírez, who
   is presently Bishop of Las Cruces in New Mexico.
12 cFLcol-4 February 1982.
13 cFLcol-7 February 1982.
14 cFLcol-27 April 1982.
15 cFLcol-28 April 1982.
16 cFcol-5/8.
17 cFLcol-12 June 1982.
18 cFLcol-29 May 1982.

CHAPTER SEVENTEEN

1 The word "Sacred" which had characterized the various Roman Congregations of the Roman Curia was dropped in 1983 with the publication of
   the new *Code of Canon Law*.
2 cFLcol.
3 George P. Schner, *The Church Renewed: The Documents of Vatican II Recon-
   sidered* (Boston: University Press of America, 1985), 1–9.
4 Marcel Lefebvre (1905–88), a member of the Congregation of the Holy
   Spirit (Spiritains), had been a missionary in Africa, served as superior
   general of his congregation, and was ultimately ordained bishop. He was
   an ardent and bitter opponent of the reforms of Vatican II and led a
   group of sympathizers after the council who sought to return to the practices of the tridentine Church, particularly in the manner of celebrating
   the Eucharist. After many years of negotiations with the Holy See, he

was excommunicated by Pope John Paul II a few years before his death, but not before he had ordained several priests and four bishops among his followers.

5 CFLcol-27 May 1984.

6 CFcol-5/6, to Robert J. Scollard, 9 April 1964.

7 CFcol-1/3, to Sister Agnes Cunningham, 19 July 1978.

8 CFcol-4/2, 25 April 1983.

9 CFLcol-3 September 1985.

10 CFcol-1/5, Carter to Donald F. McDonald, QC, 16 February 1984, copy.

11 Archdiocese of Toronto Archives, Carter to Plourde, 25 June 1984; CFcol-1/5, Flahiff to Plourde, 4 July 1984.

12 CFLcol-5 December 1986.

13 CFLcol-28 September 1987.

EPILOGUE

1 Ted Schmidt, "George Flahiff emerged as a 'gentle radical,'" *Catholic New Times* (4 February 1990), 13.

2 CFcol-31/1, letter to the author, 7 February 1996. Cardinal Bernadin died after a lengthy struggle with cancer, just nine months after writing this letter.

3 Oral communication from Sister Sheila Madden to the author, 8 November 1994.

4 Michael Higgins, "Little Things Mean a Lot," *Toronto Star Magazine*, 30 September 1989, M14.

5 "Gifelte Fish for the Archbishop," *Winnipeg Free Press*, 23 December 1970, 22.

SOURCES

The Cardinal Flahiff Collection consisting of letters, correspondence, documents, records, talks, articles, etc. of Cardinal Flahiff, is found in the General Archives of the Basilian Fathers (GABF), at the Cardinal Flahiff Basilian Centre, Toronto. The collection consists of thirty-two numbered boxes, most of which contain numbered files. This is the basic source of the material used in the present biography.

The Basilian Annals: A Yearly Record, published each year by the secretary general of the Basilian Fathers, formerly in November, now in January, contains a record of the appointments, work, anniversaries, degrees, honours, publications, and obituaries of the congregation during the previous year. The publication began in 1942.

The Basilian Newsletter, published by the secretary general of the Basilian Fathers approximately twice monthly, contains current news of the congregation, appointments, communications from the superior general, obituaries of the deceased confreres and other items of general interest to the members of the congregation.

Interviews were conducted with the members of the Flahiff family, with the many Basilians who knew Cardinal Flahiff, with colleagues in Winnipeg and among the bishops of Canada, and with many friends of the cardinal. The names of all these appear in the Acknowledgments.

The Helene Darte Collection, the source and substance of chapter 5, now forms part of the Cardinal Flahiff Collection (Box 2A).

The Cardinal Flahiff Loretto Collection will ultimately be confided to the General Archives of the Institute of the Blessed Virgin Mary (Loretto Sisters) in Toronto.

Chronology of the Life of George Bernard Flahiff

1905: born, Paris, Ontario, 26 October, to John Flahiff and Eleanor (Fleming) Flahiff.

1910–17: Sacred Heart Convent School, Paris; death of mother, 22 November 1915.

1917–20: Paris High School.

1920-1: St Jerome's College, Kitchener, Ontario.

1921–2: Paris High School.

1922–6: St Michael's College, University of Toronto; BA, Honours English and History, June 1926.

1926–7: St Basil's Novitiate, Toronto; first profession, 20 September 1927.

1927–30: St Basil's Seminary, Toronto.

1930: ordained to the priesthood, 17 August; leaves for graduate studies in Europe early September; death of father, 29 September.

1930–1: Université de Strasbourg, France.

1931–5: École des Chartes, Paris; degree: Archiviste-Paléographe, Diplôme de l'École des Chartes, June, 1935.

1935–54: Institute of Mediaeval Studies; Professor of Mediaeval History; cross appointment to the Department of History, School of Graduate Studies, University of Toronto, 1940; secretary of the institute, 1943–52.

1948: elected to the General Council of the Basilian Fathers, 6 July.

1951–4: local superior of the Basilian Fathers at the Institute House from 1 July 1951.

1954: elected superior general of the Basilian Fathers, 6 July.

1960: re-elected superior general of the Basilian Fathers, 14 June.

1961: named Archbishop of Winnipeg by Pope John xxiii, 15 March; named to Preparatory Commission on Religious Life for the Second Vatican Council (April); consecrated in St Michael's Cathedral, Toronto, 31 May; installed in See of Winnipeg, 25 June.

1962–5: attends all four sessions of the Second Vatican Council.

1967: one of four Canadian bishops delegated to first Synod of Bishops, Rome, September.

1968: named to the Roman Curia, one of seven bishops from around the world living outside of Rome, 6 January.

1969: named cardinal by Pope Paul vi, 28 March.

1971: one of four Canadian bishops delegated to second Synod of Bishops, Rome: intervention on the role of women in ministries in the Church, 11 October; intervention on social justice, 21 October.

1975: Companion of the Order of Canada, 6 December.

1978: participates in conclave which elects John Paul i, 25–27 August.

1978: participates in conclave which elects John Paul ii, 14–17 October.

1980: celebrates fifty years of priesthood, 17 August; tenders resignation as Archbishop of Winnipeg at seventy-five years of age, 26 October.

1982: resignation accepted, March; retires to the Basilian community at the University of St Michael's College, Toronto, 28 June.

1989: death, 22 August, St Michael's Hospital, Toronto; burial in St Mary's Cemetery, Winnipeg, 29 August.

Honorary Degrees
and Other Honours

Doctor of Laws, St John Fisher College, Rochester, NY, 7 June 1964.

Doctor of Laws, Seattle University, Seattle, Washington, 29 May 1965.

Centennial medal, Government of Canada, 1 July 1967.

Honorary Professor of History, University of Manitoba, Winnipeg, December 1968.

Pax Christi Award by St John's University, Collegeville, Minnesota, 25 May 1969.

Doctor of Laws, University of Notre Dame, Notre Dame, Indiana, 1 June 1969.

Doctor of Laws, University of Manitoba, Winnipeg, 23 October 1969.

Doctor of Laws, University of Windsor, Windsor, Ontario, 30 May 1970.

Doctor of Letters, St Michael's College, Winooski, Vermont, 30 May 1971.

Doctor of Divinity, University of Manitoba, 28 May 1972.

Doctor of Laws, University of Toronto, Toronto, 2 June 1972.

Doctor of Canon Law, St John's College, Winnipeg, 6 November 1973.

Doctor of Theology, St Francis-Xavier University, Antigonish, 12 May 1974.

Companion of the Order of Canada, 6 December 1975.

Docteur en Théologie, Université Laval, Québec, 16 septembre 1974.

Human Relations Award from the Canadian Council of Christians and Jews, 17 November, 1975.

Doctor of Letters, St Thomas University, Fredericton, 10 May 1976.

Doctor of Laws and Letters, University of St Thomas, Houston, Texas, 20 May 1977.

Caritas medal, Catholic Foundation of Manitoba, 8 December 1982.

Doctor of Divinity, Faculty of Theology, University of St Michael's College, Toronto, 28 November 1987.

Terminology

archbishop: the title of a bishop whose jurisdiction is that of an *archdio-cese*, or whose function is of a particular importance (e.g. delegate of the pope); the term does not indicate an extension of holy orders.

archdiocese: a *diocese* of particular importance, either because it serves as a focus of several dioceses, or because it has been designated as such for historical or other reasons.

Basilian Fathers: the name commonly used to designate the commu-nity of priests of the Congregation of St Basil, of which George Ber-nard Cardinal Flahiff was a member.

bishop: a person who has been ordained to the highest rank of holy or-ders and who usually is in charge of a particular *diocese*, or geograph-ical area, in the Church.

conclave: the strictly enclosed meeting of the cardinals in Rome for the purpose of electing the pope.

community or *religious community*: the terms used to designate a par-ticular local group of religious, men or women, as part of a larger group known as a *congregation*.

congregation: used in various senses in the present work:

1) in the canonical title of a community recognized by the Church in accordance with *canon law*, e.g., the Congregation of St Basil (*Basilian Fathers*);

2) in the titles of the various offices of the *Roman Curia*, e.g., Con-gregation of Bishops, Congregation for Christian Education, Congregation for Religious and Secular Institutes, etc.

3) to designate the meetings of cardinals between the death of one pope and the election of another, when they are temporarily in charge of governing the Church.

general chapter is the highest decision-making body of a religious congregation. It meets at regular intervals (four to six years) to elect the superior general and the *general council* for the ensuring period, and to legislate other matters concerning the congregation.

general council is elected by the *general chapter*; in the case of the Basilians it is composed of the *superior general* and four councellors; the council advises and assists the superior general in the governing of the community.

ordinary (noun): used to designate the person who holds official episcopal jurisdiction in a particular diocese, eg. Cardinal Flahiff was the ordinary of Winnipeg; the jurisdiction may be assigned temporarily to one who is not a bishop.

religious (noun): the term used to designate a person, man or woman, who lives in a religious community which professes vows of obedience, chastity and poverty; thus one speaks of religious priests as distinct from *secular priests*.

religious life: the technical term used to designate the state of those persons who live in community and take vows of obedience, chastity and poverty.

Roman Curia: the bureacracy of the Roman Catholic Church in Rome which assists the pope in the government of the Church and is composed of eleven congregations, three tribunals, four secretariats, nineteen commissions, and seven offices.

secular priests: those who do not belong to a religious community; they are usually engaged in ministry in parishes or chaplaincies in hospitals, prisons, etc.

sisters: women religious, that is, persons who profess vows and live in community, engaged in a particular mission in the Church (education, hospitals, missions, etc.); the term is synonymous with "nuns" and "women religious."

superior general: the term which designates the person elected by a religious community to govern and oversee the entire congregation; *local superior* is a person elected or appointed to govern a particular community within the congregation.

INDEX